TEA AND SCOTCH

with

BRADMAN

OTHER BOOKS BY ROLAND PERRY

Non-fiction
Elections Sur Ordinateur [Elections on Computer] (1984)
*The Programming of the President: The Hidden Power of the Computer in World
    Politics Today* (1984)
The Exile: Wilfred Burchett, Reporter of Conflict (1988)
Shane Warne, Master Spinner (1993)
Lethal Hero: The Mel Gibson Biography (1993)
The Fifth Man: The Soviet Super Spy (1994)
The Don [republished as *Don Bradman*] (1995)
Mel Gibson: Actor, Director, Producer (1995)
Bold Warnie: Shane Warne and Australia's Rise to Cricket Dominance (1998)
Waugh's Way: The Steve Waugh Story (1999)
*Captain Australia: A History of the Celebrated Captains of Australian Test
    Cricket* (2000)
*Bradman's Best: Sir Donald Bradman's Selection of the Best Team in Cricket
    History* (2001)
Bradman's Best Ashes Teams (2002)
Monash: The Outsider Who Won a War (2004)
*Last of the Cold War Spies: The Life of Michael Straight, the only American in
    Britain's Cambridge Spy Ring* (2005)
*Miller's Luck: The Life and Loves of Keith Miller, Australia's Greatest All-
    rounder* (2005)
The Ashes: A Celebration (2006)
Bradman's Invincibles: The Story of the 1948 Ashes Tour (2008)
*Sailing to the Moon: The Biography of Rolly Tasker, Australia's Greatest All-
    round Yachtsman* (2008)
*The Australian Light Horse: The Magnificent Australian Force and its Decisive
    Victories in Arabia in World War I* (2009)
The Changi Brownlow (2010)
Pacific 360° [later retitled *The Fight for Australia: From Changi and Darwin to
    Kokoda*] (2012)
Bill the Bastard: The Story of Australia's Greatest War Horse (2012)
Horrie the War Dog: The Story of Australia's Most Famous Dog (2013)
*The Queen, her Lover and the Most Notorious Spy in History: The Intriguing
    True Story of Queen Victoria's Secret* (2014)
Céleste: Courtesan, Countess, Bestselling Author (2016)
*Monash and Chauvel: How Australia's Two Greatest Generals Changed the
    Course of World History* (2017)
*ANZAC Sniper: The Extraordinary Story of Stan Savige — From Gallipoli
    Marksman to WWII General* (2018)

Fiction
Programme for a Puppet (1979)
Blood is a Stranger (1988)
Faces in the Rain (1990)
The Honourable Assassin (2015)
The Assassin on the Bangkok Express (2017)

TEA AND SCOTCH

with

BRADMAN

ROLAND PERRY

ABC
BOOKS

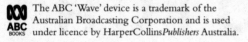

To

Neil Harvey, an inspirational cricketer and character,

&

Thos Hodgson, whose 'Tragic' love of the game does not
diminish his good humour and bonhomie,

&

husband and wife Dean Golja and Mary Finsterer,
whose creativity added much to the story.

CONTENTS

LIST OF PHOTOGRAPHS
by Dean Golja, taken at Sir Donald and Lady Bradman's
home in Adelaide in 1995

Facing page 86
We stopped for a cup of tea mid-morning, and a scotch in the living room at noon. During these breaks, we relaxed and discussed issues other than cricket. This would become a pattern over the course of preparing the biography.

Facing page 87
The Don frequently consulted *Wisden Cricketers' Almanack*, the cricketing bible, which has been published annually since 1864, and Bradman had a complete set. His reference library covered an entire wall of his study.

Facing page 134
The Don had amazing recall. He was certain that he had hit his first run ever in his maiden innings at Lord's, in 1930, to mid-off. I had it rolling to mid-on. He asked for my sources. I produced three. He squinted into the distance of 65 years and with certitude described the shot, and who ran across from where to field it. 'I remember it particularly,' he said. 'It was my first Test run at Lord's.' There could be no argument.

Facing page 135
After about two hours of questioning The Don, I asked if it would be possible for Lady Bradman to join the interview. 'She has known you since you were 11,' I said. 'That's longer than anyone.' Lady Bradman, then 85, was radiant and courteous. She warmed to the chance to contribute. I learned later than Bradman had always shielded her from the media.

Facing pages 182 and 183
In this sequence of photographs Bradman demonstrates how he was forced to play the infamous Bodyline bowling when the ball lifted sharply from the leg-side, and up into the ribcage. The 2019 Ashes team knew what it was like to face a bowler — Jofra Archer — of great speed and accuracy. But there was a big difference. When Bradman and the 1932–33 Ashes side faced Harold Larwood and co., it was with a field of six or seven close in on the leg-side. Two likely outcomes were being hit in the head or body, or popping up a catch.

Facing page 230
Bradman met his future wife, Jessie Menzies, the vivacious blue-eyed daughter of a farmer from nearby Glenquarry, in 1920, when their parents introduced them. Don was 11, Jessie ten. 'I fell in love with her at first sight,' he told me.

Facing page 231
Dean took scores of photographs from many angles over the next six hours as the first interview proceeded. The Don was oblivious of the ubiquitous camera capturing him in the longest portrait session he ever allowed. I did not want an old man in repose, as interesting as such impressions can be. The aim was to portray him as he approached 90 years — intellectually vigorous, humorous, and thoughtful, with powers of concentration that would put any monk to shame.

Introduction

When ABC Books publisher Jude McGee first approached me about writing a personal memoir of Sir Donald Bradman, I was not that enthusiastic. I had completed four books concerning him, including the biography *Don Bradman* (originally titled *The Don*). However, on reflection, I realised that there was much of his personal side that had not been explored. A sports biography always creates a dilemma: how much is to be written on the subject's story and sporting achievements, and how much on their character? How much should his or her impact on the culture, society and history be emphasised, if at all?

Bradman's long and varied record in the sporting arena, and as an administrator, was so huge that it is almost impossible to absorb unless laid out in a long narrative. I owed it to his fans to deliver in *The Don* a story on his phenomenal record. This left less space for exploring his personality, his sense of humour and his love of music; his impact on the apartheid issue; how he handled fame; the controversy over his life as a stockbroker; his prodigious output of letters; his hidden work for charities; and innumerable other areas outside cricket.

I'd had more access to him than any other journalist or writer, experiencing him both in public and in private. By the end of six years of discussions, I knew him well. We had developed what Bradman defined as a 'good friendship'. His moods and his personal characteristics had become familiar. I was aware of his strengths and foibles. Of course, his cricket exploits would still have to be covered, but this time it would be in the context of his genius, and through exploring what made the greatest sportsman of the 20th century tick.

Conversations with him were, like his batting, never dull and were often unpredictable. There was never hesitation in his organised, layered answers to questions. If he didn't have an answer, he would say so, just as if he were playing back in defence. If he had an answer, it came quickly and articulately, sometimes with the subtlety of a late cut, often surprisingly like a cover drive off a leg-cutter.

He was always friendly and obliging to deal with. Yet the nature of the relationship — biographer and subject — meant at times there had to be conflict. It was the biographer's task to delve. He might not always appreciate it. Bradman could be tough, yet never unreasonable.

Differences invariably were over publicity. If I wanted to write something about him for newspapers, he was never happy.

The reason was the direct correlation between publicity and an increase in the already huge amount of mail he received.

After 1996, I stopped writing articles about Bradman because of his complaints about the mail. He couldn't understand, nor did I try to explain to him, why his name came up nearly every day in papers in England and Australia. Mentions of him and discussions about him had been out of control since the 1927–28 cricket season when he first played for New South Wales. Part of the reason for his popularity and the fascination with him is the fact that his record has only 'grown' in the seven decades since his retirement.

Therefore, I was happy to write the memoir. I had endless notes and tapes to draw on, and it was a challenge to tackle a story that needed my personal input.

I have written 35 books of non-fiction, dramatised non-fiction, fiction in the third and first person; also film documentaries and drama scripts, articles and speeches. This was another enjoyable writing experience.

My aim in this memoir is to give a more rounded view of the man and his inevitable complexities; to address the misconceptions of the real and imagined 'Don Bradman'; and to explore the mythology surrounding major incidents in his life. I hope this will give readers a deeper understanding of a man many leading figures in Australian life believe was the nation's greatest son.

CHAPTER 1

First Impressions

I loved cricket from an early age, and the one name that dominated that sport was Donald George Bradman. He was the measure of all things excellent. 'Bradmanesque' was a term coined in that era and, approaching seven decades later, it has become overused; a cliché. Whether it be breeding roses or playing chess, or competing in any sport from marbles to marathons, when someone says he or she 'is the Bradman of' anything, Australians know exactly what is meant.

Though he had retired as a player in 1949, I only became conscious of his record, capacity and elements of his character in 1959, age 12, after reading the book *Brightly Fades the Don* by former Test player, and long-time Bradman detractor, Jack Fingleton, about the 1948 Ashes tour of England. I was then enthralled and unaware of Fingleton's at times negative attitude and account of Bradman.

Despite his fame, very few people seemed to know Bradman well. There was a mystique surrounding him. In 1994, when I first decided to write about him, there had been 57 books published on the subject, but no one had done a real biography based on interviews. I decided the project would not be worthwhile unless I was able to write the story based on face-to-face responses to questions on his life and career.

The next question was how to reach him? After pursuing several fruitless leads, a friend of mine gave me some good advice: I should write to the Bradman Museum. The museum, established in 1989, and in particular its director and curator Richard Mulvaney, had become the conduit to The Don.

Mulvaney passed on my letter to Bradman early in 1995. I was lucky — Bradman had read my latest book, *The Fifth Man*, published in 1994. He was interested. Mulvaney advised me to write directly to Bradman, which I did, and a deal was struck. I was to have just one day of interviews at Bradman's home on Holden Street, Kensington Park, in Adelaide.

*

What was the real Bradman character? Before I started his biography, I had heard rumours: he could be blunt; he didn't suffer intelligent people gladly, let alone fools. Were any of these stories accurate or just the usual myths about a famous individual? It was difficult for me to gauge. We arranged the interview through ᴉe mail, and had yet to speak in person.

I approached photographer Dean Golja to ask if he would like to accompany me. I had chosen him because he was an artistic rather than a sports photographer, which could lead to more interesting portraits.

Dean gave a surprising response: 'Bradman, Bradman,' he mused. 'I've heard that name.'

He wasn't kidding. He would not be over-awed. Only later when he did some homework did he realise what a fascinating subject he would have.

We flew to Adelaide and hired a car. As we drove to Bradman's house, I mentioned to Dean that he might have to move quickly to get his photos. At least six sports photographers had heard I was writing the biography and contacted me. They all repeated the rumours about how difficult Bradman tended to be with anyone trying to take a 'portrait' of him.

We cultivated a plan: just in case Dean was 'dismissed' after a few minutes at Bradman's house, he could explore Adelaide while the interview went on.

I was alert when we walked down the Holden Street driveway to the two-level red brick house, which was an unprepossessing minimalist design, and typical of the 1930s. I'd then had nearly 30 years' experience interviewing for books, documentaries and journalism. This was a big one, perhaps the most important encounter I'd ever have with a fellow countryman.

Lady Bradman, then 85, radiant and courteous, greeted us at the front door with the disconcerting news that 'Don' had a toothache. Dean glanced at me. Would this mean Bradman would make it even tougher for him to steal a few shots?

Lady Bradman showed us in and then disappeared. Seconds later, Bradman walked in. It was a hot day and he wore a short-sleeved shirt and grey trousers. Bespectacled Bradman was smaller in stature than the official 170 centimetres (and 65 kilograms at his fitness peak), and I put that down to old age. He had only the slightest of paunches, testimony to a mix of good living and fitness, mainly through golf, over the latter half of his then 86 years. His arms were strong and sinewy. Those forearms had thumped a cricket ball more often per innings and with more timing and power, pound for pound, than any other cricketer.

'What do you want?' he said in that familiar nasal voice, as he opened his hands to us, indicating he was at our disposal.

There was something world-weary about him in those initial moments. Yet that was about the extent of his display of irritation about more 'publicity', which was his term for all media attention.

He led us into the downstairs lounge; it was adorned with a glass case displaying ornate trophies. We sat on the floral sofa in front of an imposing portrait of him hung above the mantelpiece. It showed him seated on a deck chair in casual repose and attire, right hand on chin. His expression was attentive, yet pensive — much as it was in real life now.

There was portent in the story behind that picture. Bradman liked this oil on canvas work the moment it was unveiled. A former Test cricketer, also at the unveiling, leaned across to Bradman and whispered that the legs were too long. Bradman agreed. He later had a restorer lop off the offending limbs below the knee. The artist's signature was moved from the bottom of the painting to the top. The message was clear: better not to be the sensitive *artiste*, in any way, when dealing with The Don.

*

I began the interview with the questions that had been sent in advance. They were innocuous, to avoid putting him off before we were face to face. (I had learned to do this when I failed to interview another famous sportsman for a newspaper article years before in England. I had sent him questions. His management told me the sportsman in question was upset. The queries had been too 'hard'.)

'They were corny,' Bradman remarked on the Dorothy Dixers I had sent him.

I took this as an invitation to make tougher queries.

I asked him a question about leg-spinner Bill O'Reilly, who Bradman regarded as the finest bowler he ever faced: 'O'Reilly left posthumous tapes in which he said he did not wish to criticise you while he was alive, because, quote, he "didn't wish to piss on a national monument". What did you think about that?'

Bradman smiled wryly. 'Arh well, you know Bill,' he said, then added, 'I agree with the sentiment that you should not desecrate national monuments. And if there were a national monument to Bill, I wouldn't desecrate it, even if it were on fire.'

Dean and I laughed. It was our first experience of the sharp and quick mind of this icon of icons.

After about two hours of questioning, I asked: 'Would it be possible for Lady Bradman to join the interview?'

Bradman stared from behind glasses with close eyes that never left you; not in an intimidating way, but in a manner which signified perhaps his greatest asset: his power of concentration.

'Why?' Bradman asked.

'She has known you since you were 11,' I replied. 'That's longer than anyone.'

Bradman leaned back and, without taking his eyes off me, said: 'Jessie, could you come in here please?'

The interview continued for another hour with Lady Bradman answering questions, or chipping in a comment without deference to her husband. She warmed to the chance to contribute. I learned later that Bradman had always shielded her from the media. This was laudable, but from her responses it was easy to see that she was bright and comfortable being interviewed.

Jessie was Bradman's greatest love and asset, and he characterised it in cricketing terms by saying he and she 'formed the best partnership in life'. The analogy meant more when Bradman said it than any other person in the sport. He'd had the finest big-batting links in history, especially with Australia's Bill Ponsford. At that stage, the Bradmans had been married 63 years and had known each other 75 years.

They often both answered the same question. For instance, I asked him: 'What did you think of Douglas Jardine?' (Jardine was the England captain who conspired with his fast bowlers to destroy Bradman's career using the Bodyline tactic during the 1932–33 Ashes match series between England and Australia.)

'He was a very, very good bat,' Bradman replied. He was really saying, 'No comment,' presumably because he disliked Jardine.

'I didn't like him at all,' Jessie said, 'after what he did to Don and our boys.'

After another hour, Jessie asked what my arrangement was with the interviews.

'An interview face to face today,' I replied.

'That's not going to be nearly enough,' she said and, without even glancing at her husband, asked: 'Have you got our phone number?'

'No,' I said. 'We negotiated through the mail.'

'Well,' she said, while scribbling their number on a piece of paper, 'just give us a call whenever you want to come over and we'll arrange a lunch for you any time you want.'

I glanced at Bradman, who again did not react. At that moment, I realised that Jessie was his antennae for people and situations, or at least a back-up to his own opinions.

Dean proceeded to take scores of photographs from many angles over the next six hours as the interview proceeded. So much for the warnings. The Don was oblivious of the ubiquitous camera capturing him in the longest portrait session he ever allowed.

I did not want an old man in repose, as interesting as such impressions can be. The aim was to portray him as he approached 90 years — intellectually vigorous, humorous and thoughtful, with powers of concentration that would put any monk to shame. Dean secured what was required.

Dean later sent Bradman some of the shots. Bradman wrote back a polite letter with the comment: 'I return herewith what I consider to be the worst four …'

You could take this as bluntness or refreshing directness. Whatever it was, it sat well with his integrity, for which he said he wanted to be remembered above all. He should have no fear. Writer Raymond Chandler said 'Honesty is an art'. Bradman had it down to a fine art.

English cricket writer Sir Neville Cardus once described a Bradman innings thus: 'It was never uninteresting; he simply abstained from vanity and rhetoric.'

Such were his responses to hundreds of questions I put to him on that first day and over the ensuing months and years. His answers were button-down, logical and without a misplaced syllable. Allied to his succinct use of the language was an obsession with accuracy, which bordered on eccentricity. Australian Cricket Board staff would often send him written information for comment or approval. The Don would send some letters back. The request would be ignored; instead, there would be grammatical corrections scribbled in the margins.

*

The first interview session went an hour over the allotted time. I decided The Don had been too generous and I called a halt.

'I enjoyed that,' he said with a grin as he bounced off the sofa. 'Dean, would you like more shots?'

In his enthusiasm to help Dean with his equipment, Bradman lost his balance. He whirled his arms in an attempt to stay upright, but fell back towards the sofa. Dean dived on the sofa under him and broke the fall.

'Well caught, Dean!' was my relieved observation.

We moved to the front garden. Dean tried to get him to smile. He wouldn't. Dean tried a joke.

'Just think, Sir Don, you'll be able to tell your grandchildren you were photographed with one of Australia's great writers.'

Bradman loosened that determined jaw enough for Dean to capture him smiling.

CHAPTER 2

The Bowral Boy's Beginnings

The life of this diminutive, strong-willed survivor spanned almost the 20th century. He told me in 2000 of a book he was reading about his home town. It caused him to recall hopping on a horse used by the town's gas-lamp lighter as early as 1914, age six, and helping the man with his task in the main street. Fourteen years later — in 1928 — he burst onto the international sporting scene, never to leave it while cricket was played or discussed.

There was romance in the story of the working-class country boy made good. He was not from the privileged elite in Sydney or Melbourne. Much to his own chagrin, he left school at 14 when his carpenter father, George, could not provide the funds to further educate Bradman and his four siblings. He was intellectually hungry and inquisitive. It was a blow to stop formal training so young, and it rankled with him for life — especially,

I suspect, because he rarely met those with a similar intellect among the highly educated. Bradman had a sharp brain and worked it harder than most.

The family had two outstanding loves, music and sport, and Don was passionate about various aspects of both for most of his 92 years. He and his brother and three sisters could play at least one musical instrument. In the summer, leisure time was marked by the sounds of the violin and piano. They also all played cricket in the backyard of their home in Bowral, in the Southern Higlands of New South Wales. Physical energy was also spent on tennis and athletics. In the winter, the boys played rugby instead, and the music intensified with more time indoors.

Bradman first held a bat at age five. It was fashioned by George from a gum-tree branch. The boy was a good listener from the start, but the technique he was told to use was little more than to whack the ball at every opportunity. The country game was played for fun. Orthodoxy was not instructed for one so young. Bradman learned footwork and more refined strokes by watching other players, and by age eight was demonstrating good hand– eye coordination.

He rarely heard the cry, 'Straight bat!' If he did, he would ignore it or use the dictum instinctively; that is, when the shot required it. Otherwise Bradman learned early to manipulate shots, through the backyard or field any way he could to build a score. This was the reason that from the beginning of his cricket 'career', he was a run accumulator with one overriding aim: to win every contest, against every bowler and all opposing teams.

By age 11, the young Don was a prodigy, although it would not be recognised immediately. At the crease, he was easily transported into what later became known as the 'zone', where a batsman would build a score, in a state of semi-trance, over a long time — sometimes six hours. No one in the history of the game entered this special space with more concentration, a better temperament, greater skill or a higher run production.

Such was his early dominance at school, he was never dismissed and other schools refused to play any team with him in it. Young Don turned to other sports and was outstanding at tennis. He was the best sprinter and long-distance runner at Bowral High. But by 15, he had to make a decision on which sport he would pursue wholeheartedly. A stellar sporting career beckoned in both cricket and tennis. He chose cricket, which he enjoyed marginally more.

*

His developing cricket training and 'smarts' came from his early teen years in the local Bowral team, for which his father and uncles also played.

They wanted him to change the way he held the bat. His natural grip, with the lower or right hand forming a V on the bar handle, was seen as unorthodox.

'I tried out the other methods,' he told me. 'I even batted in some early innings with the left hand higher on the handle and the right [or lower] hand more open — that is, for making strokes that would more easily loft the ball.'

'And?'

'It didn't suit me. My natural grip acted as a brake on me lifting the ball. It made it less likely that I would be dismissed "caught".' (Being caught was the most common cause of a batsman's dismissal in all forms of the game.)

Bradman used this technique for most of his career, particularly early on. He struck few sixes in his career of about 670 innings. Instead he hit fours — 2586 in 338 First-Class innings and seven fives. His grip produced two other outcomes in attack or defence. First, the bat sloped at about 45 degrees to the ground. Second, when he hooked or cut, the wrists rolled the bat over the ball. These outcomes both ensured the ball was kept down.

He had no backlift in the technical sense. Bradman used the top hand on the batting handle to lever the bat up when playing a shot. This sped up the time for him to be ready to meet the oncoming delivery. It also took the strain off muscles in the arms and shoulders.

Did Bradman's batting technique give him advantages? Early in his career, he was criticised for playing 'cross-bat' shots when pulling balls around from the off-side to the on. Bradman reduced the alleged transgression against orthodoxy to absurdity by asking: 'How else do you score on the on-side when a ball is well outside off-stump?'

If Bradman faced a strong off-side field, he was not going to worry about playing a cross-bat shot through the on-side if that was the only way to score. However, it must be conceded that Bradman could play such shots with impunity because of his extraordinary skills. His batting methods were more effective than anything before or since.

His own moral code also largely stemmed from this time. An instance of this was the way Bradman handled loss or victory in public as captain. After-match addresses invariably included honest praise for a vanquished opponent. There was never begrudging respect, or veiled insults.

I asked Bradman where this came from.

'My parents, my uncles, my teachers and the captains at Bowral when I was a boy,' he replied.

*

Bradman met his future wife, Jessie Menzies, the vivacious blue-eyed daughter of a farmer from nearby Glenquarry, in 1920, when their parents introduced them. Don was 11, Jessie ten.

'I fell in love with her at first sight,' he told me.

I replied by citing the first stanza of the poem 'At First Sight' by Robert Graves:

Love at first sight, some say, misnaming
Discovery of twinned helplessness
Against the huge tug of procreation.

Bradman laughed. 'Not sure about that.'

A couple days later, he rang to clarify what he meant. 'I just want to say we didn't indulge in anything,' he said. 'We were very young.'

'I realise that, Sir Donald,' I said with a laugh. (I always called him 'Sir Donald', and Jessie 'Lady Bradman', until about three months into the interviewing, when he said: 'Call me Don.')

A few days later I received a note from him: '… as for your quotation of Robert Graves' poem, "At First Sight", and in relation to my first meeting with Jessie, I prefer the second stanza, which reads:

But friendship at first sight? This also
Catches fiercely at the surprised heart
So that the cheek blanches and then blushes.

'As I told you, she formed the best partnership of my life …'

During their long relationship, Jessie was a great strength for Bradman, and I doubt that without her he would have made the journey through setbacks and illnesses. Apart from her strong character and obvious intelligence, there was a charm and beauty about her; a 'charisma', before the word was hijacked by politicians, film stars and today's celebrities, and rendered meaningless. To a man and woman over the last 25 years since I started researching Bradman's biography, everyone had only positive things to say about her.

The couple had their travails outside of the scrutiny of his cricket career that were far more taxing and emotionally consuming. After the Test series of 1934 in England, during which he had been decidedly underweight, dropping to just 51 kilograms, he had severe abdominal pains that were diagnosed as appendicitis. Surgeons operated immediately. Bradman lost a lot of blood during the four-hour procedure and peritonitis set in. There were no drugs to counter it at that time and he was expected to die. On 25 September, the hospital issued a statement that Bradman was struggling for life. Blood donors were needed urgently.

The hospital had so many offers that it shut down its switchboard. Journalists in the UK and Australia prepared obituaries. Bill O'Reilly took a phone call from King George V's secretary, who asked that the King be updated with bulletins. Jessie started a month-long journey to England. By the time she reached London, Bradman had begun to recover. They stayed in the UK for several months and Bradman was told by doctors to miss the 1934–35 cricket season.

In 1936, their first child, Ross, died in infancy. This was not touched on by a considerate media, but it profoundly affected both parents, who kept their grief to themselves.

Bradman showed in his autobiography that he understood the depth of the emotional pain that Jessie was going through: 'In the lives of young parents there can scarcely be a sadder moment. The hopes and ambitions of a father for a son, fine and noble though they may be, are as naught alongside the natural love of the mother.'

Their son John was born in 1939. John contracted polio at age 11 when an epidemic swept South Australia. I contracted it during an earlier epidemic in Victoria in 1948–49. I well recall at three years of age the indignity of having to wear leg irons that I hated. I was fortunate to recover fully, and it did not hit me nearly as badly as it did John, who was in an iron frame for a year, whereas I had leg irons for just a month or two. Bradman gave away his work as a stockbroker and cricket administrator for a year to aid Jessie in John's recovery. While immobilised, John was placed in the home's lounge room, along with the piano and record player.

'One of my greatest delights over this time was my dad playing the piano for me,' John said. Music and the piano were centrepieces in the Bradman home and they played a part in John's rehabilitation.

Daughter Shirley was born in 1941 with a mild form of cerebral palsy. She was a positive character, similar to her father, and managed her disability with courage and independence. She lived in the family home until she married a local postman, whom she later divorced. I met her once, briefly, at the Bradman home when she arrived with her dog.

From 1941 until 1945, Bradman also suffered from severe fibrositis, a rheumatic disorder of fibrous tissue. It affected his spine and back, and looked likely to end his sporting career.

Decades of setbacks in private gave him and his wife a far broader and deeper perspective on life and its fragility. Bradman may have developed into the biggest legend in Australia's brief history, but his personal life grounded him, and he fell back on his immediate family and close friends as a refuge from the constant public glare.

CHAPTER 3

The Inner Sanctum

I completed the first draft of the biography over the next seven months with countless other interviews. Bradman would send me helpful items — and some of the more bizarre letters he received from around the world, names and addresses withheld.

In the middle of the writing, I had a phone call from the editor of a major British newspaper offering a sizeable amount to write a 5000-word feature on what it was like dealing with Bradman. I knew this editor, who had published freelance articles I had written on American presidential elections during the Carter–Reagan eras.

'We'd like lots of "colour",' he commented.

'Oh, I have lots and lots of colour,' I said, 'but it will all be in the book.'

'We could offer you more …'

'I couldn't do it. It would break the trust I have with Bradman.'

About a fortnight later, Bradman and I were chatting on the phone when he said: 'Had any good offers for articles lately?'

At first I didn't know what he was getting at. I had put out of my mind the British offer.

'Which one?' I asked.

'Oh, you get a lot of offers, do you?'

I was still perplexed.

'This one was for 25,000 pounds,' he prompted.

'Oh, OK. I rejected it.'

'A good thing too. We wouldn't be having any conversation if you had accepted it.'

This was both a warning, and Bradman's odd way of thanking me. After that, he loosened up his responses even more.

*

When writing the biography, I spent time poring over the *Wisden Cricketers' Almanack* books at the Melbourne Cricket Club library at the MCG. (A new edition of *Wisden* has been published annually since 1864.) Several times, Bradman offered to look things up in his own set of *Wisden*. He had one of only two private sets in the world. (The other owner was John Paul Getty II, who loved cricket, but there might be more now.)

At first, I was hesitant. Could I really ask the *great man* to in effect act as a research assistant?

'I really don't want you to go to any trouble,' I said.

'It's no trouble. I enjoy it. Do you want me to help or not?'

This remark made it clear he wanted to dig for me. This saved me much labour. Bradman revelled in helping me find information.

At the end of the project, he asked if he could read my biography of him, which was not part of our original arrangement. We had agreed that it was to be 'unauthorised'. No one would interfere with the editorial.

'I only want to check the manuscript for factual errors,' The Don explained.

I agreed, having come to know him as not precious about fair criticism. I sent the book overnight to him. A day later, I received a phone call. He had read it — all 250,000 words. What's more, he had typed four pages of comments on yellow legal-pad paper.

I was stunned. In my experience, no editor had ever been through such a sizeable manuscript so fast. Of course, he knew the terrain. It was *his* life. Yet his attention to information he had never seen before was remarkable, as was his energy. I was not yet aware of his capacity to watch sport or work through a night.

He asked if I could I make another trip to Adelaide to discuss the manuscript. I arrived a few days later. Anticipating Lady Bradman's hospitality, I brought flowers. Don greeted me at the door when I arrived, at 9.30 a.m.

'Oh, thanks a lot,' he said, reaching for the flowers.

'They're for Jessie.'

'Oh,' he said. 'Why doesn't anyone ever bring me flowers? They're always for Jessie.'

These and other such blasé and bizarre comments always had me a fraction baffled. Was he serious or not?

The Don bounced upstairs, past alcoves displaying trophies and his favourite portrait of himself executing a cover drive, and into the inner sanctum — the small Bradman study, with which I became familiar on the trips to Holden Street. It was dominated by a cricket reference library, featuring the *Wisden* yearbooks, and covered an entire wall. We sat opposite each other at a card table, each with a copy of the manuscript, and began sifting through his 80 points. I was relieved to find he had mainly picked up literals and typing errors. He made no reference — as anticipated — to the 'editorial' that considered his character and style, except to say he took exception to being called a 'hard-headed little pessimist' by a journalist.

'What's this "little" business?' he asked.

We continued to plough through his notes.

'Now, point 14, you have me going out to bat at Leeds flanked by two *bury* policemen,' he said, looking over his glasses at me like a benign schoolmaster. 'You mean *burly*, don't you?'

The Don loved a malapropism: 'Point 24. You've got here that I "did it for prosperity". You mean *posterity*, don't you?'

He was reminded of a dinner party he had attended where a barrister was 'pontificating' about how well he cornered witnesses in the box.

'He said he liked to go for the jocular,' Bradman said. 'He meant jugular and he wasn't joking.'

We stopped for a cup of tea mid-morning, and a scotch in the living room at noon. During these breaks, we relaxed and discussed issues other than cricket. The Bradmans proved to be a well-informed couple on everything from politics to the republican debate going on at the time (1995).

By now, The Don's amazing recall was coming into play. He was certain that he had hit his first run ever in his maiden innings at Lord's, in 1930, to mid-off. I had it rolling to mid-on. He asked for my sources. I produced three. He squinted into the distance of 65 years and with certitude described the shot, and who ran across from where to field it.

'I remember it particularly,' he said. 'It was my first Test run at Lord's.'

There could be no argument.

Bradman's Test average of 99.94, or, rounded off, a century every time he went out to bat, was well known. *Un*known was his average from the time he first played competitively at 11 years until his first full season of cricket at 16 years. I checked several sources and came up with 166, an indication for anyone who had cared to check his early efforts that the Boy from Bowral might just be extraordinary. The Don, *point 35*, questioned this.

'I think you've given me one too many innings,' he said, indicating a particular match for Bowral when he was 14. Again, the question: 'What are your sources?' The Don listened. Unconvinced, he stood up, wandered over to his library and pulled out a tiny 1922–23 scorebook. He was correct, once more. We made our re-calculations and arrived at the same figure, which will one day be the answer to a Trivial Pursuit question: 187.

The Don also queried the position of one hit made in his record as the fastest century maker in any game of cricket anywhere in the world. Bradman had moved from 54 to 154 in just 12 minutes in a 1931 match between a combined Blue Mountains team and the Lithgow Pottery Cricket Club. He noticed that in the three (then eight-ball) overs he took to score the runs, I had one scoring shot in incorrect sequence. The correct list of shots was: 6, 6, 4, 2, 4, 4, 6, 1 (first over, 33 runs); 6, 4, 4, 6, 6, 4, 6, 4 (second over, 40 runs); and 6, 6, 1, 4, 4, 6 (third over, 27 runs).

This was an example of his acute numeracy, the intellectual root of his need as a young man to break every record that counted in batting at First-Class and Test levels. This capacity to play with, build and surmount 'the numbers' accentuated the public's fascination with the statistics of cricket in Australia in the 1920s and 1930s. It had begun with the great Bill Ponsford, the Australian and Victorian opener, who had mastered the universe of big innings a few years before Bradman came on the First-Class scene. Together in the 1930 and 1934 Ashes in England, they became the mega-scorers of cricket, setting records that would last decades and change the face of the game. No longer was a big hundred the aim in the sport. The bar had been set at 200, 300, 400 and beyond by these two. Nine decades later, in the rare event of an Australian marching towards or over a double hundred, people will turn up at the venue, or switch on TV sets and radios to tune in and ogle the spectacle. Only a close finish in a Test will garner more viewers and listeners.

*

As ever on my visits to Adelaide, Lady Bradman's hospitality was evident at lunch on that final day of reviewing the biography. She brought in help to prepare a three-course lunch, complete with excellent wines, as she had on other occasions.

At one point, The Don struggled to remove a cork from a wine bottle. I motioned to help. He waved me away as if I had insulted him: he was strong enough to do it.

Once during the meal, when Jessie had left the room, he told a mildly risqué farm joke. I can't recall it exactly. It had something to do with servicing a sow. The convivial atmosphere elicited glimpses of Don the country boy.

Bradman and I coasted through the remaining points in the manuscript in the afternoon, and discussed many things, including Lady Bradman's health. She had suffered for years from chronic leukaemia. The Don's deep love and respect for her courage and character came up, as it had in several previous discussions.

That memorable day with the Bradmans ended with more scotch and cups of tea in the evening, followed by another three-course meal, and more wine. A taxi arrived to pick me up. Bradman thumped the car's bonnet in a last gesture of farewell. As we drove away, the driver asked: 'Was that who I thought it was?'

I only needed to say, 'Yes.'

That last day dealing with the biography was one of several occasions that we drank alcohol together. Bradman loved his drink, particularly his wines, and, just like with anything else he applied himself to, he was very good at it. In retirement, he had long buried his wowser image of the 1930s. But from discussions with many of his friends, I learned he was never a heavy imbiber. I like my wines and scotch too, but did not have his constitution, and have never been a big drinker. Twice after convivial evenings at his home, Bradman, 37 years my senior, seemed a lot steadier than me as he led me out to the waiting taxi.

I once related this anecdote in a speech to a Probus Club meeting and it went down like a lead balloon. I never mentioned it again. The myths about Bradman being a teetotaller abounded. Showing that he enjoyed alcohol seemed in some eyes to besmirch his character.

He did not drink until he retired from cricket in 1949 at age 40. He had dedicated his mind and body to representing his country to the best of his ability, which was far above everyone else. He had earned the right to let his guard down over fitness disciplines.

Yet somehow, that particular audience, and probably his vast numbers of fans, did not wish his image changed or modified to reality. They envisaged an abstemious, rigid figure, which was just not the real Bradman.

After writing 35 books and 17 full or quasi biographies, I have learned you often can't change mythology, whether it be dealing with John Monash, Lawrence of Arabia, Queen Victoria, Harry Chauvel, Celeste (Mogador) Venard, Stan Savige, KGB masterspy Yuri Ivanovitch Modin, Lord Rothschild, Mel Gibson, John Curtin, Wilfred Burchett, Rolly Tasker, Keith Miller, Steve Waugh, Shane Warne, Don Bradman or the war horse Bill the Bastard. All an author can do is write with integrity about the subject.

The reader can either accept the bedrock facts or stay with the mythology.

CHAPTER 4

Bradman versus the Great Depression

Nelson Mandela once remarked that Bradman was 'one for the divinities'. The Don himself was uncomfortable with such epithets, as was his son, John, who said when Don died that his dad should not be seen as a 'religious figure'. But why would Mandela, a sports lover all his life, make such an observation, endorsed by the bulk of Australia and the cricketing world?

The complete answer could not be his ranking alongside Muhammad Ali by many international expert analysts as the greatest sportsperson of the 20th century. It certainly is *a* factor, but not *the* factor in bestowing a kind of sainthood on Bradman. The fact that his two-decade record at the top of his chosen sport placed him statistically superior to the rest of the best does not translate to deification, hero-worship or immortality. It's not enough.

Nor is the fact that he was around for most of the century. Legends and saints are more often than not created from those who die young. Consider Jesus Christ, Alexander the Great, or even Diana, Princess of Wales. Bradman lived three times longer than them and proved a durable, positive and awe-inspiring identity. Instead of dropping off as a hero after he retired from cricket at 40, his status grew, and never stopped growing.

It wasn't for want of trying *not* to be hero-worshipped. There are plenty of media people who have experienced the wrath of Bradman for an indiscretion or an invasion of his precious privacy. Instead of ingratiating himself with members of the Fourth Estate, he eschewed them. This is not in the rulebook of those who seek fame. Pandering to media requests at every opportunity is among the top dictates for achieving conventional recognition and status. Yet it is the media that has pandered to him. For more than 70 years, the Bradman 'mystique' developed around his inaccessibility. His name and anything vaguely associated with it was cause for a news item with a photo and footage. Writing a piece or making a documentary about excellence in sport? Make sure there is reference to The Don. A brilliant new Indian cricketer? Prepare a radio broadcast or an internet item and be sure to include comparative figures for when they were both 12 years old, with photos. A popularity contest? Put Bradman in it to spice it up.

So is there a clue to his 'divinity' or everlasting fame here? Become famous at something — anything — and then shut yourself off from the world for the rest of your life so that the mystery about you grows? We saw it happen with former British Foreign Office spy and espionage fiction writer John le Carré. He finally cracked after 20 years as a ghost walking around Cornwall and Hampstead Heath and became a media 'personality' and 'raconteur'. He was human, after all, and enjoyed fame as much as anyone else.

But not Bradman. It took him decades to appear on commercial TV, first on Channel 7's *World of Sport* with Doug Ring in the 1960s and 30 years later on Channel 9. He hated the whole ordeal of exposure, made worse for him in 1996 at age 87 when still recovering from a stroke.

In one way, he was closer to 1930s screen actress Greta Garbo, who unwillingly created an enigma by 'retiring' youngish as a film star and stating she wanted to be alone. Yet Bradman did not retire from cricket. He was a key administrator (as a state and national selector and member of various boards) until he was well into his seventies. He could hardly be alone and without influence. But he still preferred the backroom to the media room. It wasn't that he couldn't handle the media. Nobody did it better when it came to a succinct thought, direct statement or good photo opportunity if it had to be had. It was just that he thought the media limelight was mostly superfluous, to be used as a vehicle for a message, not for ego-boosting.

Bradman chose stockbroking as his profession. At 26, he disappeared (when he wasn't playing cricket) into the confidential grey world of stocks and shares. If you wished to avoid media attention, it was as good as the morgue, and nearly as unpublic as the upper echelons of banking.

This attempt to become anonymous failed to give him privacy; instead, it enhanced his aura until his image was seen by many commentators to be akin to an Australian version of royalty.

There were differences. The British royals were more or less born to it. Bradman's elevation was due to substance. He earned it. The royals had to exude that doubtful trait of 'charm'. Bradman's charm was that apart from exhibiting all the normal niceties at public events, he was always transparently *him*. He seemed incapable of small talk — another reason for avoiding, if he could, functions, where small-talking champions aired their skills.

Perhaps the only royals he was really like were the Duke of Edinburgh, Prince Philip, and his daughter, and particularly the latter. Bradman, like Princess Anne, was capable of telling media people to 'naff off'. This endeared him (and her) to the media more. In a manner, this attitude embodied what intrinsic royal 'power' was about. The media were there to serve as a vehicle for a comment, not one to boost adulation. As long as this power was not abused, at least not in public, it would be maintained.

A key divergence here is the royals needed the media in order to survive. Without media support, or without a continual presence through the media, the British royals might have been reduced to smaller habitation and riding bikes, like their counterparts in Holland. Bradman never needed the media; it needed him.

*

Bradman avoided politics. Both major parties wanted him. Labor Party officials listened to his accent, took into account his roots and thought he was ideal for them. The conservatives looked at his two-decade job as an Adelaide stockbroker, noticed how all 'classes' of Australian society admired him, and claimed him as one of them. Bradman gave a decided No to becoming a politician, although he did flirt with being a diplomat — as Australia's high commissioner to the UK. By not becoming a political partisan, Bradman enhanced or at least maintained his image as the 'greatest Australian ever born'. Where, say, half the population might admire a Gough Whitlam, the other half for reasons of political sympathy would not. Thus Bradman by the end of the 20th century was far more universally popular — polls suggest at least twice as popular — as any politician from Billy Hughes to Bob Hawke and John Howard.

*

The substance beneath the mythology was created by the perfect coincidence between Bradman's incredible feats with the bat and Australia's decline into a miserable economic depression that lasted from the late 1920s to the mid-1930s, a seven-year period.

In 1927, Prime Minister Stanley Bruce moved his office to the new Federal Parliament in Canberra and announced that Australia 'was on the threshold of achievement'. This remark was a good argument for those critics who suggested politicians based in Canberra would be isolated from the real world. Yet when it was uttered, the world looked not rosy but not ugly to the average

Australian, who was unaware of the impact of overborrowing in London by Australia and especially New South Wales.

Bradman, at this moment of false national optimism, was unknown outside those following Grade cricket in Sydney. At 18, he had made his debut at the St George Club with a run-a-minute innings of 110 before being run out. Yet his first season (an aggregate of 289 runs at an average of 48.16 in six completed innings) was not world-shattering. The fact that he made 320 not out for his country team Bowral in 1927 was simply not newsworthy, even in Sydney.

In late October 1928, the price of wheat and wool (both then essential to Australia's prosperity) fell through the floor. Bruce's 'threshold of achievement' was suddenly, shockingly, the edge of an abyss. Right on cue, young Don, now 20, crashed a compelling double for NSW versus Queensland at Brisbane's Exhibition Ground, scoring 131 and 133 not out. In a flash, the unknown was being talked about as a prospect to make the Test team to play against Percy Chapman's English tourists. He made it and scored a century in his second Test.

In January 1929, a loan issue for the Commonwealth of Australia collapsed with 84 per cent of it not taken up but left in the hands of underwriters. Precisely at that moment, Bradman cracked a formidable 340 not out for NSW versus Victoria at Sydney, a feat that was reported on the front page of every Australian paper right up against items about the ramifications of the loan collapse.

In the Test arena, England was giving a weak Australian attack a walloping, mainly due to Wally Hammond with the bat (who scored a massive 905 runs in the 1928–29 Tests at an average of 113.12 from nine innings). The only consistent hope in the wake of this onslaught was Bradman's form. Spectators jammed all the grounds to see him and will him on against the English. He and Australia were at once the underdog.

Yet there was another dimension to the feeling among fans. English financiers were dictating to Australia how to manage its economy. This amounted to deflationary measures and an increase in the cost of borrowing — a squeeze that was putting enormous numbers of Australians out of work. The England players were symbolic of the pressure being put on the 'colonials'. They were heckled. Douglas Jardine, then a most accomplished bat, was a particular target. His harlequin cap and neck choker seemed to the fans to represent the image of the British establishment.

At the time of Bradman's 340 — a score that signalled this gifted newcomer would challenge Hammond as world champion run-plunderer — the economic crisis became personal for him. He lost his job at Deer Westbrook's Sydney real-estate office. It had been set up to sell housing estates, but this type of operation went flat in the sudden 'recession'. (It was yet to be labelled a Depression.) Bradman, who had no qualification apart from his real-estate work, felt the humiliating experience of being, not a creator of magic statistics, but an unprepossessing statistic himself. Unemployment in the first quarter of 1929 rose from 9.3 per cent to an alarming 12.1 per cent. Wherever Bradman went around Sydney, he saw men out of work and food lines everywhere. It worried him. But he was fortunate that Mick Simmons' sports store employed him. He hated the job of chief front-of-shop glad-hander, but was grateful for work. It took the pressure off.

He celebrated by being the match-winner against England with 123 and 37 not out in the Fifth Test at Melbourne. The crowd was near hysterical at this result. For a few precious days, the nation could submerge the mental anguish over the bleak immediate future and celebrate. England had been defeated. Bradman was proving the champion the fans had predicted (and prayed) he would be. By the end of the series, only Hammond had performed better.

Through 1929, the recession deteriorated into the Great Depression, triggered by the Wall Street Crash. Wool and wheat prices fell to rock bottom. Overseas loans from England, the monetary lifeblood of an overextended nation, evaporated. A countrywide drought added an uncontrollable physical element to the deplorable conditions in the country.

At the beginning of the 1929–30 season, Australia's export revenues were plummeting. Half of it (heading for under 100 million pounds) would be used to service foreign debt, which meant that much less was available for loans. The banks restricted the amount of money on offer. Interest rates climbed. Taxes were imposed on non-essential items, like cricket bats and tennis racquets. The squeeze threatened Mick Simmons. Bradman wondered if he would be out of work again.

Instead of panicking, he went out and made runs. Fans flocked even to Second-Grade games in the bush to see him. Saturday afternoons at St George were a lockout. So were Shield games. He cranked up for First-Class matches, including 157 against a touring Marylebone Cricket Club side. Then he smashed a breathtaking double hundred, and a century, in the trial game, to decide the team for the 1930 Ashes tour of England. It was exhilarating.

The fans — the masses of people from every walk of life who filled arenas around the country — felt somehow symbiotically linked to this unassuming youthful new champion. They had cheered for him before he had been proven at the highest level, screamed when he was dropped from the Test side for one game, applauded as he caught up with their dreams. Everyone from battlers to bankers felt a part of his rise and rise. They looked in the mirror and saw a bit of hope, a reflection of Bradman in all of them. They had willed him on, prayed for him and talked up what he would do in England in the upcoming 1930 Ashes. Figures and averages began to spill onto the sports pages in the country, in Sydney and across the nation. In five categories of the game in 1929–30 from Second Grade to First Class, Bradman was averaging more than a hundred every time he batted. No one had done anything like this, not even the great Victor Trumper nor the English champion W.G. Grace. In a desperate, dispiriting summer, here was someone to take the collective mind off the continual bad news as businesses crashed, farmers committed suicide and dole lines stretched around the blocks in every city.

And finally, in early January 1930, just as everyone dreaded entering another fearful year of economic malaise, he performed in such a way that it put him in a dimension all his own. The location was Sydney; the opponents Queensland. Bradman smashed and accumulated 452 not out in 415 minutes.

It was an act of sporting obliteration at once both brutal and poetic; the highest score by anyone anywhere in First-Class cricket. This innings was beyond any dream by anyone except the performer himself. More importantly, it was a show that inspired and made everyone who saw it, or read or heard about it, proud that one of their own, a country kid at that, could reach such perfection. He didn't give a chance, not one in just under seven hours of precision carving-up of the opposition. What's more, he wanted to go on to 600. He was miffed that his skipper, Alan Kippax, declared when he was setting himself to do it. Bradman's hunger was mindboggling, his powers of concentration as high as a human could get them, and his stamina formidable.

*

Australians began to speculate seriously now that Bradman might just challenge the might of England in their own backyard. And while this was being discussed in innumerable pubs, churches, businesses, homes and schools, the economic disaster subsuming the country was momentarily, here and there, forgotten. At one of the lowest points in a fledgling nation's short history, he was a ray of hope. There was nothing else, certainly not on a national, unifying level, that could deliver the same.

When Bradman reached England for the first time, those moments of distraction fused into a long-running drama for Australia as millions followed the fortunes of Bill Woodfull's team. They read with anger that, despite Bradman opening the tour under the cathedral at Worcester with a big double hundred,

English critics were applying psychological warfare tactics by suggesting the down-under hero was flawed in his batting technique. Australian indignation was reserved more for this than the squalor of the now well-set Depression.

Bradman, aware of but unaffected by praise or attacks, launched on and on. At The Oval against Surrey, he silenced one of his biggest critics, the county's captain, Percy Fender, by making 252 not out in a dazzling 290 minutes. Only the rain stopped Bradman going on to 400. It was a portent of things to come.

And they came in a torrent of run-making that may never be bettered in Test cricket. He scored 974 runs from seven innings at an average of 139.14. It was a performance that more or less matched, say, the combined Test averages of Ian Chappell, Neil Harvey and Stan McCabe, or in another instance, Arthur Morris, Lindsay Hassett and Bill Ponsford. Instead of his career superiority of being nearly twice as good statistically as the rest of the greats of the game, he was, in that one glorious English summer, worth three top batsmen from any era.

In that huge aggregate, he hit four different kinds of innings that could truly be called unsurpassable exhibitions of each batting 'genre'. In the first Test at Trent Bridge, he hit a fighting 131 in 260 minutes, which was hailed as one of the finest ever rear-guard performances in the final, uphill innings of a Test (lost by Australia). In the Second Test at Lord's, he hit 254 in 320 minutes. Bradman himself claimed it as technically the best innings he ever played. In the Fourth Test at Leeds, he scored 334 — 309 of them in a day, a feat yet to be equalled in Test history. Its supremacy was in the speed of accumulation — the fastest first-day pre-lunch century ever, and 220 by tea. At The Oval, he hit a series-winning 232 — a pressure knock on a difficult wicket against a strong attack that included a hostile Harold Larwood.

At the precise moment in July 1930 that he was reaching the heights with that triple hundred, Sir Otto Niemeyer, a director of the Bank of England, was in Australia advising its leaders to 'balance its budgets', stop raising loans and cut back on expenditure on public works. This was accepted in a supine way by the Australian establishment, including James Scullin's ruling Labor government. It led to a further spiral into the Depression's void.

Bradman came home the conquering hero and gave the local collective psyche an immeasurable boost, especially as Otto Niemeyer and his English banker and financier companions were increasingly blamed (over the next few years) for the nation's plight.

Right at the depth of the Depression, Bradman had dispensed hope, pride and inspiration. He had also humiliated the rulers of the British Empire, something that no other foreigner, in peace or wartime, had been able to do in several hundred years.

CHAPTER 5

My First-hand Experience of Bradman the Competitor

Discussions over the Bradman biography didn't end with the review of the manuscript. Towards the end of 1995, I visited the Bradmans to show them my choice for the book's front cover. Lady Bradman liked it. I had chosen a non-clichéd shot of him at age 20, waiting to bat in a Shield game for NSW in which he scored a triple century. His casual cross-legged stance and enigmatic gaze spelled both cool determination and pensiveness. It was a look that meant despair and disaster for a thousand bowlers. I judged it out of 1500 photos as the most telling portrait of Bradman, the great competitor.

We were in the billiards room that he built into the house in 1934. Bradman didn't really react to the photo. He asked me if I played billiards.

'I've only played a few times,' I replied. 'I'm not good.'

'Doesn't matter,' Bradman said, reaching for cues to chalk.

'I'm really hopeless,' I protested, and then related a story of how I had been having tennis lessons at London's Queen's Club in 1984. American champion John McEnroe walked into the locker rooms and struck up a conversation. Discovering I was Australian, he asked: 'Would you like to have a game? My practice partner has not turned up.'

I told him I was there to receive tennis lessons and I was not really up to giving him any sort of game.

'Aw, c'mon,' McEnroe said, 'all Aussies play tennis.'

'No, really. You wouldn't get a decent game out of me.'

McEnroe shrugged and walked out of the locker room.

About 15 minutes later, I was on the court with my coach, a Pakistani female pro. McEnroe strolled past with someone he'd found to have a hit with. He called out: 'Hey, Roland, I see what you mean!'

As I related this to Bradman, he had already placed a cue in my hand. He wasn't interested. He was already in competition mode. And this was where he thrived, in a game with someone to beat, even obliterate if possible. In this case, it was possible. It would surely be Bradman versus Bradman, and I had to play the man who had beaten the world's greatest ever billiards player, Australian Walter Lindrum. Bradman proceeded to win three games with ease, and twice pocketed two balls with one shot.

I watched in awe as he demonstrated his uncanny skills. He focused so hard that I limited my observations to 'Shot!' on innumerable occasions. I was glad he insisted on the game. I was able to witness two of the factors that made Bradman stand out as the greatest sportsman of the 20th century — his incredible hand–eye coordination and his power of concentration. I liked the way he kept going regardless of the ineptness of the 'competition'. That was the way he played cricket and all sports. He did not slacken off and toy with any opposition. He gave them the highest respect by crushing them. It wasn't the way everyone played sport, but it was Bradman's way. He performed for the enjoyment too, but it centred on winning.

*

Bradman's reticence when he saw my choice of front-cover image became clear when the book's editor at Pan Macmillan, Amanda Hemmings, sent him a copy of the proposed cover. I unwisely forgot to phone him to talk about it. Bradman wrote to Hemmings to complain about the chosen photo, saying that his pads needed a clean-up, he was wearing a NSW jacket and he appeared 'gloomy'.

I rang Don and explained my choice, saying his pads could be air-brushed. Further, the fact that he was wearing a NSW blazer was irrelevant. Everyone who knew his name associated it first with representing Australia. (I suspected that he would rather be associated with South Australia than NSW.) I argued that rather than gloomy, he looked determined.

Having had many discussions with him, I realised he was unconvinced.

'What's more, the editor said you look sexy,' I said as a last resort.

'She's 50 years too late,' he quipped. It was the argument-breaker. The photo was in. That wry wit, which kept him sane through an eternity of adulation and attacks, was always lurking.

*

Early in November 1995, Jessie's leukaemia, which she had lived with for some time, worsened. Bradman wrote several concerned letters to me. I decided not to bother him with news about the book, but a week later I realised that Bradman was interested in what kind of publicity it generated.

He sent me a note: 'A friend told me he heard your interview with Philip Satchell [ABC Radio Adelaide]. Regrettably I missed it. But I am told you handled Satchell with aplomb and put him in his place. I must confess he is not one of my favourite interviewers.'

After that, I sent him reviews, good and bad.

Bradman responded to one less-than-flattering review: 'Any fool can criticise, and many do. I am surprised that it has been so poorly written. In the days of [English commentators] Robertson-Glasgow and Cardus one could be carved up with style and panache. They could write ... In varying degrees I have been taking it on the chin for over 60 years. It's not funny.'

There was always the odd miserable hack willing to make a spurious attack on The Don. A couple of them made 'nice little earners' over decades attacking him. They would usually be published. After all, he was the tallest poppy Australia ever had. Despite 'taking it on the chin', there were times when

45

Bradman hit back. Former Fairfax executive Bob Mansfield was once told by Bradman to fire the writer of a pernicious piece. Mansfield agreed that the article was bad and said he would have obliged him if he could. But the writer didn't work for Fairfax any more.

Around Christmas 1995, Bradman had a stroke. He didn't tell me at first. But his writing was shaky. That definitive signature was barely recognisable. Within two months, he was fighting to come to terms with the physical setback: 'I am afraid the publicity surrounding the book has brought an avalanche of requests for signatures and other things but I am immune because it has been going on for 50 years. Currently the big problem is of course my stroke which has prevented me attending to mail etc. but thankfully I've had good secretarial support.

'Worse than this however is the terrible worry over Jessie. She is standing up to her chemo remarkably but it is cruel and if this is the price she has to pay for keeping alive one wonders if it is worthwhile. Old age is not funny.'

*

I had offered Bradman copies of the biography. At first he said he didn't need any, but then he wrote to ask me if he could have five to give to friends as Christmas presents.

'I'd appreciate it if you signed them,' he wrote.

Soon afterwards I was in Adelaide and delivered the books in person. I was about to write my signature on an early blank page, when he stopped me.

'What are you writing it there for?' he asked. 'You're an author, aren't you? You should always write it on the title page.'

Chastened, I did so and have never again signed a book on other than the title page, except for one occasion when a woman insisted I sign on the very first page. 'Write something funny,' she ordered.

I obliged, writing 'something funny' with my signature underneath.

'That's not funny,' she said grimly.

I had to agree.

CHAPTER 6

Fender Bender

Bradman's genius as a cricketer, and his universal appeal in a time when heroes were much needed during the Great Depression, elevated him to an unassailable position in the pantheon of Australia's famous. His dignified, calm-in-any-crisis demeanour, based on steely resolve, determination and a capacity for the big match-winning effort, magnified an image that became embedded in the national psyche. While General John Monash was a far more *important* figure in the nation's history, people never actually witnessed him 'winning'. Monash had excelled in the ultimate combat of war, yet it was not 'combat' like that on the pitch in front of packed crowds. Spectators *saw* Bradman's brilliance. They read about it in the press and heard about it on the radio; they rejoiced in his ability to destroy the XI representing the mother country, the United

Kingdom, then still the hub of the most powerful empire on earth.

*

Monash himself had known the value of a sporting hero to his soldiers. His Australian Army took on 39 German divisions — one million enemy soldiers — in the last 100 days of the war and defeated every one of them. When he and his digger army began to win every battle, Monash, a keen amateur psychologist and an early follower of Sigmund Freud, said: 'I fed them on victory.'

This was no idle, chest-beating phraseology by a military martinet. He knew the psyche of his men. They ate, drank and slept competition. They bet on anything from horse races to scorpion fights in the desert sands during the Middle East Theatre. Winning was everything. There were no second prizes in the heroics of Australian fighting males, more than 300,000 of them, in the 1914–18 conflict. Sporting analogies were what they knew and understood.

Even though Bradman did not perform at his peak until a decade after World War I, his name would be used as a military code for strength and invincibility in the next terrible conflict, World War II.

*

In the Depression years of the late 1920s and first half of the 1930s, Bradman was someone the public could rely on to entertain them, whether at Test, state or local club level. Even at the latter, the crowds were too big for the grounds he played at. A Kensington Park local, Doug Bigelow, told me in 1995 of Saturday afternoons at the grounds when Bradman was playing at the Kensington Oval: 'The word would get around that Bradman was batting and 5000 or 6000 fans would turn up. Many could not get a look in and there would be literally thousands wandering the streets. He would get a score; he averaged nearly 90 even in club games ... and when he got out, everyone would go home! I stayed. I was a kid and felt sorry for the other batsmen!'

Even people with scant interest in cricket, like my father, then aged 13, joined the throng at the MCG to see Bradman perform against England during the Bodyline series.

Bradman's appeal was universal. It was the same in England on every Ashes tour. In the UK in 1948, when he turned 40 and was past his best, counties begged him to play against them. His appearance often meant the difference of a season's profit or loss for the county concerned.

In Australia in the early 1930s, punters bet on the grand horse Phar Lap for a near-certain win. Bradman was an even surer bet to entertain, and his career lasted two decades at the top (excluding World War II, which robbed him of five or six years at his peak).

*

After the first few interview sessions in the lounge room, we would chat in the upstairs study. I would get to Adelaide early and we would work through the morning and into the afternoon for a five- to six-hour stint. I used a tape recorder for most interviews, but still took notes.

Once during the interviews for the biography, I mentioned to him the old chestnut, almost certainly apocryphal, about the English coach who abused a school boy for the 'ugly' way he held a bat.

'But that's the way Don Bradman does it,' the boy retorted.

The coach was cornered, but managed to respond: 'Well, just think of how many more runs Bradman would have made had he held the bat the right way!'

Bradman smiled. 'That joke emerged in 1930 in England,' he said, 'when I was criticised for my alleged unorthodoxy by Percy Fender.'

Fender, a former England player who was still playing county cricket as captain of Surrey, was one of the best tacticians and most knowledgeable cricketers of the era. During the 1928–29 Ashes in Australia, he covered the Ashes as a journalist and rebuked Bradman for his inventive batting and unorthodox style, saying he would fail in England as a result. Fender reckoned the youthful Australian was formidable on quick, bouncy wickets, judging him a fine hooker and cutter. But on slower English wickets, where the ball moved around in a heavier atmosphere brought on by cloud and smog, he would be found wanting.

Bradman had made a more than promising debut in Test cricket with two centuries in four Tests at an average of 66. English observers saw it as possibly a portent of things to come. They wished to unsettle his mind before he established himself.

The young Australian had a score to settle when he toured the UK in 1930.

*

When Bradman toured England in 1930 and began piling on the centuries and doubles, Fender modified his appraisal, conceding that Bradman was 'brilliant' at scoring yet 'unsound' in his technique.

Fender noted that Bradman 'did not correct mistakes or look as if he were trying to'. He kept making the adverse remarks early in the season in which Bradman rushed towards the much-vaunted 1000 runs before the end of May. The confrontation between these two came at London's The Oval under the gasometer on Saturday, 24 May 1930, in a game between the Australians and Surrey. By this time, Bradman had notched 670 runs at 111.66 per innings. It was a flying start to a season, but Fender had kept carping.

I asked Bradman for his mindset in that game.

'There have always been psychological games before series commence,' he replied. 'British reporters were out to unsettle us any way they could. Fender was the chief offender.'

'You wanted to make a point?'

'After his last comment, I thought it best not to make any mistakes against Surrey.' (Here, again I wondered if this was the serious or droll Bradman.)

'Were you aware of this game on the schedule?'

'Not more than any of the other games. Remember, I had 36 innings [that season]. Some of the matches were literally back to back.'

'But the press was making something of the confrontation. Journalists were suggesting you were out for revenge.'

'Not revenge. I'm not sure it [the approach Bradman had] was any more than the other big games against the counties, particularly Yorkshire.'

By contrast, Fender was determined to stop the little Aussie battler in his tracks.

*

Bradman strode across the field to the pitch. There were no shoulder rolls, jumps, runs or stretches. The crowd had packed into The Oval for a glimpse of this new batting phenomenon. Bradman took block and surveyed the field. Fender called over Douglas Jardine and fast bowler MJC Allom for a three-way tête-à-tête. Bradman dropped to his haunches as if to register impatience, then he stood, cross-legged, and watched Fender move in two fielders close on the leg side.

'You had a shaky start?' I asked Bradman.

'I played and missed several times, yes.'

'You were nervous?'

'No.'

'Keyed-up? Toey?'

'No. I never had nerves when a game got underway.'

'Was there stress in the build-up before games like that?'

'No time for that. As I said, we moved from one town or city to the next.'

Bradman made a cautious 50 in 90 minutes, slow for him. He stepped up the pace, striking the next 50 in 50 minutes. He had driven Fender himself out of the attack with fours either side of the wicket in one over. Neither Fender nor Jardine clapped Bradman's hundred.

As Allom turned to run, the umpire's arm went up to stop him. The cheeky little bastard from down under was taking block again and making Surrey *wait for him*. Bradman was just 21 years of age and acting as if he were a professional in his mid-thirties against an old foe. It was a signal of things to come.

He hammered Fender out of the attack for a second time. At tea, the whippersnapper was 142 not out, having struck 114 between lunch and tea, his first century in a session for the tour. Bradman had won the day and settled the argument about his ability.

Ashen-faced, Fender rang the changes after tea as he had in the previous session, but to no avail.

'Was this one of your more satisfying performances?' I asked Bradman.

'I had not actually given a chance, so it was satisfying, yes.'

'You wanted to rub Fender's face in it?'

'I wanted the biggest score I could manage.'

'Crushing an opponent sends a message?'

'It shows respect to the other party. Throwing your wicket away was never an option in circumstances like that.'

Bradman moved in for the kill, cutting like a master surgeon in a hurry, but always with clinical control. The Surrey bowlers kept feeding him outside off-stump, waiting for him to tire and mistime one. But he had reached a somehow controlled fever-pitch at the crease. He was still hungry. This was a massive display. No balls were now reaching the keeper. Bradman was flaying the bowling, but still with his strong technique intact. In this session, he displayed every major stroke in the cricket manual and some that were not. But whatever he did, he meant. All Allom, Jardine and Fender could do was look on in silent awe. Bradman represented a new dimension in the game, and they were watching its blossoming.

And Fender? He seemed to do a lot more leather-chasing than the other fielders. Many witnesses believed Bradman was sliding balls past him intentionally, making the fatigued skipper run and puff. Was it true or an optical illusion brought on by Fender's continued abuse of the newcomer? Bradman was capable of such a cricket 'lesson'. He had remained quiet in response to all critics (and would remain so over the decades). His reply came in the form of magnificent batting displays, and this answer to Fender was one for the ages.

But did he purposely set out to embarrass Fender in the field?

'No,' Bradman said, 'it's simply not true. I was concentrating on making runs as fast as possible without concern for any particular fielder.'

'But when you were established and into your second hundred runs [which took just 80 minutes], several reporters suggested ...'

'No. Think of the situation. I was a junior member of the team. Fender was a senior England player and captain of Surrey. I'd never even spoken to him. Only the captains spoke to each other in those days. There was no fraternising after the game as there is now.'

'So the only way to shove back his criticism at him, make a fool of him, if you like, was to do it with the bat? You have said that most of your last hundred was off Fender …'

'Well, as I said earlier, it was not revenge. If I concerned myself with answering critics, I'd have been exhausted! I just went out to do my best. On that day, I had the good fortune to strike form on a good wicket.'

When Bradman passed 150, the crowd applauded. Fender and Jardine examined their boots or gazed at the looming gasometer next to the ground — anywhere but at the young Australian. They did not clap. At 200, many in the crowd stood and applauded. Fender and Jardine again did not react. When Bradman reached 252 not out, it rained a half-hour before stumps. Fender hurried off the field without even a look of acknowledgement at his diminutive conqueror, who had delivered the Surreyman his biggest humiliation in a decade as skipper. The crowd cheered. Some spectators ran onto the field to congratulate Bradman, but Jardine strolled past as if nothing had happened.

'Looking back on that innings, what comes to mind?' I asked Bradman.

'The fact that I could not go on to at least a triple hundred,' he replied with his trademark half-grin. 'The rain caused the game to be abandoned.'

*

Bradman went on to the huge tally of 2960 First-Class runs in England in 1930. His 974 in the Ashes series is likely to fall at some point if the five-day Test format is retained. The 2960 in a First-Class season by a tourist anywhere, and his aggregate of 4368 runs in a calendar year (1930), at an average of around 100 an innings, are unlikely to be surpassed.

And Percy Fender? He never criticised Bradman in public again after the Surrey match. But the embarrassment at Bradman's batting retort would not be forgotten by him or Douglas Jardine.

CHAPTER 7

A Philosophic View

Bradman's ability to make big scores at will, and on average with twice the capacity of the best of the rest in history, has been discussed by everyone interested in cricket, including kings and philosophers. Brian O'Shaughnessy, an Australian expatriate who was regarded as one of England's best and most radical modern philosophers, dwelled on Bradman in his book *Consciousness and the World* when examining human skills, and the power we have over our limbs to achieve goals using those skills. He said: 'I was using Sir Donald as an example in which the distinction was almost negated — so great did his power of choice seem to be.'

In his book, the philosopher noted:

The great batsman Donald Bradman signalled his arrival in England, in 1930, 1934, 1938, with innings of 236, 206,

258; and at the age of thirty nine in 1948 relented to the extent of notching a mere 107. Each of these innings were played at Worcester, they were the first first-class innings in each tour, and he made four tours in all. And yet cricket is supposedly noteworthy for its marvellous 'uncertainty'! But this was the man who hit over 300 in a day in a Test match against the truly great bowling of Larwood and Tate, and without taking any risks. And it was he of whom Constantine wrote, on witnessing his 254 in the Lord's Test Match in 1930: 'it was like an angel batting'. Indeed, it was Bradman who said of McCabe, who played three innings of genius in Test Matches, that he had the impression that he 'played beyond his means'. And it is entirely credible to claim that he did, and that Bradman did not do this. After all, we are talking surely of the greatest sportsman who ever lived.

O'Shaughnessy here touched on the distinctions Bradman had over other leaders and batsmen, related to his willpower, determination and single-mindedness.

Along with O'Shaughnessy's philosophical analysis, I would add other characteristics that set Bradman apart: his own expressed philosophy; an exceptional innate pragmatic psychology; a strong lateral thinking capacity; courage; technique; knowledge of the game; natural athleticism; leadership skills; and intelligence. Woven together, they provide at least part of the answer to Don Bradman's sporting uniqueness and genius.

During long interviews of up to eight hours, he never wavered, or seemed to tire. The answers were sometimes long and layered, but never complicated, and I can't recall an 'um' or an 'arh' to punctuate them. Our discussions occurred when he was in his late eighties. It wasn't difficult to imagine what he was like when concentrating at anything — including batting — from age 11 to 40. Yet he differed from other batsmen like Geoffrey Boycott, Len Hutton, Ken Barrington and Bill Lawry, all outstanding with touches of brilliance, who could stay at the crease for long periods, minimising mistakes. Bradman pulsated, pushed on and accelerated in his mammoth scores, whereas these four outstanding players, with their faultless, textbook techniques, more often than not simply accumulated runs. Bradman was as error-conscious as anyone who ever played the game and he measured his grand performances by the least number of batting mistakes, but always at an attacking rate.

His aim always was to win and in the most entertaining way possible. This approach dictated his overriding thoughts on the game. Cricketers must give the paying public the best value for money possible. Everything must be done to keep fans coming through the gates, especially in the modern era where there is so much competition for people's attention every minute from other sports and entertainment on TV, radio and the internet. It is no wonder that he loved watching Garry Sobers, Shane Warne and Adam Gilchrist. (In more recent years, he would have enjoyed the power and brilliance of Steve Smith, David Warner and Virat Kohli.)

*

Bradman's modest manner has been noted by all those who observed him at close quarters. I was aware of it in the late 1990s, when Bradman was in his nineties. Sixty-five years earlier, when Bradman was in his twenties, the English journalist William Pollock noted: 'He is not at all swell-headed. On the contrary he has almost a horror of saying or doing anything that might lead people to say that he is conceited or putting on side. He was very nearly fastidiously sensitive in this manner.'

Evidence of this innate lack of self-regard and arrogance is documented in all his writings. In his autobiography *Farewell to Cricket*, he wrote of his magnificent innings at Leeds in 1930: 'The match was memorable because of my own score of 334, at that time a world record score in Test cricket, a feat later to be excelled by Leonard Hutton.'

Apart from a couple of extra lines about him judging it not as good as his previous one at Lord's, that was it.

In his later published tour diary, he said: 'Archie [Jackson] is out for 1. I followed and at stumps was 309 not out, breaking the previous highest score in Anglo-Australian Tests. Reached my 2000 runs for the season. To hotel in the evening for dinner and wrote letters, thence to bed.'

Perchance to dream about the day? I doubt it. Bradman would be moving on to the next challenge in his reverie. So there it was. The best one day's batting in Test history reduced to a line or two, by an executioner more interested in the mechanics of his performance than a measure of greatness. Bradman was certainly no narcissist like some of his major critics, underachievers by comparison in terms of the game itself. He was neither in love with his efforts or his words about them. Such self-description, enshrined in his diaries, makes the laconic characters played by actor Clint Eastwood seem garrulous by comparison.

*

We did actually talk about Bradman's dreams. In 1995, when discussing his first-ever Ashes century in England in 1930, he said: 'I still have nightmares about it.'

He was referring to how he got out on the last day of the match at Trent Bridge, Nottingham. Australia reached 229 after a stand of 77 but then McCabe was caught for a forceful 49. Australia was four wickets down. At 267 Bradman's mate Walter Robbins came on to bowl leg-spin. Australia was now just 113 short of victory, with Bradman in control.

Then *quelle horreur*! Robins, workmanlike spinner rather than a great one, bowled the ball of his life; the one he would dine out on forever. It was a wrong'un, the ball that spins from right to left to the right-hander, the opposite to the regular leg-break. Bradman was caught, like not a rabbit but a kangaroo, in the headlights of a lorry, and bowled, off-stump, the delivery of which Shane Warne would be justly proud, given the moment and the opponent. Bradman, known for giving keepers nothing to do because he hit everything, did not play a shot.

'It was the only time in my career that I got out not playing a shot,' Bradman told me.

It was a delivery in a million, for a batsman in a billion.

On a comparatively minute scale, I was dismissed leg before wicket (LBW) to a wrong'un from Melbourne Grammar leg-spinner and future district player David Beer in a school match in 1965, after struggling like a fish out of water. While it didn't bring nightmares, it gave me a few daymares. I had my heart set on a century and fell 96 short. I felt comforted by Bradman's discomfort. He too was nagged for a long time by a mis-stroke to a tweaker and it made the great man accessible. He too was tormented by failure.

This reminded me of the genius John Monash's own fallibility. He failed Latin at university and school, whereas I scored 99.5 in my final Latin exam at school. Admittedly that score was out of 200, and my compassionate teacher, Mr Walker, gave me a pass. But it gave me a sliver of access to Monash's gigantic intellect and mind.

This satisfaction recalled the adage espoused by British prime minister Benjamin Disraeli: 'The failures of great people are the consolation of dunces.'

My disappointment in that 1965 school match was caused by, first, a need to score runs for my own glory, with thoughts about victory for my school a close second. Bradman's reason for being plagued so much for so long was more admirable.

'We could have won,' he said with mild indignation at my question of why his dismissal had upset him so much.

This was what had tortured him for so long. *He could have won another Ashes Test for Australia.* Bradman felt he had made such an egregious error in not picking the wrong'un that he had let down his team, his nation and himself.

CHAPTER 8

The Red Baron

Several of the cricket events and moments Bradman and I discussed needed face-to-face interviews. This was sometimes because we had to check facts in *Wisden* and other archives. On other occasions, one or both of us thought the issue was important enough for a meeting. For instance, Bradman thought the 1948 tour needed it; I believed Bodyline needed closer examination.

Bodyline was a tactic designed by England captain Douglas Jardine in order to cripple Bradman's scoring by delivering short balls at the head and torso rather than to the wicket. The method was within the rules, but well outside the spirit of the game. It caused the biggest upheaval in the history of cricket.

We discussed going in search of Bodyline's roots. I flew to Adelaide and we went through the *Wisden* yearbooks dating back to 1924. The phone rang, and Jessie reported from downstairs: 'Don, it's Paul Keating's secretary on the line. He wants to chat.'

Bradman, his eyes on an open *Wisden*, replied: 'Tell him to call back tomorrow at 2 p.m. please.'

I smiled to myself. Bradman would not be diverted from his current endeavour. I suspect only Queen Elizabeth II could have broken his concentration.

We continued to probe for the first recorded instance of Bodyline; or, to be more exact, the first time an articulate 'victim' had experienced it. That victim was Nathaniel Mayer Victor Rothschild, the Third Baron, whom I had named in my book *The Fifth Man* as one of the top seven KGB-recruited British double agents. (Rothschild's double agency was in 2018 verified by KGB documents.)

Rothschild was a man of many parts. According to US analysis, he had the highest-recorded IQ in tests that were given to leading personnel from the US, UK, France and Germany during World War II. It stood at an immodest 184. Not surprisingly, he was a polymath. He was the scion of the grand banking family of Europe, but that was just the tip of his interests, which covered biology, history, nuclear energy and politics. It helped that Bradman had read my book on the brilliant British baron. It gave him an extra pep in his research when I told him that Rothschild had been pulverised by a Bodyline attack.

We found the record of the county game in 1929 when the 18-year-old Rothschild, still at Harrow School and playing for Northamptonshire, faced up to the Nottingham speedsters, ex-miners Harold Larwood and Bill Voce. Having located the date of the match, we were then able to research newspaper reports of the game, which added to my interview with Rothschild's sister, Miriam, who was able to pass on some first-hand experience of the game.

Rothschild survived a torrid first over of bouncers from left-arm Voce, who had five fielders crouched close to the wicket, waiting like vultures for a catch. Rothschild had three choices when Voce charged at him: duck and risk being hit; fend off the ball, which meant a probable catch to one of the vultures; or attempt an aggressive counter-stroke, usually the hook. This again risked him being hit, or caught by two fielders on the boundary.

Somehow, the novice batsman had negotiated the over without being struck. Now he had to face Larwood, England's fastest bowler, who could deliver at around 160 km/h. He was an even greater intimidator using the same tactic, which relied on accurate deliveries aimed at the left of the batsman (on leg-stump) and lifting sharply into the body. There was nowhere to hide from the red leather missile.

Showing raw courage, Rothschild took thumps on the chest and shoulder, rather than pop up a catch. He lasted an hour and scored 36 before succumbing to the barrage, which left him with a mosaic of multi-coloured welts and imprints from the ball's raised stitching. When a teammate asked the shaken Rothschild what he thought of the tactic — then called 'fast leg theory' — he replied ruefully: 'You mean fast, leg, chest and head theory.'

'I wonder if Harold had a crystal ball,' Bradman quipped during this discussion.

I asked for clarification.

'Perhaps they knew that Victor would be a traitor ...'

I laughed and replied: 'No, I reckon those men from the pits just wanted to knock around, legitimately, a very rich member of the British upper class. It was thuggish behaviour and they got away with it.'

In that August 1929 county game, Larwood and Voce collected 15 wickets in the first recorded sustained use of the tactic that came to be known as Bodyline. Notts skipper Arthur Carr did not call on it more than a few times a season. This avoided the game's then ruling body, the Marylebone Cricket Club (MCC), taking action against it, despite Rothschild protesting in writing.

Circumstances changed in 1930. The 21-year-old Bradman carved up English bowlers in the lead-up to the Ashes series. He targeted Larwood in the Tests and derailed the Nottingham Express. His paltry four wickets cost him 73 runs apiece. Against all odds, Australia took the Ashes and Bradman's dominance humiliated the seat of Empire. It had to strike back. But how?

The MCC wished to appoint a new England captain who did not carry the scars of 1930. It used Fender and former Test skipper Plum Warner (the Oxford University-educated son of the former attorney-general of Trinidad) to try to persuade Douglas Jardine (an Oxford-educated lawyer) to lead England on the next Ashes tour down under. In May 1932, these three establishment figures met for lunch at Lord's to discuss the England captaincy and the Bradman issue. The telephone numbers Bradman scored in Tests against the West Indies and South Africa in the Australian summers of 1930–31 and 1931–32 were demoralising.

The sharp, aquiline-featured Jardine thought Bradman 'could score a thousand in a series' on Australia's harder pitches.

Warner, who would manage the 1932–33 tour, offered Jardine the leadership. Jardine declined, saying he had 'better things to do in the winter than suffer the heat, flies and ill-humoured crowds'. Warner then enlisted Jardine's father, who knew much about heat, flies and crowds. MR Jardine was the former advocate general of Bombay. He persuaded his son to do his duty 'for King and Country' and lead the tour.

The new skipper consulted Arthur Carr, who explained that fast leg theory should be used as a shock rather than a stock tactic. They arranged a meeting with Larwood and Voce in London in August 1932. Jardine found Larwood confident he could 'bowl on the leg-stump and make the ball come up into the body so that Bradman had to play his shots to leg'. His accuracy had improved and his stamina was good.

Larwood recalled Bradman 'flinching' when hit at The Oval in the final Test of the 1930 series. It made no difference that Bradman had been struck on the forearm in difficult conditions while carving out a brilliant 98 in the pre-lunch session en route to a series-winning 232. The 'flinch' would be Jardine's whispered justification for the attack on him.

CHAPTER 9

Jardine's Vicious, Brilliant Tactics

While Bradman's demise was being plotted, he was on a honeymoon cum cricket tour with his wife, Jessie, in North America, sightseeing, meeting Babe Ruth the champion baseballer, and Hollywood stars such as Clark Gable, Jean Harlow, Boris Karloff and Leslie Howard. After 49 matches in 76 days, in which he scored 3779 runs at an average of 102.1, Bradman returned to Australia fatigued and dogged by a mystery illness. One contributing factor here was the state of his teeth, which were in a poor condition due to his own neglect, not an unusual situation in that era. They were giving him much agony at the start of the 1932–33 season. He kept it quiet, hoping that the pain could be managed through the summer.

On top of this, a dispute with the Australian Board of Control made it uncertain Bradman would be a starter in the Ashes series.

Bradman had a contract to write for Kerry Packer's grandfather Clyde Packer, who owned the Sydney *Sun* newspaper. The Cricket Board didn't mind him commentating on Sydney's 2UE radio for a neat thousand pounds a year, enough to build a two-storey home in a major capital city. Apparently, it was unconcerned with his words disappearing into the ether, a quarter of a century before television in Australia. But words on paper and circulated to a wide audience was too much. Bradman was ordered to desist.

'I had a contract and that was it,' he told me. 'I would honour it, even if it meant not playing in the series.'

To Bradman, his word was his bond, and his signature on a contract was binding.

It hung over his head when he travelled to Perth in October 1932 to play in a 'Combined Australian XI' against England. Jardine didn't select his three exponents of fast leg theory — Larwood, Voce and Yorkshire's Bill Bowes. The Australians were caught on a sticky wicket. The left-arm Yorkshire spinner Hedley Verity dismissed Bradman twice cheaply and England won easily. Jardine now had the advantage over the opposition, even before his grand plan was revealed.

He noted The Don's demeanour. Gone was the youthful self-confidence of England in 1930. He was underweight as a result of his illness and teeth problem, and tentative. The crush of expectations on Bradman, the weariness after his American trip, and the illness that no doctor could diagnose were having an effect on his mental and physical state.

His contractual tangles, however, were eventually resolved. Clyde Packer told him: 'You must play, Don.'

'You can force me to write,' Bradman replied, 'but there is nothing in the contract which forces me to play.'

'Well, Don, we are asking you to forget writing for the time being.'

'If you put it that way, I will accept and play. But I want it understood that at any time I am prepared to give up playing and honour my contract with you.'

Clyde Packer released him from his agreement.

'Would you have stood out of the series?' I asked. 'Or was it bluff?'

'I would stick by my principles. I was recently married and without a proper job. I needed the income.'

*

Prior to England's next encounter with Bradman and the rest of the Australian XI in Melbourne in mid-November, Jardine played up Verity's importance, suggesting the spinner was his wildcard for the Ashes, but later surprised everyone by omitting him and selecting an all-pace line-up. Jardine himself did not play. Instead, he went trout fishing on the Kiewa River in country Victoria — but not before leaving instructions for his fast bowlers.

When Bradman came to the wicket in a tense atmosphere at the MCG, Larwood set his field with five men close and two men out for the hook — all on the leg-side. Bradman was unsettled, never having experienced this set-up, and was dismissed by

Larwood. The Nottingham Express was back on track and ecstatic. It was payback for all the beltings Bradman had given him in every encounter since 1928.

Jardine learned of Larwood's success by phone. He was thrilled.

The tactic was then dubbed 'Bodyline' by the press for the first time. Fast leg theory had a more pertinent name.

A week later, on 25 November, Bradman was in the fray for NSW against the confident tourists. Jardine was proving a master strategist. He left Larwood out of the game, saving him for the First Test that would begin just three days after this match.

Bradman contracted flu just before the NSW game and managed only 18 (LBW to Maurice Tate) and bowled for 23 by Voce in a Bodyline burst. Five of England's six main bowlers had dismissed him in the lead-up to the Tests. England had a grip on the urn of burnt bails, for which these two countries fought so hard, even before the 1932–33 Ashes began.

Bradman's flu worsened and so did the state of his teeth. It all added up to him being physically and mentally run-down. He missed the First Test at Sydney, and decided on the spur of the moment to have his teeth attended to. This meant — as was common practice in those days — having all his teeth removed and replaced with dentures. Bradman opted to have the surgery over the last two days of the First Test. He then disappeared with Jessie to a remote beach cottage on the NSW coast to recover from his flu and to accustom himself to the dentures.

When I probed Bradman about this, he thought it 'better to keep quiet about it'. He did not wish to appear as if he were making excuses for his poor form early in the 1932–33 season. But the issue over his teeth and general condition must have had an impact. He never had such an ordinary patch at the beginning of his 20 First-Class seasons.

*

Meanwhile, Larwood dominated the First Test, taking ten wickets. A spectator brought rare mirth to the match by calling out to Jardine to 'leave our flies alone' as he gave the Aussie salute. Yet the England captain would not let up on the Australian batsmen, who capitulated.

Bradman decided that there was no way Bodyline could be defeated through a series unless countermeasures could be devised.

While Bradman recovered and prepared himself for the Second Test, he came up with a plan.

'I decided to play some tennis shots,' Bradman noted.

He would run across the crease and attempt to hook and cut from unorthodox positions. Only this batting genius, with his lightning footwork and amazing eye, could attempt this against Larwood and Voce. Nothing else looked like working for a full series.

He had thought through a method to overcome Bodyline at the risk of being branded a coward for pulling away to square-leg or easing towards point to play shots. In that era, and until the 21st century, any batsman who slipped a back foot even a centimetre towards square-leg was deemed to lack courage. Until the 1980s, a tail-ender would be called a 'bunny' and excused from a fast attack because of the golden rule that speedsters did not bowl bouncers at them.

In the modern era, his methods of moving away left or right of the pitch and playing up-and-under shots are standard in games of 20 overs a side. It is nothing now to see players such as David Warner and Steve Smith, and switch-hitters and reverse-sweepers such as Glenn Maxwell, stepping square of the wicket to play tennis shots. Bradman could lay claim to their innovation here, seven or eight decades before it became fashionable. In the modern era, if you have not got the skill-set for such shots, you are unlikely to be selected. The unorthodox techniques have also seeped into Test cricket.

In late 1932, Bradman was prepared to ignore the unwritten rules of orthodox batsmanship that had stood for a hundred years. He was not going to just ease towards square leg. This audacious cricketer was prepared to move even a metre from his stumps, and on both sides of the wicket. It shocked the cricket world and pleased his adversaries. Bradman was afraid, the old-timers squeaked; he's gutless, cried his enemies.

He would have been inhuman had he not been afraid, but it was not fear that drove him to such movements, seen as drastic at the time. With the benefit of hindsight, Bradman was the original Twenty20-style shotmaker.

*

He came back for the sell-out Melbourne Second Test over the New Year leading into 1933. After a shock first-ball duck in the first innings, he made a superb unbeaten century. Australia won.

Yet Bodyline was taking its toll on the other Australian bats, who did not have Bradman's capabilities. They were getting hit or out to awkward deliveries.

In the nine-day break before the Third Test at Adelaide, the press built it up as a grudge match. The police turned up at the Test, keeping their mounted troops and foot squads outside the ground. Mid-afternoon on the second day of the game, in front of a capacity crowd, Australia began its first innings and Bradman was soon at the wicket. As he was greeted by tremendous applause, lines of police began curling into position around the ground. He hadn't been at the wicket long when Jardine, wearing his silk scarf, signalled Bodyline positions for his fielders. The crowd booed and jeered.

Again, one moment of humour punctuated the electric atmosphere in a lull before Larwood delivered. A flock of seagulls flew overhead.

'There's Jardine at mid-off,' a spectator yelled, 'go for him!'

Moments later, Larwood bowled a bouncer that crashed into Australian skipper Bill Woodfull's chest. Woodfull dropped his bat and staggered from the wicket. The spectators erupted. It seemed they might invade the ground. Jardine sidled up to Larwood to offer support. 'Well bowled, Harold,' he said.

Bradman was out for just eight, caught in the leg-trap off Larwood. The crowd was incensed, but with another paceman, Gubby Allen, refusing to bowl Bodyline, there was some respite.

Had Jardine used Voce with Larwood, then fans may have turned into a dangerous mob. The courageous Woodfull (the schoolmaster son of a preacher) battled through to the tea break. England manager Plum Warner visited him in the dressing room, where the Australian captain uttered the immortal words:

'There are two teams out there. One is trying to play cricket and one is not. It is too great a game for spoiling by the tactics your team is adopting. I don't approve of them. It might be better if I do not play the game.'

The 'I' here was the captain and his team.

Later in the day, Australian keeper Bert Oldfield had his skull fractured by Larwood. The crowd reacted by counting down from ten, indicating it might attack him.

Only a double hundred from Bradman in his second innings could save Australia. He brought gasps from spectators as he pulled away from the wicket to cut Larwood and reached 50 in quick time. Larwood was removed from the bowling crease. Bradman had won another battle using the precursor to the modern Twenty20 method. But the mental effort had unbalanced his normal cool demeanour. His control, which checked rushes of blood, deserted him. He hit Verity for six — his first in Test cricket — then tried another and was caught for 66. Australia was thrashed.

After play, the Board of Control sent a telegram to the MCC, which said the tactics were 'unsportsmanlike'.

'Unless stopped at once,' the telegram stated, 'it is likely to upset friendly relations between Britain and Australia.'

CHAPTER 10

Nash's Lash of Revenge

After the game, the Australian camp argued about how they should fight back. With two Tests to play, the Ashes were still not lost. Some players, including hard-hitting batsman Vic Richardson, grandfather to the Chappell brothers, wanted Australia to select bowlers who could deliver Bodyline.

On the field during the Adelaide Test, he had said: 'I'd give 'em bloody Bodyline if I was captain.'

Off the field, he was more circumspect, but still adamant when he told the press: 'I would throw it right back at them right away.'

Paceman and champion footballer Laurie Nash — an athletic Merv Hughes of his day — was mentioned as the type to fight fire with fire. Nash was a dashing centre halfback for the Swans in their Aussie Rules premiership of 1933. He played his cricket sometimes as if he were still on the footy field.

Jack Fingleton, Australia's opener, and the first to wear extra padding to face Bodyline, supported a counterattack. 'The best of all [at using it] would have been Laurie Nash,' he said. Fingleton thought Nash would have had no scruples if he were ordered to set a Bodyline field and aim at the batsman's chest and head.

Nash was not enthusiastic. 'I would have bowled it if asked,' he said, 'but I disagreed with it. It was my policy to play cricket.'

The fastest bowler in the country, Aboriginal Eddie Gilbert from Queensland, was another name that came up. He was short and wiry with long arms, and adept at the javelin. Gilbert had a chest-on, whipping action from only four paces that some considered suspect. But a chucker or not, he was swift enough to knock the bat out of Bradman's hands and dismiss him for a duck when they faced each other in 1931, in the first of several memorable tussles.

The press picked up on the retaliatory theme, but Woodfull would not hear of it. He was supported by leg-spinner Bill O'Reilly and Bradman. They thought the game would be reduced to thuggery if both teams used Bodyline.

Bradman warned: 'It would lead to both sides stacking its team with speed merchants, hell-bent on breaking ribs on a bad day and heads on a good one. Shot-making such as driving, cutting and glancing would be out. Only the hook and pull to leg would be left. Spinners would not be chosen. Apart from anything else, the game would be greatly reduced as a spectacle.'

Bradman was also concerned that Bodyline would be copied at lower levels of the game, where many lesser batsmen would be injured, even killed.

*

Without time to mount an effective counterstrategy, a shellshocked Australia went down 4:1 for the series. Bradman had the best batting record with an average of 56.57. His unorthodox tactics had been the only method that worked. Yet he had been reduced to half his usual effectiveness. Jardine and his pacemen had won back the Ashes by a nefarious but clever scheme within the laws of cricket, for which they were feted in England. The question was whether Bodyline was in the 'spirit of the game'.

Bodyline as a tactic had repercussions. The talented West Indies fast bowlers Manny Martindale and Learie Constantine used the tactic a few months later in a Test in England. Now the English batsmen suffered. Martindale split Wally Hammond's chin. The champion batsman said he wouldn't play again if Bodyline was not outlawed. A grim Jardine scored his only Test century in facing Bodyline, while Larwood and Voce continued to use it in the 1933 English county games. More battered batsmen complained.

By the time Australia turned up for the Ashes tour of 1934, Bodyline was outlawed, and Jardine had been dumped by the MCC as skipper. Its main exponents, Larwood and Voce, were told they would not be chosen for their country if they didn't apologise for using Bodyline. This was hypocritical, given that the MCC had supported Jardine in Australia. Larwood refused and never bowled for England again. Voce agreed to apologise. He would live to fight in another Ashes series.

After an indifferent first half of the 1934 tour through illness, Bradman's capacity to craft a massive score returned. He hit 304 at Leeds and 244 at The Oval in each of the final two Tests, and Australia won the series.

Soon after these efforts, he collapsed with peritonitis — the mystery illness — and was fortunate to survive an operation.

*

Bradman fully recovered in time for the next Ashes in Australia in 1936–37. Now, at 28, he was Australian captain, and Gubby Allen, the bowler who had refused to bowl Bodyline, was England's skipper. The series restored the goodwill that had been lost between the two teams during 1932–33, but came close to turning nasty again during the Fifth and deciding Test at Melbourne.

The series was two-all. In the week before the Test, Laurie Nash, playing for Victoria against England, let go a barrage of short-pitched bowling ('bumpers'). Allen and Hammond protested to the Board of Control and demanded that Nash not be picked to play in the final Test.

Bradman, sensing panic in the England camp, pushed for Nash's selection. The Board refused to name him in the team of 12. Bradman suggested it name 13, with Nash in the squad. The Board reluctantly agreed.

Allen and Hammond were furious. They demanded a meeting with Bradman, which took place at the Windsor Hotel in Melbourne. Over lunch, Allen said Nash could not be chosen, otherwise there would be a 'bumper war'. He threatened to unleash Voce.

Bradman replied, 'No Englishman will ever dictate who is selected for Australia.'

An agreement was reached where Bradman promised that there would not be a bumper war, although some would be allowed. Hours later, Bradman fronted the Board and put his case for Nash being in the final 12; that is, one less than the original squad.

When Bradman left the Board meeting, there was a heated debate on whether to accede to his request. One director posed the question of who was more powerful, Bradman or the Board. The room fell silent. There was a fear that Bradman might stand down if he didn't get his way.

That evening, the Board announced the final 12. Nash was in it. The intriguing question now was: would he carry the drinks as 12th man, or actually play in the XI?

On the morning of the match, Bradman won the toss and decided to bat. The skippers exchanged team sheets, which confirmed Nash's inclusion in the Australian XI.

'Are you going to have a go at us?' Allen asked angrily.

Bradman repeated there would be no bumper war.

He dominated Australia's innings of 604, scoring 169 to follow his 270 and 212 in the two previous Tests. When England batted, Nash bowled fast, if erratically. He let go only a handful of bumpers, yet his fiery manner put England off. Bradman had learned much about the nuances of intimidation since the Bodyline series. Australia won and retained the Ashes for the next 16 years.

While the ill feeling generated between the two countries in 1932–33 has long since passed, the rivalry that Bodyline accentuated is very much alive. The tactic was banned, but intimidation became a permanent part of Test cricket as its legacy.

Since then, both sides — and the other Test-playing nations — have bred bowlers to target key opposition batsmen.

CHAPTER 11

The Creed to Play By

Don Bradman had a creed for the game, which he adhered to his entire life. He wrote it down for Sam Loxton, one of his 1948 Invincibles, and one of his closest mates from sport:

> When considering the stature of an athlete or for that matter, any other person, I set great store in certain qualities which I believe are essential in addition to skill.
>
> They are that a person conducts his or her life with dignity, with integrity and, most of all, with modesty. These are totally compatible with pride, ambition and competitiveness.
>
> I love to see people with personality and character, but I resent utterly the philosophy of those misguided people who

think arrogance is a necessary virtue. It is only endured by the public not enjoyed.

This was a clear enunciation of a doctrine he had had ever since he was about to embark on his first Ashes tour in 1930. Facing a big crowd at the Empire Theatre in his home town of Bowral, he said: 'First my parents taught me to be a cricketer off the field as well as on. It was not "Did you win?" but "Did you play the game?" that made the man.'

It was a variation on other lesser clichés such as 'Manners maketh the man' or 'Clothes maketh the man'.

His comments then at age 21 were the precursor to the high-minded articulation of 18 years later. He could hardly write with such profundity if he had not a grand record of behaviour and performance behind him after a two-decade career in the public eye as the ultimate role model. Even in 1930, the Christian name 'Donald', invariably shortened to 'Don', was by far the most adopted of any name since Federation in 1901. His efforts in 1930 set a very high bar for a country in Depression and looking for guidance and leadership from its public figures. There was none among its political leaders. That year, former prime minister Billy Hughes called Bradman 'the greatest Australian ever born'.

'How did you feel about being called that?' I asked him in a long afternoon phone interview in May 1995.

'I was 21 years old,' Bradman replied. 'I was just a cricketer. And anyway he was just trying to get up the nose of General Monash. They were not close, you know.'

'You saw it as premature?'

'Just not valid to refer to a sportsman that way. Monash was the most famous man in the country in the 1920s, and with good reason, and Hughes was jealous of him. After Monash, there were others.'

'Such as?'

'Nancy Bird Walton [the aviator]. She achieved so much and she was a fine ambassador too.'

But there was a lot more that prime ministers and the population saw in Bradman. His image had 'values' written all over it. He performed in the way all mums and dads would have wanted their sons and daughters to: in a modest manner, with integrity.

A not-so-trivial instance of this was the way one behaved after being given out wrongly by an umpire. Everyone who has ever played cricket — whether in the street or park or right up to the highest level — has faced the moment when he or she thought the umpire's decision was incorrect. The hardest thing to do was to not show any negative emotion; to not remonstrate with the opposition; to walk back to the pavilion and not complain to team-mates. This was sometimes a tougher test of character and moral courage than anything done with the bat. It sorted out the whingers from the non-whingers.

Bradman set an example here, and rarely mentioned a wrongful dismissal, and then usually years after the event. An instance was when he was given out at 232, caught behind off Larwood in the Fifth Test of the 1930 Ashes. He claimed decades later that he had not touched it. Given he is not on record as having commented like that on another occasion, you could put your house on the veracity of his complaint, especially as he had such a big score on such an important occasion. (Whingers usually complained as an excuse for a low score.)

*

Bradman was set against sledging, but would tolerate a humorous comment as long as it was not uttered to unsettle an opponent on the field.

'You've said you would not put up with sledging ...' I said in a discussion on the game's values, in mid-1996.

'It's a very poor aspect that has crept into the game since the 1960s,' he replied.

'What would you, as skipper, have done to a sledger?'

'I'd have warned him. If he repeated the offence, he'd be dropped for the next game.'

'The story goes that Bill O'Reilly was bowling to England's Len Hutton, and Hutton, not a powerful driver of the ball, hit one that rolled gently to mid-off. O'Reilly applauded sarcastically and said: "Well done, Len. I didn't know you had the strength!" Would you call that a sledge?'

'I hadn't heard that one. It wasn't said while I was captain.'

'But was it a sledge?'

'It depends on how it was said. Bill was a witty fellow at times. It would be a borderline case. The worst sledge of all came, not from a player, but a spectator — [American comedian] Groucho Marks — in the 1930s,' Bradman said. 'He was watching a Test at Lord's. Halfway through the first session, he asked: "When does the game start?"'

After the biography was published in late 1995, our talks changed from me asking questions to more discussions about the game, although I would always throw in queries, either prepared or spontaneous.

When our chat turned to sledging again, Bradman asked me about my experiences at my modest levels of the game. I hadn't played much since I lived in England in the mid-1970s and played for Chelsea's The Alibi Club against *Private Eye*, the satirical magazine. I heard no sledging at all in Australia and England until 1975, by which time I had stopped playing. I didn't play again for nearly a quarter of a century, until 1998 — in the Lady Bradman Cup at Bowral, organised by Thos Hodgson. A generation on, a mild form of sledging had crept into even a friendly competition. It surprised me.

'I didn't like it,' I told Bradman, 'but I rolled with it. In a game for Hodgson's team against a NSW University XI of cricketers who'd all played at club level, I was batting above my weight and trying to hold out for a draw. Hodgson was my partner. I had hung around for a long time until I lost patience and skied a ball. The fielding team's captain circled under it.

'"Run two!" I called. "He'll drop it for sure!" The captain spilled the catch. I was greeted with silence by the fielding team. I made it through to stumps for a not out and we forced a draw. But no one spoke to me after the game.'

'That'll teach you,' Bradman said with a grin.

'It did. I realised that there were still teams who didn't indulge in sledging, although they seemed few and far between.'

*

It was very much an Australian characteristic to play the game as hard as possible, but within the rules and the spirit of the game.

Did Bradman ever 'walk' (leave the crease, thus giving himself out) when there was debate over a dismissal — a low catch, for example?

'I left it to the umpires if I was uncertain. You of course left it to them for stumpings, LBWs and run outs.'

'If you feathered one through to the keeper, and was given not out, did you walk?'

'Again, I left it to the umpires. One way or another, over a career these things evened out.'

I related an incident in a school match when I was very keen to be promoted from Scotch College's Under 14Bs to the Under 14As. We were playing against St Kevin's College in Melbourne. I needed a 50. I was on 28. The day was very windy. More than once, the wind removed a bail. I played a ball down the leg side and stepped back. I felt my heel may have made the faintest contact with the base of the leg stump. I ran one and looked back at the wicket. The bail was on the ground.

The St Kevin's keeper pointed to the bail, but not in suspicion. No one appealed. The umpire put the bail back on the stumps. The game went on. I reached 50 and was picked in the 14As the next week. This incident had stayed in my mind for six decades.

'Did I do the right thing?' I asked Bradman.

'If you were in two minds,' Bradman said with a smile, 'then you did the right thing. There has to be an appeal [in any unclear situation].'

The world is divided unevenly into walkers and non-walkers. I was a non-walker. I agreed with Bradman. The good and bad luck evened out over time. Today's technology to detect the accuracy of a dismissal or otherwise circumvents the moral issue of conscience, to a point. Batsmen still hang around at the crease, some unsure, some in desperate hope, when a ball is feathered to the keeper, or a low catch is made. Gone are the days up until the 1960s when a batsman might ask the catcher if he had snaffled it or not, and then walk off on the catcher's word.

*

The modern game has fewer standards. The old adages about the game, such as 'it's not cricket' and 'playing with a straight bat', do not have the currency they had a half-century ago. Now there is a thin line between winning at all costs and keeping it as a game. Moments of exuberance or belligerence receive more TV coverage than a great catch.

A big factor in the change is obviously money and professionalism. The competition is fiercer as players perform for their livelihood. Here Bradman admitted to me that he was caught in a 'time warp'. He came from era as a player and administrator where the game was a sport, more amateur than professional in Australia. He believed it was important that players should find work that would sustain them and their families after cricket.

Bradman was at the end of his long period as the nation's top cricket official. Despite better payments being earned in the game by the late 1970s, he still could not countenance the game being a substitute for a job. Bradman was suddenly behind the times.

There was evidence to support his view that cricketers should prepare for an 'after-life'. A sad instance of sportsmen not coping with life after the end of a sporting career has been graphically illustrated by the high suicide rate among professional county cricketers in the UK, many of whom suffer mental anguish on retirement from the game. Some had known no other existence, and had nothing to fall back on for a living after touring around England with mates in a comfortable bubble of minor prestige and fame on the cricket circuit.

Bradman's certitude about having a job to provide for the after-cricket life hit its own wall of reality in 1970 when the possibility of easier plane travel caused the number of games played at Test level to increase. Players grumbled, rightly, for more pay if they were to represent their states and nation away from home more often.

Keith Stackpole, a crowd-pulling shotmaker who opened for Australia in the 1970s, recalled complaining to a Board official that the conditions under which he'd played in India were poor. The official, reflecting the attitude of Bradman, said: 'If you don't like it, there are plenty of others who will want to take your place.'

The popular 'Stacky', a strong asset to the game, and a player ahead of his time, was hurt by the remark and retired soon afterwards.

That kind of rebuff was rife. Kerry Packer received it too when his brusque style of business dealing was rejected by the 'old-school' Cricket Board when he wanted to buy the TV rights for Test cricket. He didn't help his cause by reportedly saying jokingly to the Board members: 'We have established what you are, gentlemen; all we have to do now is negotiate the price.'

Bradman was right about players needing to find an occupation for the cricket afterlife. But he was from another era and stubborn about maintaining cricket and its values in the face of massive change after a century of the status quo.

He was also correct in attempting to keep a gold standard, so eloquently expressed by England's Lord Harris, in Bradman's favourite quote, which began with: 'You do well to love it, because it is more free from anything sordid, anything dishonourable, than any game in the world.'

That sentiment has been diminished by betting, match-fixing and drugs. But the rest of Harris's observation still holds true: 'To play it keenly honourably, generously, self-sacrificingly, is a moral in itself, and the classroom is God's air and sunshine; protect it from anything that would sully it, so it may grow in favour with all men.'

Another favourite Bradman axiom, which he used often when addressing young players in particular, was 'to leave the game in better shape than you found it. Remember, you are simply the custodians of it, and its standards.'

CHAPTER 12

Winning the Captaincy

The circumstances and fortunes of Bradman's life in the build-up to the 1936–37 Ashes series fluctuated more than at any other time. Before the series, Bradman's form was arguably the strongest in his career. His last seven innings in First-Class cricket had been 233, 357, 31, 0, 1, 369 and, the most important one in every observer's eyes, 212. This had been made for the Rest of Australia, which he captained against Vic Richardson's Australian side that had returned victorious from a tour of South Africa in 1935–36. Bradman had missed that tour because he had been ill and was recovering from his medical issues.

This Sydney game, beginning on 9 October 1936, was the biggest showdown in internal Australian cricket and would destine the nation's cricket for the next two decades. The Board was not going to hand Bradman the captaincy without him proving himself. It could not, in the face of public opinion, just take it off the successful Richardson. The nation's top sporting job had to be earned.

It left Bradman with several challenges. He had to outplay Richardson in the leadership stakes, and he had to take on two bowlers who were not fond of him. They happened to be the best spin combination in the world at the time — Bill O'Reilly and Clarrie Grimmett. A big part of their attitude and dislike was the way Bradman treated these two in cricket combat. He set out to obliterate them, simply because they were the best in the spin business.

'There was nothing personal in it from my point of view,' Bradman said. 'There was no animosity and even if there were, I'd have put it out of my mind.'

He thrived on these moments, perhaps more than any other sportsman in any sport, and especially his own. In modern terms, he 'targeted' the best of any opposition and set out to defeat them, first by getting on top and then by destroying them. He had done this throughout his eight-year First-Class career. An example was Percy Fender in the 1930 game; another was the way he went after Larwood in the 1928–29 and 1930 Ashes, and crushed him to the point where the Nottingham Express had run out of steam. Larwood said he would refuse to tour Australia unless he could use Bodyline tactics to overcome his major tormentor.

Before Bradman's First-Class career, he had gone out of his way as a 17-year-old to hammer O'Reilly in the legendary Bowral versus Wingello clash of 1924. Bradman scored 234 in 167 minutes in a soul-destroying performance that made

O'Reilly think about giving away the game when he was just on the verge of New South Wales selection. Rivalry had lingered on for 12 years, and O'Reilly obsessed over it. In two discussions I had with the spinner a decade apart, he had brought it up each time. He was not bitter about Bradman, but his pride had been battered and he would never forget it. When I asked O'Reilly about the Australia versus The Rest of Australia (really two even teams with 22 players vying for 11 places) game in 1936, he became irritated. The memory had been seared into his psyche and it showed he was just as competitive as Bradman but on the losing end of most of their encounters.

By contrast, Bradman salivated over them. The competition exhilarated him.

'He [O'Reilly] was the best bowler I ever saw or played against,' Bradman told me. 'It was the greatest challenge to combat him and see him out of an attack.'

*

The so-called 'Test Trial' began with 'Australia' piling up 363. Richardson only managed 26, which meant first blood to Bradman. The South Australian leg-spinner Frank Ward took 7 for 127 in easily the best bowling effort by 'The Rest'. Then it batted and Bradman delivered one of his most devastating performances ever outside of Tests. He sliced, diced and drove O'Reilly out of the attack on four occasions and Grimmett on two in compiling 212 in just 202 minutes. The demolition complete, he began lofting the ball and threw his wicket away.

He hit two sixes and 24 fours. The Rest ended on 385 and then Australia, demoralised by Bradman's onslaught, was rolled for 180. The Rest then wrapped up the game, winning easily by six wickets. Ward took another five wickets, giving him 12 for the match.

Richardson's team had been humiliated and its grand South African efforts diminished. When faced with such fierce and brilliant opposition from one player, it had fallen apart in the field. Bradman was the cruel measure of just how good Richardson's squad had been.

On 13 October, just after The Rest had won, the England team, captained by Gubby Allen, docked at Fremantle.

As the team disembarked, a wharfie yelled: 'Hey Gubby, did you hear Bradman's score in the trial game?'

'Yes,' Allen replied, 'but who was he playing?'

It was a lame response, given the Australian bowling line-up, but the war of words had begun. Yet there was no argument, and all bets were effectively settled concerning who would lead Australia in the forthcoming Ashes. The Board had no choice but to dump 42-year-old Richardson, who had averaged 23.53 in 19 Tests, and replace him with 28-year-old Bradman, who had an average of just under 100. At that point, however, Richardson had proved himself as a skipper, and had been a popular father figure for the team. Bradman was an unknown quantity in that role. He was easily the number-one cricketer in the world, but that did not mean he would be a good captain.

Everyone in the 1936–37 national side was pleased to have Bradman in the team, which meant they were all likely to be winners. Yet many would have been unsure about his potential as a leader. He was not a nurturer. He was never going to be a psychologist in terms of 'minding' players. The attention the media and public gave Bradman also caused resentment with some batsmen that had festered as jealousy. Bradman had not just mastered all Australian bowlers, he had humbled them, and this fostered a negative attitude with a handful.

Off the pitch, Bradman was not a glad-hander or back-slapper like Shane Warne in a later era. Warne received most media and public attention, but only one or two in the national side were envious. 'Warnie' jollied up most of his team-mates and was an indiscreet 'Jack-the-lad' womaniser off the field, which made him popular in the locker-room jocular sense. But it also made him vulnerable to media exploitation and helped ruin his chances of captaining Australia.

Bradman believed that if players had made it to Test level, they should be able to sort out issues and deal with pressure. If not, they would not last long. He believed in leading from the front and by batting that led to victory. Being personally popular with the players was ephemeral in his mind. Performance counted; victory counted most.

*

Gubby Allen and all his team knew that they were doomed if the form Bradman was in carried through the five Tests. They were in for a painful shellacking under Australia's hot sun. But then fate and fortune played a hand and changed the Ashes landscape. On

29 October, Don and Jessie lost their son Ross a couple of days after his birth, which was devastating for them both. Bradman was in no shape to play for South Australia against the touring MCC team that day.

Flags were hung at half-mast at the Adelaide Oval.

Bradman did not have a chance to play again until mid-November, for his state against Victoria. He was ill with gastroenteritis, but still managed to reach 150 with little trouble. He'd told cricket writer Sir Neville Cardus that he was no longer fit enough to endure the longer stays at the wicket demanded by double and triple hundreds. Seemingly true to his word, he started lofting balls into the deep and was eventually caught for 192.

In 1995, in a phone discussion over the 1936–37 series, his first as Australian captain, I asked what was his state of mind, just before the Tests, given his personal loss?

'The cricket was therapeutic in that one has to focus on the job at hand,' he replied. Though he was reviewing a very sad situation of 60 years earlier, he spoke as if it were a more recent experience. 'I couldn't do that in Adelaide. I could in Melbourne. While a tragedy such as that never leaves you, it was not going to have an impact on my performances as batsman or captain.'

A much more prosaic factor impacted on his form: the weather. In the opening Test at Brisbane, he made a cavalier 38 in the first innings. When Australia was set 381 to win and after torrential rain was in on a gluepot, Bradman made a second ball duck and Australia collapsed for just 58 in 12.3 overs.

England had won handsomely and nine days later moved down to Sydney for the Second Test with hopes higher. Hammond spent most of two days compiling 231. Then it poured again and Australia was caught on another sticky. This time Bradman went one worse and made a golden duck and the team were all out for 80.

In the follow-on, he had patches of looking like the player who had in the previous year compiled double and triple hundreds. But he lifted his head when hooking at a long hop from Verity, which lobbed into his stumps. He was out for 82. Australia was beaten by an innings and 22 runs. They were two–nil down and on the brink of an ignominious Ashes defeat.

The criticism came from everywhere. Jardine in England was saying, 'I told you so. He is not up to being captain.' Cardus saw Bradman 'riddled with fallibility' and suggested the stroke he played against Verity was 'not fit for public view. It spoke of little hope, little resource.'

Bradman chortled when I quoted this to him.

'Cardus was right that it should not have been played in public or anywhere else. The rest was hyperbole, well written as ever!'

I asked what happened. 'Was it similar to that moment in 1930 when Robins bowled you for 131?'

'No. I played a shot against Hedley. I missed the ball.'

'So the knives were out after Sydney?'

'It was understandable. We were on the brink of a series defeat. I had not proved my capacity as captain.'

'But the weather had been the big factor …'

'Yes, but it usually evens out over five Tests, as it did in this series.'

Bradman was quickly the scapegoat for the national 'disgrace' of being beaten by the 'Poms' again, especially when everyone from the wharfie who challenged Allen at Fremantle to the prime minister had expected to beat the tourists. Journalists began to speculate on Bradman's leadership skills. There was talk of restoring Vic Richardson to the captaincy, which, if averages were considered, would have robbed Australia of about 150 runs in the Test, given that Richardson would score 46 and Bradman would not get his 200 from two innings. This was not going to happen and would have been a retrograde move. The Board would not make the change. Nor would Bradman resign.

The criticism bled into whispered comments about the new skipper not receiving support from all of his squad. Former Test spinner Arthur Mailey wrote: 'Some members of the team have not been giving Bradman the cooperation that a captain is entitled to expect. There is definitely, has been for some time, an important section of the team that has not seen eye to eye with Bradman, either on or off the field.'

The main antagonists were Bill O'Reilly and Jack Fingleton. O'Reilly was by nature a stirrer, and he simply didn't like Bradman. The way the bowler had been humiliated in combat only exacerbated his attitude. Big Bill had been used to dominance at the pitch, and the consequent respect. And Bradman was not a drinker, a factor that marked his character down in O'Reilly's eyes. Fingleton had an axe to grind ever since Bradman had suggested, when asked by selectors, that Bill Brown would be a better opener in the UK in 1934. Fingleton missed out on a trip he wanted badly. It left him embittered. The fact that Bradman's judgement proved accurate was no sop for an opener scorned.

Some rumours suggested that there was a split in the team over religion, with the Catholics in the side — O'Reilly, Fingleton, Fleetwood-Smith, McCabe and O'Brien — pitted against Bradman, who had once been a Mason.

'This was utterly false,' Bradman commented to me on more than one occasion when the non-issue was raised. 'There was never such a divide in any team I was in. It was perpetrated by religious bigots outside the side.'

Former captain Bill Woodfull in private told others that O'Reilly and Fingleton had wanted Stan McCabe to replace Bradman as captain.

'That may or may not have been true,' Bradman remarked, 'and there was some justification for all sorts of suggestions at the time. I simply had to do a lot better, if the weather would let me!'

CHAPTER 13

At the Abyss

Australia's dreadful summer continued when the two teams confronted each other again on New Year's Day 1937. Rain the day before meant the wicket was expected to present problems, but Bradman had no hesitation in batting when he won the toss. He threw his hands high, smiled and registered his relief after the bad luck with toss and weather in the first two Tests. But his joy was short-lived. Brown was dismissed caught behind off Voce for a single, and Bradman was soon marching out in front of a huge Melbourne crowd of 79,000. Most had come to see The Don begin what was hoped would be Australia's fightback. He may not have been popular with every player in the team, and naturally every England team member wished to see the back of him. But the vast majority of the spectators and the population at large wished him success.

Bradman was given a dome-lifting reception all the way to the centre. The sun was out. The oval was a sea of green. The MCG, more stadium and 'Cauldron' than picturesque cricket arena, was not his favourite venue to bat at — he put Lord's, Adelaide and Sydney ahead of it — but it was by far his happiest hunting ground. In Tests and other First-Class innings to that date, he had scored ten centuries, including 357 against Victoria the season before. Bradman was originally from New South Wales, and was living in South Australia, but his status overrode state boundaries. He was a national hero. Victorians loved him. He guaranteed value for money and grand entertainment at the nation's biggest stadium. He was also a sentimental favourite, especially against England after the last Ashes series in Australia — Bodyline — four years earlier.

The big audience's rapture was palpable. Cardus noted: '[The] roar told not only of hero worship but of supplication,' which was not Bradman's favourite state for fans, or anyone. Yet he appreciated their excited anticipation.

Allen knew of Bradman's respect for left-armer Hedley Verity. He brought the spinner on. Verity's first delivery was an 'arm ball', which did not turn and went straight on. Bradman, on 13 after half an hour of looking untroubled, anticipated a turn and mistimed a pull that dollied to Robins, placed forward of the square leg umpire. The spectators' excitement turned to dismay. Their shock and disappointment gave way to a befuddled silence as Bradman tucked his bat under his arm and strode off. The coliseum raised a belated, desultory applause as he disappeared into the pavilion.

Bradman had scored just 133 in his first five innings of the series. For the statisticians, accountants and numbers nuts in the crowd and around the nation, this was an omen. Hadn't he come good in England in 1934 with that same number of 133 runs on the board in the corresponding first five innings of that Ashes? It gave them hope, and at least they had this when all else was failing.

Cardus, demonstrating admirable extrasensory perception from outside the dressing room, 'felt the spirit of defeatism in the Australian ranks. I thought in fact the rubber was ours now.' The Australian batting was 'tame and feminine. Even the running between the wickets suggested hungry men starving for crumbs of singles.'

Australia reached 6 for 181 as rain caused a premature end to the day's play. Allen told his diary that his team was 'in an impregnable position' concerning the result of the series.

But once more, Melbourne's fickle weather played a part. There was a torrential downpour overnight. The uncovered wicket presented a gluepot the next morning, Saturday.

Another bumper crowd turned up to watch the gloom. Play was not allowed to resume until after lunch. Bradman let his batsmen struggle up to 9 for 200 before declaring.

'You said this was the "appropriate psychological moment" [to declare]. Why?'

'Two hundred was a tough target on this pitch. I also wanted to send a signal to the opposition that I thought it was an awful strip. I'd already told Gubby in the morning inspection I thought it was the worst wicket I'd ever seen. To let the innings linger on and fold added nothing to us.'

103

In effect, Bradman was saying, 'Right, now you have a go.' He characterised it as the beginning of a 'sensational battle of tactics'.

First, he wanted to get England on the disgraceful pitch before it began to dry out.

Did he think his luck had changed at this point?

'The weather had been woeful but because we'd batted first, we had a slight advantage. That was all.'

England was quickly 2 for 14, but steadied with Maurice Leyland and the in-form Hammond at the wicket.

'Their batting was superb,' Bradman commented. 'Could not have been better under the conditions.'

The wicket remained terrible, with balls popping up or skidding low. English *Daily Express* writer William Pollock noted: 'You didn't want cricketers on that pitch. You wanted the Crazy Gang, Mickey Mouse, Einstein and Euclid.'

Bradman crowded the batsmen, but they resisted stubbornly. There would be no attempt to hammer their way out of trouble. It was a matter of staying at the crease. Tactically, Bradman was in a useful position. He checked the weather forecast that predicted uncertain conditions for Sunday, which in Melbourne meant it might rain or might not. Good weather was said to be on the way for the next two or three days after that. He believed that if he could dismiss England for under or about the Australian score, and the wicket improved, then after the Sunday rest day, he could build a big second innings, and go for a win late in the game. At least, that was the scenario in his mind until England's sudden collapse, when Len Darling took two spectacular catches to see off Hammond and Leyland.

The score was 4 for 68. Some England players were urging Allen to declare 132 runs short of Australia's score. Allen's fear was that Bradman, the risk-taker, would counter by immediately declaring without another run on the board. But Allen was not a gambler. He almost had the Ashes in his keeping. Why risk all?

Allen watched Bradman through binoculars. His face, Allen wrote, was inscrutable. He seemed to be enjoying the moment. 'How could the little blighter be so calm?'

Allen let the game drift. England deteriorated to 7 for 76.

Bradman had to reset his thinking and planning.

'We did not want to bat again on that horror,' he said, 'so I asked the bowlers to do what was anathema to them — try *not* to take wickets.'

He sidled up to them and gave instructions. The innings dragged on. The bowlers delivered very ordinary balls wide of the wicket and the odd lollipop. The England bats had been told to drop anchor and stay for as long as possible, eking out runs, which was playing into Bradman's hands. He placed more men on the boundary and fewer close to the wicket.

'Every moment I was afraid Allen would see through my tactics,' Bradman said. He dared not look to the pavilion and hoped the England skipper would not declare. The charade continued for another half-hour. O'Reilly seemed to be conforming to his captain's wishes, but still managed to remove Joe Hardstaff and Verity. England was 9 for 76.

Then, the penny dropped for Allen. He became wise to his opposite number's cunning and decided to close the innings with 50 minutes play left for the day.

The England bats left the field. Bradman approached the umpires.

'What's Allen doing?' he asked them.

'We take it he has declared,' one replied.

'Well, he didn't actually say so,' Bradman pointed out, as his players mingled around to see what was happening.

'I see what you mean,' umpire Borthwick said. 'I'll go and confirm it.'

Bradman kept his team on the field while Borthwick found Allen in the England dressing room.

'Of course I've declared!' Allen spat back at the umpire. 'That little blighter ...!'

Borthwick hurried back onto the ground and signalled to Bradman that he had to bring his team in. The Australians sauntered off. Five minutes had been wasted before the ten minutes allotted for the changeover. That left 35 minutes of play before the scheduled close.

Bradman's willingness to throw the dice surfaced, along with a logic that had evaded all captains in the Ashes since the first-ever Test. He decided to reverse the batting order as rain threatened and the light failed. His tail-enders would be sent in as openers to endure the spitting, diving, jumping, running balls. The new men at the top of the order were Bill O'Reilly and Chuck Fleetwood-Smith. O'Reilly shook his head in dismay, but understood the approach straightaway. Fleetwood-Smith, averaging 9, took a fraction more convincing of the move.

'Why?' he asked Bradman.

'Chuck, the only way you can get out on this wicket is to hit the ball,' the skipper replied. 'You can't hit it on a good one, so you've no chance on this.'

Bradman then demonstrated the forward prod that each man was instructed to play every delivery, with the front foot stretching down the wicket as far as possible.

The big crowd broke into applause at the appearance of these two walking out in the late afternoon, and a titter ran around the stadium. O'Reilly obeyed the captain's directive, but was a fraction too early with his push to the first ball from Voce. He popped back an easy caught and bowled. The spectators now laughed as the greatest bowler in the world trudged off, muttering to himself.

'No one dared say "well batted" to Bill,' Bradman recalled, 'but I told him he had fulfilled his role. Better Bill O'Reilly than Bill Brown.'

Frank Ward was in next and a few minutes later a cloud burst and ended a limited but intriguing day. The crowd wandered off. Bradman was still 'alive' and because of this, Australia was in the better position.

CHAPTER 14

Fight Back at the Double

Sunday was overcast and cool. The wicket dried considerably without further rain. On day three of the game, Monday, 4 January 1937, Ward and Fleetwood-Smith resumed, this time in front of nearly 88,000 spectators, a world record.

Cardus noted that 'a gigantic crowd was in, sunning itself in placid contentment, men, women, children, sitting, standing, craning their necks, sitting on steps, even hanging onto rails'.

The gates were shut before play began. Thousands more people were still streaming from Richmond Station and the city, unaware that they would be locked out.

It was a daunting moment for two bunnies starting the day with such a monster crowd packed to the rafters and beyond at the biggest stadium. The fans, however, were amused with every delivery defended, or, more correctly, every one not hit.

Voce quickly put Fleetwood-Smith out of his misery and had him caught by Verity. It was the first ball the batsman had hit. Bradman's blunt assessment had been accurate.

Australia had lost 2 for just 3, a score that would normally make fans tremble. But not this time. They had read the papers and made their own assessment. Bradman the shrewd had played the right card. The wicket would improve by the precious hour and the longer he was in the dressing room, for once, the better Australia's chances became.

Bradman sent in Keith Rigg to accompany Ward, and they shared the strike and crawled the score up to 38 in a vital hour. Verity then had Ward caught for 18. All the almost 176,000 eyes at the ground scanned the MCG scoreboard as the next name was slotted in. It started with 'BR', but was Brown, not Bradman. Muted applause greeted this fine player. The mob wanted The Don, but he had set his new line-up and would stay with it. Time and the weather were now on his side. The Australian lead was 162 and there were seven wickets in hand.

Critics attacked him for not facing up to the conditions and batting with a normal line-up.

'Some were unkind enough to suggest I was avoiding batting on a wet wicket,' Bradman noted. 'Of course I was. What was the sense in losing your batsmen on such a pitch? My decision was in the team's interest, and that of winning.'

At 74, Voce had Brown (20) caught. The fans flicked their attention from the pavilion to the scoreboard again. Its operators were none the wiser, for Bradman had not given them his batting order, in a tactical move to keep the opposition wondering. The lean, sprightly figure making his way steadfastly to the wicket was not Bradman but Fingleton, the second of the openers. The applause was scattered and belated. Some wondered if Bradman was ill.

At 2.49 p.m., Rigg (47) fell at 97. The parochial crowd clapped him all the way back to the pavilion for a gallant effort. The noise didn't abate, and built to a crescendo as the BRADMAN nameplate was slid into the scoreboard panel. He strode out with that usual confident gait and concentrated demeanour. Half the side was out, but the lead was 221 and several key batsmen were intact. In his mind, there was still a very big job to be done.

*

At this point in our phone discussion, Bradman had to make a private call and we decided to continue on the following day this recall of the make-or-break Third Test in the 1936–37 series. That gave me time to formulate some follow-up questions. When we resumed the chat, I reminded him of where we had left off. He was coming into bat with a series on the line. If he failed in this innings, Australia would lose the game and the symbolic urn of ashes.

Bradman had already told me he was nerve-free whenever he reached the crease. Did he feel the pressure? After all, apart from the series, his captaincy would be lost, probably, if he failed in this innings with the bat.

'There were still two and a half days to play,' Bradman noted, as if that was enough of an explanation. In other words, there was no rush, therefore, in his mind, no panic or nerves.

'How many runs did you need to feel comfortable?'

'A lead of 400 was in my mind, but I would only be content with 500. Hammond was in fine form and England had a strong batting line-up apart from him. The wicket would improve to a good one, if there was no more rain.'

The crowd hushed to silence with the first ball he faced. There was relief in the applause as he pushed the first ball through mid-wicket for two. Bradman batted confidently, but he had started that way in the first innings. Yet there was a difference. He was notably using defence more, as was Fingleton, who looked immovable. They both nudged and drove enough to energise the score.

At 18 runs, Bradman reached a personal milestone — 4000 runs in Tests. Rain put up umbrellas and sent the players off the field three times. He and Fingleton needed all their considerable powers of awareness and deliberation with these interruptions. Restarts were always the batsman's enemy. Yet the breaks worked against the fielding side too. The ball was slippery, making it hard to grip, and Verity suffered.

'Despite the weather,' Victorian state cricketer Percy Beames said, 'no one left the ground. In fact, people were still clamouring to get in.'

Bradman played a superb cover drive to reach 50, and the spectators stood and clapped. This was the Bradman they wanted. He was 56 not out at stumps with Fingleton on 39. These two may have been unfriendly away from cricket, but they were united in their fight to defeat England, which now looked more likely than not. Australia was 5 for 194, giving it a lead of 318.

*

On the fourth day of play, Tuesday, 5 January 1937, with the state of Victoria back at work, another thumping crowd of 70,000 turned up, hoping for their champion to go on to the century and a long-waited 'kill'. It had been four years since England had gone down at Melbourne during the Bodyline series. Bradman had then scored a first-ball duck in the first innings and a match-winning 103 in the second.

Allen had noted in his diary that Bradman seemed fatigued and even ill in the previous five innings. So the England skipper decided to tire him out rather than dismiss him. Allen put the field in defensive positions on the boundary to force him to take singles. Bradman, his face still inscrutable, took the bait and dashed the singles. His score mounted with further twos, threes and fours. He climbed into the 90s at lunch with Fingleton not far behind and the lead nearly 400, Bradman's first target level. He was batting his opponents out of the game and soon after lunch brought up his century with a brilliant cut for four off Voce. It had taken him 193 minutes, which was good for anyone but him.

The Melbourne audience stood and cheered. This was what they desired; what they had paid the freight for. England players slumped to the ground and waited several minutes for the din to quieten down. Bradman took block again, and this brought another burst of clapping. He was reminding all viewers, particularly those on the field, that he was set on a big innings. He celebrated with his quick one-two-one down the wicket to drive England bowler Jim Sims through mid-off for four. He followed this with a vicious pull for another boundary. The crowd was now alight and loving it. Sims responded with a good delivery that beat the bat for the first time on the day, and Bradman was reminded of his own axiom of not getting carried away.

Fingleton wandered up the wicket to him and had a quiet word, perhaps reminding him they needed another hundred runs to be safe. Bradman gave a half-nod of acknowledgement to his partner, who was not going to attempt anything so rash. His gritty performance and patience was a counterpoint to Bradman's growing 'touch'. He maintained his aggression to be 164 not out at tea, with Fingleton closing in on a century.

No bowler held up Bradman except Verity, who bowled unchanged in the second session and kept him earth-bound with unerring accuracy.

'Nothing but consummate length and flight could have checked Bradman, in circumstances made for Bradman,' Cardus wrote. 'Verity's length dropped with the persistence of water on a rock. I began to look for stalactites hanging down to earth.'

Fingleton kept his wicket intact at one end 'not obviously thinking of runs, which came to him as a sort of interest on time accumulated at the wicket'. Yet he was again the perfect foil for Bradman, whose approach had changed from the first five innings. Bradman was now the supreme leader rather than the adventurous lone ranger, constructing a team win rather than a record score. He had found the right balance between captaincy and batsmanship.

After tea, he stepped up his rate again with Verity still providing the only brake. Allen came on with the score at 324.

Bradman got on the back foot and hammered him through mid-off for four. The England skipper feared this form, which he had witnessed in 1930 and 1934 when Bradman had won series against superior England teams.

Fingleton reached his century to big applause, which was in appreciation for his application. He would never be a crowd-puller, but he was a fine, determined opener.

At 5.15 p.m., Bradman reached his double hundred in 354 minutes. The crowd reacted even more than when he reached his century, and the England players fell to earth again, quicker this time. It was a sign of the general capitulation. Allen shook his counterpart's hand and smiled. It registered resignation.

But Bradman was not about to call a halt. While the England players lay on the ground, Bradman took block for the third time in the innings. It had always been his ploy to send a message to any opposition. He was going on; there would be no letting up short of a complete demolition.

Fingleton gave up the ghost of his most important innings ever at 136 and was caught behind off Sims. The partnership was 346, a world Test record for the sixth wicket. It had taken 364 minutes. The score was 6 for 443. Australia led by 567.

Bradman did not drop his guard with the loss of his partner. But he did cut loose with some fierce cuts and pulls, reaching 248 by stumps and a commendable 192 for the day. He had been at the wicket 399 minutes.

Australia was 6 for 500 at stumps, with McCabe on 14 not out. The score appealed to Bradman's love of numbers. The Melbourne fans, more than satisfied with what they had witnessed, left to catch trams and trains; 1937 at least looked promising.

Cardus and other observers began to backtrack their commentary a fraction: 'Bradman escaped from a vein of ill-luck; our bowlers had not been beating him technically; he had been getting out to unreal, inexplicable strokes. The big score cleared the air.'

Bradman had once more played outside his physical limitations, willing his body on. He contracted a heavy flu and batted listlessly on Wednesday, day four, reaching 270 before skiing a shot to Allen at wide mid-on. Thus ended his longest-ever innings in Test cricket of 458 minutes and 375 balls. He hit 22 fours. He was ninth out and the final tally of 564 put Australia 688 ahead.

England batted for a draw and was dismissed for 323 just before lunch on the fifth day. Hammond managed 51, and Leyland was left 111 not out. Australia's 365-run win put the series at 2:1 to England. But Bradman's confidence was up. In the Fourth Test he made 212, and in the Fifth 169, and Australia was victorious in both. Australia won the Ashes 3:2 and became the only team to win a five-match series after losing the first two games.

It was and still is the greatest comeback in the history of Test cricket.

CHAPTER 15

First Love

During face-to-face meetings early in 1995, I asked Bradman about a situation that always intrigues when dealing with successful sportspeople: what was his state of mind before a game and during it? Most batsmen at the very top admit to having been nervous before batting, especially if there was a long wait to perform. Was Bradman ever nervous?

'No,' he said. 'I was tense, and could not wait for a match to start and to be out there. But once it was underway, that tension dissipated. This was supplanted by an exhilaration.'

'Excitement, joy?'

'I loved batting, getting into an innings.'

'You were often "in the zone" — as Steve Waugh calls it — when you played those big innings. How did you feel afterwards?'

'After the long ones I had to come down a long way. I had a reaction.'

'Meaning what? After heightened adrenaline?'

'I think so.'

Few others in sport — in fact, in any public performance area — had such a long way back mentally to reach normality. Bradman was a 'pocket rocket' with energy to burn, but not a big man. As stated, his capacity to go beyond normal human bounds of mental and physical endeavour, which cricket demands for longer periods than any other sport, was exceptional. To avoid a flatness, or even depression after his prolonged rushes batting all day, he had to unwind. Music drew him gradually back to earth.

Where millions were in awe of him as a superstar, his heroes were not sportsmen, but conductors, composers, singers and musicians. He listened to his favourite composers, including Brahms, Mozart, Mendelssohn, Elgar, Beethoven, Rachmaninoff, Dvorak, Tchaikovsky, Schubert, Ravel and Debussy; in fact, just about all the greats.

Bradman's tastes were eclectic. He played and enjoyed listening to works from musicals such as evergreens *Oklahoma!* and *Annie Get Your Gun*. He liked John Barry's compositions, but was not overly enchanted by the James Bond theme or music. Bradman laughed when I asked him what he thought of The Beatles and The Rolling Stones.

'Put it this way,' he said, 'I wouldn't spend time sitting down and listening to them. But they must have some merit; they're so popular.'

Bradman enjoyed the singing of Bing Crosby. Former comedian Harry Secombe, an accomplished tenor, was admired for his performance of 'If I Ruled the World'. He liked baritones, such as Paul Robeson performing 'Ol' Man River', and his Adelaide-based friend Kamahl delivering a range of favourites.

(In 1995, when my biography on Bradman first appeared, I was about to be interviewed by ABC broadcaster Jim Maxwell when the phone rang in the Sydney studio. Maxwell handed it to me. Thinking the deep drawl of the caller was a prankster, I was about to dismiss it when the voice said, 'No, it's really me, Kamahl. I am a friend of Sir Donald's.' He wanted to have lunch to talk about Bradman and my biography.)

*

Bradman came from a musical environment. As a youngster, he sang as a soprano in the choir of Bowral's Church of St Simon and St Jude, and he pumped the organ for Sunday services. His father played the violin. His sister Lilian, an excellent pianist and teacher, influenced him to play the piano, by all accounts, well. She inspired Bradman's love of music.

Bradman's love developed on his first tour of England in 1930. His diary is replete with entries about musical events, concerts and theatre. At age 21, he visited the headquarters of the record producer His Master's Voice, when captain Bill Woodfull was given a portable gramophone. On the evening of 25 June, Bradman was delighted to meet Dame Nellie Melba, the celebrated Australian soprano. The next evening, he enjoyed the light opera *Bitter Sweet* at His Majesty's Theatre.

Each tour thereafter, he relaxed with the grand musical and theatrical entertainment available in England, and never missed the chance for a musical evening in Australia.

Fellow Australian cricketer Doug Ring recalled Bradman's insatiable desire for such entertainment on the 1948 tour and later when he was a selector and administrator. Ring had a couple of tickets to see Handel's *Messiah* at Brisbane in 1950. None of the Ashes team members were interested in going with him. However, Bradman heard about it and wanted to come.

'We were ushered to our seats, at the front,' the affable Ring recounted in a TV interview on Channel 7's *World of Sport* program in 1963. 'We were invited backstage because the conductor Eugene Goossens wanted to talk with Don. He [Goossens] surprised us with his knowledge [of cricket], but Bradman wanted to talk about music. He had serious comprehension of it.'

Ring enjoyed the music of the brilliant harmonica player Larry Adler.

'He and Don were good friends,' Ring said. 'Larry performed at musical evenings at his [Bradman's] home.'

(Ring, for the record, managed the first-ever TV interview with Bradman, which was arranged at Parliament House in Melbourne by Sam Loxton. It was broadcast on *World of Sport* and ran 22 minutes. Channel 7's manager, Ron Casey, sold the rights worldwide. Perhaps only characters such as Ring and Loxton could have convinced Bradman to sit down in front of the cameras. They were both easygoing types who enjoyed a laugh, and were not overawed by him.)

*

Of the classical composers, Chopin was at the top of Bradman's list with the third movement of his 'Piano Sonata No. 3 in B minor' being his favourite work.

Professor Mary Finsterer, who in 2014 helped me put on an event about Bradman that included musical interludes, summed up the third movement of Chopin's Piano Sonata No. 3 this way: 'The whole sonata is a long, sophisticated, complex and esoteric work — very much for aficionados of this composer. As always with Chopin, the melodies are hauntingly beautiful. This particular third movement is extremely slow and serene. It's not technically difficult, but very meditative and philosophical.'

It was just what Bradman required to come down from the dizzy heights that only he scaled regularly. Bradman, who was an exceptional sight reader, loved the movement so much he gamely tackled it at the piano, a John Brinsmead that he bought in early 1948, and on which his children learned to play. This sonata was a challenge for him, but he ploughed on undeterred, even if he hit the occasional wrong note. To the untrained ear, he was very good; to the professional, he was his usual courageous, diligent self at anything he tried.

'I heard him play Chopin,' Arthur Morris told me. 'Don went by the principle that practice makes perfect; in this case, imperfect, but still very, very good ... [and] enjoyable, especially with that composer.'

While recovering from his near-death experience with peritonitis in England in 1934, he and Jessie were hosted by the Duke of Portland at Welbeck Abbey. The day after their arrival, he heard Bradman playing the piano 'very beautifully in the [Abbey's] Gothic Hall. It seemed to me nearly as well as he batted.'

The duke complimented him on his skills.

'I enjoy playing the piano better than anything in the world,' Bradman replied, 'and now thank to goodness shall have plenty of time for it, for I have been forbidden to play cricket.'

*

'How long would you take to unwind [with this music] after, say, the triple centuries?' I asked Bradman.

'At least two hours,' he said.

'Alone?'

'If Jessie was with me, she might sit for a while, but generally alone, yes.'

It was a case of one genius coming down to earth with the aid of another. Those few cricketers who have performed at this level (Hammond, Hobbs and Ponsford come to mind) will know what the feeling was like to concentrate and make as few errors as possible for six to ten hours in front of tens of thousands of spectators in an international contest. The mental exhaustion from willing the mind to concentrate so hard would be matched by the muscle fatigue of arms, legs and back. Others may have consumed alcohol to normalise afterwards; some may have gone straight to bed. Bradman had his solitary style, which eschewed adulation and congratulations.

English writer R.C. Robertson-Glasgow said famously of him: 'Poetry and murder lived in him together.' He should have added 'musical endeavour'. I believe, from the way Bradman spoke, music was the most important aspect of his non-working career. If he wasn't listening to it intently, he was playing the piano to relax and drift into a less exacting headspace and world.

*

On 9 July 2014, I produced, with a highly talented team, an alumni event for Monash University called 'Bradman, Mandela and Apartheid', about what I regard as Bradman's finest moment beyond cricket: his dealings over the apartheid issue (you can watch a video of the 'Bradman, Mandela and Apartheid' event on Vimeo (https://vimeo.com/108080613). 'Event' in this case meant a narration by me with musical interludes and interaction with a leading actor. No matter what the standard of the script, good or otherwise, this occasion was lifted enormously by the composer, conductor and (former) Chair of Composition at Monash University, Professor Mary Finsterer; the magnificent singing by the soprano Merlyn Quaife, AO; the versatile acting of Monash academic and performer Dr Felix Nobis; and a wonderful ensemble from the Sir Zelman Cowen School of Music.

To prepare the show, I worked closely with Professor Finsterer on what pieces of music should be included, based on Bradman's favourite works (classical and otherwise) and songs about the man himself. It was a tough task. The alumni show was just an hour long. We had to pick only a handful of composers, an impossible task.

I laid out what I saw as Bradman's favourites, based on several discussions with him, and left it to a serious professional. Finsterer is one of Australia's best operatic and orchestral composers, and was therefore a fitting person to put in charge of arranging and performing the works and loves of Bradman. Having worked with her on other projects, including a similar event about General Sir John Monash, I had full confidence in her expert judgement.

In the end, she chose the third movement of Chopin's Piano Sonata No. 3 in B minor (this of course had to be included); Schubert's 'An die Musik'; and Ravel's 'Jeux d'eau'. In addition, Merlyn Quaife sang the best-ever rendition, operatic or otherwise, of the snappy fox-trot number 'Our Don Bradman' by Jack O'Hagan. It was a hit around Australia after Bradman's record-breaking 1930 Ashes tour of England. Merlyn also excelled in an unmatched performance of Bradman's own composition 'Every Day is a Rainbow Day for Me', which Finsterer lifted with an operatic version.

I had fun in the performance interacting as Bradman with Felix Nobis, who demonstrated outstanding thespian dexterity and versatility by performing as R.C. Robertson-Glasgow, Lord (Colin) Cowdrey, Jessie Bradman, Neville Cardus, Meredith Burgmann, John Vorster and Nelson Mandela.

I had wanted a composition from Georges Bizet's *Carmen*, which Bradman and I had discussed. He was as much enraptured by the music as he was Bizet's life. The grand French composer had battled all his career, and had died of a heart attack at 38, unaware of the massive hit *Carmen* would become.

This touched Bradman.

'To struggle so long and not to receive the plaudits would be devastating,' he said. 'But then again, such a creative would receive his own rewards from the process [of creating].'

*

Bradman loved the soprano voice. Jessie, who had sparked his love of classical music, was herself a fine soprano, and had sung with her two siblings as 'The Menzies Sisters'. His favourite soprano was Elisabeth Schwarzkopf, yet he delighted most in hearing his gifted granddaughter Greta perform in her teens.

Greta has since gone on to become one of the nation's most sought-after and talented singers. I have watched her perform several times, including at a Lord's evening event in London in 2013 during the Ashes. One of her assets was an apparent lack of nerves when getting up on stage.

'I think you have your grandfather's gene,' I said to her once.

She looked surprised and pleased. 'You're right!' she replied.

CHAPTER 16

The Quick Learner

Bradman came from an era where no one in Australia could live by earnings from sport alone. He always believed that players should develop a trade or profession or business away from the game; something to fall back on when they left cricket. He felt they were better-developed people if they managed it. Sportspeople were more rounded if they stayed in touch with the real world.

In 1934, Bradman had an offer from Adelaide's dapper-dressing commercial leviathan Harry Hodgetts to join his Grenfell Street stockbroking firm. Hodgetts had seen Bradman close up as a cricketer and was aware he had a mind for calculation, planning and strategy. He saw that Bradman was discreet and thoughtful; mature for his 25 years — all traits that were essential in the conservative world of stocks, shares and other people's money.

'I wasn't overjoyed at the first thoughts about it,' Jessie said, when I brought her into that first interview in 1995. 'It meant uprooting from family, friends and a way of life in Sydney I enjoyed. But we took it as a challenge and we adjusted well.'

Bradman had second thoughts too. At that stage, he'd had offers to play professional cricket in England, and he was earning a modest sum as a journalist.

Journalism was a viable career choice for him. Bradman's writings were astute, accurate and well-structured. He could have adapted to developing the flair in articles that sell papers. But 'flair' and 'sensationalism' would not have come naturally to him. His analytical mind would not allow him to pull out a 'hooking' paragraph to grip an audience. Bradman had humour, which he injected on occasions, but there was a brutal frankness and logic about him, which never offended me, but did others, and this may have worked in journalism. When he later covered Ashes series in the UK in 1953 and 1956, he boosted sales for the papers that carried his byline. People read his articles. It was Bradman communicating, and his superior comprehension of the game came through.

He was hard-working, a feature that had not always befallen cricket correspondents, especially ex-stars of the game. Some of that period and later preferred to prop up bars than diligently tap typewriters. But his pieces did not set the cricket world alight. Nor did they stretch his strategic brain.

Broking offered more. The concept of a good, fixed income in a six-year deal, with the chance of advancement, was the most sensible opportunity put to him in his career thus far. Not to mention Hodgetts was a member of the Cricket Board and Bradman trusted him. It was an offer Don couldn't refuse.

'Those other offers didn't seem to lead anywhere long term,' he said. 'No offence.'

'I fully understand,' I replied. 'The average author in Australia earns about $7000 a year [1990s figure].'

Bradman had been grateful for employment ever since he left school in 1922, age 14, with a good Intermediate Certificate from Bowral High School. He had known at one point what it was like to be unemployed. The Depression shook him and everyone who experienced it. Work in broking appeared to offer substance. He would be able to extend his natural bent for arithmetic calculations. Bradman would have lessons in accounting, and he would trust to memory everything he could about companies on the Australian market.

'How did you go about grasping the business?'

'Hodgetts at first had me meeting clients and finding out what they wanted; how they wished to invest and in what.'

If the clients didn't know what they wanted, Bradman would take them to the more established of the firm's partners, members and employees. All the while, he built up his knowledge. He was a quick learner.

'I worked weekends, going over company reports and prospectuses, until I felt I knew what I was doing.'

How long did it take him to be confident about the job?

'It took about six months to find my feet,' Bradman said.

Hodgetts encouraged him to distinguish between speculative scrips and solid stocks, as well as understand the Stock Exchange's workings. Bradman himself felt an early affinity to the solid blue-chip stocks, and was wary of new miners, which seemed to fit Hodgetts' own careful approach in the hush-hush, padded-carpet world of stockbroking.

Hodgetts was as shrewd as his natty pin-striped suits inferred. He had a well-fed look of prosperity, a useful image for a broker of that era. It indicated that he was doing well with his broker fees and his own investments, suggesting his clients would also do nicely. He knew that having the most famous sportsperson in the country working for him would attract the curious, and, from among them, new clients. Bradman was always clean-cut and his integrity as a cricketer and person was obvious. Sports store managers in Sydney had had the same idea in using him as 'front-of-store', where people walked off the street and feigned interest in cricket bats or tennis balls just to glad-hand him. Yet Bradman never had his heart in that work. There was something more serious about doing it in a broker's office where gravitas and the rituals around money and investment were revered.

Hodgetts mentored Bradman and encouraged him to network, which was not the young man's inclination. Hodgetts couldn't hope to get him into the Adelaide Club, which was even snottier and more selective than the Melbourne Club in the 1930s. (A mere cricketer in the organisation? The son of a carpenter from rural New South Wales? Good God! Never!) However, Hodgetts could ease the new chap into the next best thing: the Mount Osmond Golf Club, with its arcane rules, enforced to the letter; its setting in rolling hills and its grand views over the city. It didn't hurt that Bradman was already an impressive golfer, despite his cricket-like swing of the club and ungainly feet positioning. He enjoyed the game and was more than competitive.

'Never let a potential client lose badly,' Hodgetts told him, aware of Bradman's killer instinct and willingness to crush any opponent.

Furthermore, the broker jockeyed behind the scenes to have Bradman made captain of the South Australian state side, and a state selector. There was more harrumphing from the establishment. What, its members asked, were his qualifications for such prestigious local positions? At these protestations, Hodgetts was able to wave the words of commendation for Bradman's selectorial skills and efforts as vice-captain on tour in the UK in 1934. He was well up to all of it, Bill Woodfull said. The skipper reported to the Board on Bradman's quiet influence on strategy, willingness to perform when unwell, and his magnificent batting performances, with 304 at Leeds and 244 at the Oval, which did much to give Australia a 2:1 Ashes victory.

'Don could be the best tactical and strategic leader ever,' Woodfull told Hodgetts in private, 'if he is nurtured and given the chance.'

It suited Hodgetts to boost Bradman further. After a year, he helped to manoeuvre him into the captaincy of the Australian team for the 1936–37 defence of the Ashes. There had to be influential backing for change, but Bradman also played his part by performing at his best to secure the leadership position.

War intervened in 1939. When France surrendered to Germany on 22 June 1940, Britain stood alone against Hitler and his Nazi war machine that intended to control all of Europe, including

Russia. Bradman was among tens of thousands of Australians who reacted by enlisting in the armed forces. He was passed fit for air-crew duty in the RAAF and attended training courses. In July 1940, his broking duties were put on hold and even cricket would only see him in a few Saturday games and fundraisers.

The army decided to use Bradman for publicity purposes. He was promoted to lieutenant and transferred to Frankston, Victoria, to begin a fitness program for forces going to North Africa. Bradman pushed himself too hard as usual in a variety of sports, including cricket, and during physical exertions.

First, medical checks found his eyesight was failing. He was hospitalised for two weeks. Then his back strain, which had kept him out of tour games in the UK in 1938, returned. In the early months of 1941, he was in and out of hospital. In May 1941, he experienced excruciating back spasms. The pain spread to the muscles and nerves of his right arm. Bradman was so debilitated that Jessie had to shave him, when she already was preoccupied with daughter Shirley, who was a few weeks old, and two-year-old John.

In June 1941, an army medical board invalided him out of the armed services. The Bradman family retreated to the Mittagong, New South Wales, home of Jessie's parents for the remainder of the year for rest and recreation. He was in such a bad way, he could not be sure about ever returning to broking, let alone cricket.

CHAPTER 17

The Downfall of Harry Hodgetts

While Bradman was ailing, his boss, Harry Hodgetts, was expanding. He invested his own and some clients' funds in underwriting a hotel complex in Darwin. But losses in 1941 from a Broken Hill agent's business failure, and from speculation in wheat futures, hit Hodgetts hard. Then, on 19 February 1942, Japanese forces bombed Darwin with more weaponry and fire power than they had Pearl Harbor, Hawaii, two months earlier. Australia's northernmost city and Hodgetts' underwriting of bricks-and-mortar investments were hit badly.

He scrambled to cover his losses by using funds from his clients' accounts. This was a desperate, fraudulent move. He was also relying on loans and guarantees from friends. He had even pledged his Adelaide Club debentures as security for a loan. Meanwhile, his bank overdraft soared to more than 100,000 pounds.

In 1942, John Curtin's federal government tightened wartime controls over stock-exchange transactions. Hodgetts had lobbied against them. When enacted, they helped deny him the chance to trade out of his predicament. His only hope would be a boom period that would allow him to restore the clients' funds without anyone being the wiser. But boom years were not possible during war, and the broking firm began a slow, hidden spiral downwards.

Oblivious of all this, Bradman returned to the Hodgetts firm in April 1942, relieved that he was earning a living again after two years away. He was not yet well enough to play any sport through the rest of 1942. In December, he managed a few gentle holes of golf at a time, which was therapy for his back. This continued into 1943. Bradman was able to concentrate more on the broking business than ever before, without the distractions of cricket.

Bradman, now 34, was looking to the future. Hodgetts had not made him a partner in his firm, which surprised Bradman and others. Bradman had been instrumental in growing the firm's client base to nearly 4000 in the years 1935 to 1940. He had moved beyond his early public relations role to one as a broker who gave sound advice and was trusted by all. This lack of promotion made Bradman think he might have to branch out on his own at some time in the future. In May 1943 and after a year back at Hodgetts & Co., he became a member of the Adelaide Exchange in his own right when he bought a seat for 330 pounds, but remained working for Hodgetts.

'It was a kind of insurance,' Bradman said during a tea break in the kitchen of his Holden Street home, with Jessie present, in May 1995.

'I suppose it was a more prophetic move than you could have realised ...?'

'Oh yes,' he said with a wry expression.

Bradman was uncomfortable going over this period. The time of convalescence, which had temporarily crippled him and resulted in a significant loss of earnings, was troubling to review. Furthermore, a financial scandal concerning his boss gave him some pain to revisit.

*

By early 1945, Australia seemed safe from invasion, although its armed services were still at war with Japan. This caused people to think about loosening up their investments. They began to liquidate shares to buy land, business, cars and other goods. There was promise of a post-war boom. But then there were delays in payments from Hodgetts. He didn't have the funds to meet the sudden extra demands. No longer could he prop up his business by juggling clients' funds. He could not any more rob Peter to pay Paul.

On 2 June 1945, the Adelaide broking world received one of its biggest ever shocks. Hodgetts informed the Exchange that he was 'unable to meet his commitments'. In plain language, he was broke. He, and by association his firm, were bankrupt.

An affidavit filed in the Adelaide Bankruptcy Court showed Hodgetts' deficiencies at 82,854 pounds. Some 238 unsecured creditors were named, with debts totalling 102,926 pounds. Solicitor Guy Fischer lost 34,567 pounds. Test cricketer Arthur Richardson (no relation to Victor) lost his life savings and Bradman himself was owed 762 pounds. The whole affair was a tragedy of *Mayor of Casterbridge* proportions in parochial Adelaide.

'We were all in shock,' Jessie remarked.

Don nodded. 'Despite his folly, we felt very sorry for Harry. We believe he was a good man who got caught up in unfortunate circumstances.'

The Exchange moved with commendable speed from the point of view of stopping the rot that could set in to a fragile broking world over Hodgetts' demise. The President of the Exchange and the Official Receiver met with Bradman. They suggested, as an Exchange member, he could start his own firm if he wished, with certain conditions. First, he would have to submit a list of the Hodgetts firm's outstanding settlements to the Exchange. Second, he could not automatically take over the entire client list; instead, he would have to write to as many as he wished, inviting them to be represented by his new firm. Third, Bradman would have to apply to the committee of the Exchange to register his new firm's name. The President would ensure that this was granted quickly.

Bradman consulted fellow broker and Hodgetts employee Len Bullock, who agreed to join him in this venture. He then spoke with Jessie, knowing it would be an additional burden for her.

'I had no hesitation in supporting Don,' she said. 'It meant employment and being his own boss, which I endorsed.'

Therein lay the nub of the proposition. If Bradman rolled over with the firm's dissolution and left all the clients he had helped bring to the firm, he would be unemployed at a time he could least afford it, with his health issues and a growing family.

Bradman agreed to the Exchange's conditions. He wrote to hundreds of clients, offering them his services, and took a small suite of offices in Cowra Chambers at the same address as before, 23 Grenfell Street. It reminded visitors of a solicitor's tiny wood-panelled office. Bradman's desk was meticulously neat and reflected his logical and uncluttered mind. Jessie joined the firm to do secretarial work, making a grand total of three employees: Bradman, Jessie and Bullock.

The firm opened its doors for business as Don Bradman & Co. on 5 June, just three days after Hodgetts had declared he was bankrupt. The Exchange's footwork, faster than Bradman's batting against Bill O'Reilly, meant that initially, to the outside world, Hodgetts had disappeared. In its place in a flash was a firm with the most marketable name in Australia.

There was some initial objection from competitors that Bradman should have paid for the 'goodwill' of the business, a premium built up over time. But the Hodgetts company name had been severely damaged and any goodwill was diminishing because of his fraudulent activity. Another complaint centred around the claim that it usually took a month for a receiver to decide whether a company could trade its way out of trouble in order to best service the interests of its creditors. But the receiver had no doubt that the Hodgetts business was in such a mess, it was too late to salvage. Hodgetts himself had supplied enough information to support the claim that it was irredeemably insolvent.

There was further disgruntlement over whether the client list should have been put out to tender. Then other brokers could have bid for it. The return from that could have been distributed to creditors. But the flaw in that argument was that the clients would not be consulted over which broker they wanted. Under that arrangement, the Exchange would be dictating to whom a client's business went, which would have been unacceptable to most of them. Broking was a most personal thing, more than it is today; the bond and trust between broker and client is almost sacrosanct. Money was involved. Lifetime savings were often at stake. No one wanted an incompetent or slack broker. Hodgetts' clients would not have appreciated being told to accept a new, unknown controller of their investments.

As it was, Bradman's letter gave them the choice. They could go with him, or elsewhere.

Furthermore, the unfortunate big losers among the creditors would have received at most only a few pence in the pound for their losses. There was no way that a rival broker to Hodgetts would have remotely compensated the clients for their ex-stockbroker's criminal behaviour.

Another factor was the Exchange's need to move on fast to avoid bad public relations over a long, drawn-out period. Putting the Hodgetts list up for sale, like a carcass for vultures, would have been an agonising process for all concerned, which the Exchange Committee and official receiver did not want. They wished minimum disruption to the Exchange's image of probity.

Naturally Bradman drew most rumours over the affair, and his detractors worked overtime to besmirch him. The most common line of attack was that Bradman 'must have known' about Hodgetts' problems. But none of the staff did. Bradman was not a partner in the firm. He suffered because of the false rumours that drew his integrity into question.

This inaccuracy was revived 55 years later, after Bradman died, and still lingers with a few 'fake-news' journalists, and other Adelaide gossipmongers.

CHAPTER 18

Opportunity Knocks and Knockers

A month after the revelation about Hodgetts' failure, the official receiver's report was submitted to the Bankruptcy Court. Police arrested 63-year-old Harry Hodgetts at his Kensington Park home and he was charged with three counts of fraud. The news was soon Australia wide. One reporter who sat in on the case wrote that Hodgetts now had 'iron-grey hair and tired features'.

Hodgetts pleaded guilty to 'fraudulent conversion and false pretences'. The judge passing sentence agreed with the defence counsel's plea that Hodgetts had not set out to commit fraud, that he had truly believed he could trade his way out of his trouble. Yet Hodgetts was still given a five-year jail term. He broke down and cried. (He spent three years in prison and was released early on compassionate grounds. He died from cancer just a year later, on 4 October 1949.)

Prim and proper Adelaide, 'the City of Churches', was stunned; the affair filled the papers, even pushing Australia's struggle to hold and defeat the Japanese on Bougainville off the front pages. General MacArthur's drive to 'return to the Philippines' from whence he had run in 1941 was even relegated to a minor item on page three in the Adelaide *Advertiser*.

'It was a sad and distressing time,' Jessie remarked, 'especially when the press learned of some of Hodgetts' [high-profile] personal clients, including the nation's former Governor-General Lord Gowrie and his wife. They were, and remained, personal friends of ours.'

The Gowries' portfolios were reported to have been made nearly worthless and they were thinking about suing their agent, the Commonwealth Bank of Australia, for the recovery of lost assets. Even the funds of the Royal Institution for the Blind had been misappropriated.

Yet despite Hodgetts' 'goodwill' being reduced to nought, many of the firm's old clients responded to Bradman's letter and went back to him.

'Within weeks we, a small team, had just about all we could handle,' Bradman said.

Institutions from the weightier end of town gave his business the appropriate nod, and bankers offered support. Bradman the broker was in business and it was soon going well. Through dint of much labour, inside a year he was putting on staff. In 18 months, his client list had expanded well beyond Hodgetts' old list.

Bradman was once more in the public arena, making big scores in an Ashes series in Australia. In a dashing post-war, post-illness comeback, he began with 187 in the Brisbane First Test of the 1946–47 series.

There were some consequences for this renewed exposure after seven years out of the limelight. The firm was subject to strict regular audits. Two upset members of the Exchange, who had been hungry to access the Hodgetts list, organised a photo journalist to take a shot of the sign outside Bradman's office — 'Don Bradman & Co., Stock, Share and Investment Broker'. The picture showed a group of men in the foreground, including an earnest-looking, pipe-smoking army sergeant, and a knot of suited, hatted gentlemen. Bradman was summoned before an Exchange committee, which investigated whether or not the newspaper photo was 'advertising'. He explained to the committee that he had no control over what the press did. He certainly did not ask them to take a photo of his business.

'It happened because of the jealousies of one or two members,' Bradman said, 'and because of the way the business was progressing.'

*

Bradman was his usual conscientious self and would not let anyone else — not even his experienced fellow broker and employee, Len Bullock — make the tougher decisions. Even when it came to things such as going onto the floor of the Exchange for bigger clients to buy and sell shares late in the day's trading, which tended to be more frenetic, Bradman would simply do it himself.

'If an expected price was not met,' Bradman told me, 'I did not wish any of my staff subordinates to take the blame.'

Unsaid was the fact that clients were most unlikely to confront Bradman for a miscalculation over a buy or sell. On top of that, all clients got to know Bradman's diligence and integrity over money. Broking has always been built on trust, and he provided it.

In 1954, after two decades as a broker, Bradman at 46 was finding the stress too much. He retired and handed over the operation to Bullock in a smooth transition. Bradman was not aware of course, but he still had another 46 years to live. Stresses and strains to come would test his mettle and constitution ever more.

*

Bradman remained a consultant for Bullock's firm and took up directorships with companies, which together brought him a similar income to his broking operations, but with less stress. Over the next 25 years, these included Endeavour Ltd; Centurion Ltd; Tecalemit Aust Pty Ltd; Kelvinator Aust Ltd; Argo Investments; Bounty Investments Ltd; Leo Investments Ltd; and F.H. Faulding & Co. Ltd. He was also an alternative director of Uniroyal Holdings Ltd, chairman of Wakefield Investments, and on the local advisory board of Mutual Acceptance Ltd.

Some groups, such as Argo and Wakefield, had him consult until he was well into his eighties. He was respected for his knowledge of the stock market, his astute analysis, his corporate background and his contacts, both locally and internationally. Bradman's reputation and his name were assets nearly as much in the UK as Australia. Many an English top-line cricketer had gone on to become successful businessmen, and they all knew and respected Bradman.

He kept a close relationship with members of the Reserve Bank. Most prime ministers had a strong link to him, starting with Bob Menzies and including Bob Hawke, Paul Keating and John Howard. I was amused when two of them phoned while we were working on some aspect of my books.

'Call back tomorrow,' he said to them or their secretaries, with a bluntness that only he could get away with. This was not done for my benefit. Nor was it meant to be in any way discourteous. Bradman was concentrating on an issue and he did not wish to be distracted.

He had experienced the worst of the 1930 Depression and used to discuss inflation (which he hated) and other fiscal matters with prime ministers and leaders from both political parties. All of them ranked him highly in his comprehension and attitude. It was a factor behind every prime minister from Billy Hughes to John Howard judging him 'the greatest Australian ever born'.

He wrote copiously to the Reserve Bank chairmen, dispensing advice, often gratuitously. If they did not reply, he might let the prime minister of the day know, which always elicited a prompt response. The Reserve Bank vault of Bradman letters and replies would make interesting reading, although they have remained locked away.

CHAPTER 19

The Final Challenge

Of all our discussions on a variety of topics, Bradman had most satisfaction in reviewing the 1948 Ashes tour, the most successful tour by any team in the history of the game.

Bradman asked if I could come to Adelaide for this interview, and it made me comprehend it was important to document the tour from his point of view. He had covered the tour in a few chapters of his autobiography, *Farewell to Cricket*. Yet it needed a fresh, deeper view. I was so intrigued. I could see a separate book, apart from the biography, looming. There had been five or six tomes from those who covered the tour, including the aforementioned readable efforts by Bill O'Reilly and Jack Fingleton, along with England's John Arlott and others. But none had interviewed Bradman for them. The captain's perspective on the most successful tour of any sport, let alone cricket, was

143

missing. The thoughts of the engineer, the genius behind that phenomenal success, had yet to be documented.

The Australians went through an entire 34 matches, including five Tests, without losing one of them. We covered it in detail over two long sessions, mainly in his upstairs study so we could access *Wisden*, his diaries and other sources.

In 1999, four years after the biography *The Don* was published, I suggested that I would write a full account of the 1948 tour from his perspective. He was pleased, but we both agreed that it had to be published on a date that marked another decade since the tour, which meant 2008, and 60 years.

'That would make me 100,' Bradman remarked. 'I doubt I'll be around then.'

We talked about the books already published on the tour. None seemed to do justice to the enormous significance of the Australians' achievement under his leadership. But as Bradman pointed out, 'No one could envisage how the tour would stand out given the passage of time.'

This was a fair point, and now with shorter tours, the success of the 1948 side will stand for all time as something that cannot be replicated or bettered.

I was fortunate enough to be in a position to get Bradman's personal views. The resultant book, *Bradman's Invincibles*, was published by Hachette Australia in 2008.

*

Bradman was never a certain starter for this tour. His injuries, particularly his back issues and fibrositis, had laid him low during the war years, and had recurred during the recent five Test series versus India in 1947–48. By early in 1948, he was still uncertain about touring. The easy option was to retire as the greatest cricketer ever. He was averaging more than a hundred every time he batted in Tests, and he had dominated England in six out of seven Ashes series since 1928–29. Bradman had few peers in the history of sports leadership. He was eager to move on and put more time into his business and family life.

At first, the thought of another gruelling Ashes campaign in England, with non-stop cricket and functions over half a year, not to mention the months of boat travel to and from the UK, seemed unattractive. But there was pressure from Australia and England at all levels of sport and politics for him to lead the Australians one final time.

Bradman was big on duty. It was put to him that he would be 'doing the right thing' by the post–World War II battered seat of the British Empire if he turned up at London's Tilbury Docks. This caused him to re-consider his position.

And in his thoughts, but never expressed even privately, was one very last grand challenge: to lead a team through the northern summer of 1948 without a single loss. It had never been done in the 80 years of campaigns by all cricket nations since Charles Lawrence led an all-Aboriginal team the length and breadth of England in 1868 but was beaten in many of their matches.

Going through undefeated was the nearest thing to mission impossible in sport. The bookies and pundits were certain that if the home team didn't manage to challenge the tourists in a Test, then one of the counties or representative teams, such as 'The Gentlemen', would topple the Australians in the 34-match schedule. Poor weather, a collective lapse of form, a let-down period after a big Test win, or even a cunning ambush with a Test-standard England team in a 'festival' match would inflict at least one defeat. It had happened every other tour on scores of occasions to the Australians, South Africans, Indians, New Zealanders and West Indians.

Bradman had failed to achieve the freakish feat when captain of the last Ashes tour a decade earlier. Yet he thrived on sporting challenges, whether it was scoring below par on every golf course he competed on in South Australia and Victoria; taking on world billiards champion Walter Lindrum at his peak; beating Don Turnbull, the South Australian squash champion, in a state title in his (Bradman's) first-ever official competition; defeating several Wimbledon tennis players of his era in 'friendlies'; or coming out on top against every bowler he ever faced at every level of cricket over 30 years.

In the end, this final test was too alluring. He decided to tour.

British commentator John Arlott observed that Bradman 'planned the 1948 season with the precision of a General in a major military campaign'. Yet Bradman kept it simple. He singled out his top bowler, the brilliant 'Atomic' Ray Lindwall, for special nurturing and guidance in the build-up to the Tests, with the aim of letting him loose in the Ashes. The main target was England's best bat, Len Hutton, who had scored 364 in the final Ashes Test of 1938 to break Bradman's Test record and set up the biggest win in history.

Bradman wanted no repeats. He asked the dashing all-rounder Keith Miller to open the bowling with Lindwall. They were directed to blast out the home team's strong batting line-up. Lindwall delivered the most effective bouncer in history next to that of the West Indies' Malcolm Marshall in the 1980s. It was slung at a terrifying pace, while never rising above throat level.

'It was the most lethal delivery in cricket,' England batsman Colin Cowdrey observed.

'You never knew when it was coming,' fellow bat Tom Graveney recalled, 'and that was what made you nervous. On top of that Lindwall had the best swinging yorker [full-pitched delivery at the toes] I ever faced.'

But as the old saying goes, 'Man makes plans, God laughs.' Lindwall pulled a thigh muscle and limped his way through the first two Tests. Miller aggravated a back injury sustained in a wrestling match during the war. Suddenly Australia's much-vaunted opening bowling combination looked fragile. Yet Bradman was well served by two unheralded left-arm medium pacers, Bill Johnston and Ernie Toshack, who stepped up a notch to keep the pressure on the opposition.

The Australian batting line-up was strong and consistent, led by Arthur Morris and Bradman. They were supported by Sid Barnes, Lindsay Hassett and, later in the series, teenager Neil Harvey. They built big scores, giving the shaky (Toshack also damaged his knee), yet still penetrating bowling line-up time to dismiss England twice.

Mid-season, Australia led the Ashes 2:0 with England being on top in a draw at Manchester in the Third Test. Everything was set-up for a huge encounter in the Fourth Test at Leeds. England was in fine form with a chance to get back in the series; Bradman was playing his last big game at a ground at which he had scored two triple centuries and a century in his three previous Tests there in 1930, 1934 and 1938.

Yorkshire fans were ecstatic over England's big first innings score of 496, with Cyril Washbrook (146), Bill Edrich (111) and Hutton (81) all performing at their best. Yet none expected other than a forceful response from the Australians.

*

When Bradman entered the arena in front of 40,000 spectators in the first innings after Morris had been dismissed for six, he was cheered by an honour guard of spectators all the way to the wicket and, as English cricket writer E.W. Swanton later commented, was 'greeted like an emperor'.

But when he was bowled for just 33, the roar from the crowd was one of delight, shock and dismay. Many had seen every one of his Test innings at Leeds. There was a first-innings fallibility in him after all. An Emperor with pads he may have been, but no deity.

Australia needed something special and this came from Harvey (112) in perhaps the finest first-up Ashes innings of all time; Miller (58) in a dashing cameo; and Sam Loxton, who slammed 93 in the manner of a Twenty20 innings by David Warner. Australia smashed its way to 458.

Fifteen minutes into the final day, England pumped hard to declare its second innings closed at 8 for 365. England skipper Norman Yardley had batted on so he could use the heavy roller before play on a pitch that was already taking spin. Australia was left with 404 to make in less than a day on a turning wicket. No team in the history of Test cricket had come remotely near such a target.

Opener Arthur Morris was irritated by the papers telling him the game would be over by lunch. He was motivated to 'prove them wrong'.

CHAPTER 20

Triumph

Don Bradman and Arthur Morris were similar characters. They were both taciturn, undemonstrative types with dry senses of humour. At the crease, they had few peers in skill, determination and powers of concentration. They would need everything functioning perfectly, and some luck to reach the massive target. Until then, the highest score in Australia in a final innings to win was 332. In England, it was a mere 263, and that was in 1902.

'I read that you were pessimistic about getting the runs on the last day,' I said to Bradman. 'I understand that anyone facing such a task on a last-day wicket against a good attack would hardly be optimistic. What did you think?'

'I had discussions with Bill Ferguson [the team scorer] and that night [before the final day] he told me that such a score had never been achieved in a Test before. He actually pulled out figures for all First-Class cricket to show that it was a rare achievement.'

'Did that put you off?'

'Bill knew me pretty well. We loved to discuss the numbers. I started as a scorer for Bowral [at age 11].'

'You have had a passion for the statistics, the numbers ...'

'Yes.'

'You wrote in your diary that night: "We are set 400 to win and I fear we may be defeated." The next morning you told Ferguson: "I think we are going to lose the game. It's too many runs for any team to make in such a short time."'

'I'd call that realism rather than pessimism. But whatever way you slice it, there was a grand challenge ... 'When you consider our batting line-up, it was not out of the realms of possibility. Half the team would have to contribute something substantial, and it had to be done in partnerships.'

*

In the second innings, he was in at 1 for 57. It was 1 p.m. Australia had 347 to get in 257 minutes. People gathered at the gate for him and formed another, final passage to the wicket. If anything, the crowd, according to Bill O'Reilly, was cheering even louder than in the first innings.

As he crossed the turf on his unhurried march to the pitch, he was now the lonely figure for the last time in his career at his favourite ground for fans. Moments such as these inspired English commentator H.S. Altham to write:

In the many pictures I have stored in my mind from the burnt-out Junes of forty years, there is none more compelling than that of Bradman's small, serenely-moving figure in its big-peaked green cap coming out of the pavilion shadows into the sunshine, with the concentration, ardour and apprehension of surrounding thousands centred upon, and the destiny of a Test match in his hands.

Did the crowd reaction touch him?

'No. I was most appreciative of their reaction. It always lifted me. But I had a job to do.'

'Did you have a plan?'

'Well,' he chuckled, 'I didn't want to lose … There was no definitive plan. I had to get myself in first. Arthur was in very good touch, and that was comforting.'

'When did you think you had a chance of winning?'

'I didn't think about it. My mind was on beating the clock. If we did that, we were still alive.'

Australia reached halfway at 1 for 202. Morris had a century. Bradman was on 79. They had 165 minutes to get the next 202. Then the first real threat came. Bradman held his side as if he had strained it. It was an onset of fibrositis, which had debilitated him since the war years. He told Morris to take most of the strike.

'Did you think of retiring hurt?'

'I would have had to if it got worse. But it was a spasm. I had them often and it passed.'

There was another irritant in the lack of a sight-screen. Leeds did not have them. Both batsmen were having trouble picking up the ball in the glare. It was hot and sunny. Men were removing their jackets. It left a multi-coloured blur behind the bowler's arm.

'It was like looking at a draughts board,' Bradman recalled.

He reached his century with 15 fours in 145 minutes and raised his bat.

'Reports said you smiled for the first time in the day. Did you think you had it won at tea? The score was 1 for 288.'

'We managed 167 in the second session. The calculations were encouraging. We needed 116 in the last session. A win was now possible.'

Left-hander Morris and Bradman were very good friends. They supported each other in the partnership of 301 in 217 minutes until Morris (182) was out for a fine knock, perhaps the best of the 1948 Ashes to that point. Bradman was on 143. Just 46 were needed. Miller came and went for 12. Neil Harvey and Bradman (173 not out) completed the formalities that brought victory at 3 for 404. Australia was 3:0 up and the series was secured.

'Was this the finest come-from-behind win in your experience?' I asked.

'I believe so. You would not have been able to bet on it at the start of the final day.'

The Leeds Test was one of the stand-out international matches in cricket history. Victory gave Australia the series and the Ashes.

*

Bradman then focused on winning big at The Oval. The urban ground under the gasometer at Kennington, South London, had been on his mind for a decade since the crushing by England there in 1938. He had injured his ankle, preventing him from countering Hutton's record score, which added to his frustration. The experience had given him nightmares. At last he had a chance to purge the memory and gain revenge.

Lindwall, at his whirlwind best, delivered what Bradman thought was one of the most devastating pace performances he ever saw in taking six wickets for 20. England managed just 52. Bradman scored his famous duck in his last-ever Test knock. Had he scored four runs he would have ended with a Test average of exactly 100. Many observers thought this must have devastated him. Yet in our conversations, it was barely a disappointment. It was clear that, rather than individual achievement, his main aim was to win well, which the Australians did, thanks to Lindwall's bowling, and Morris, in the form of his life, carving a magnificent 196.

*

Australia won the 1948 Ashes 4:0 and then went on to reach Bradman's last great challenge of going through the summer undefeated. Thirty years later, at a 1978 reunion of the team, NSW cricket administrator Bob Radford was the first to dub the team 'the Invincibles'. More than seven decades on, 1948 seems even more remarkable. It will remain a unique achievement ...

Just how good were the Invincibles? Most would agree that it was the finest cricket unit in history until 1948. Since then, others to impress have been Peter May's England side of 1956; Ali

Bacher's South African side of 1969–70; the West Indies under Clive Lloyd and later Viv Richards in the 1980s; Steve Waugh's combination in 2001; and Ricky Ponting's 2006–07 Ashes squad.

One thing is certain. Bradman's 1948 side invites favourable comparison with the best teams into the 21st century, which speaks volumes in itself for the Invincibles.

CHAPTER 21

The Leader

Bradman was not a natural leader. There was something so individualistic in his make-up or persona that it may have been better to leave him alone to dominate the game without the burdens of captaincy. This too could be said of Sachin Tendulkar, whose quiet yet deceptively strong manner also did not signal a capacity as a skipper. Bradman didn't seek the Australian captaincy and, from our chats, I believe he would have accepted continuing to play under others. But when duty called, he responded. He led from the front with his performances as captain, but developed a high tactical and strategic ability. He applied himself to this challenge with his usual perseverance and diligence.

Bradman led Australia in 24 Tests, for 15 wins, three losses and six draws for a win ratio of 62.5 per cent, which is high among leaders who had skippered in at least 20 Tests. He took on the captaincy of Australia in his 29th Test and applied the same skill-set to leadership as he did to making himself the best batsman of all time. His performances, statistically at least, improved once he took on the top job. Bradman's average while captain in his last 24 Tests (101.51) was higher than in his first 28 games (98.69). He scored 14 centuries while skipper at a better rate than his 15 before that.

He was skipper in five series. Four of them were won decisively. Two of the five teams he led — in 1936–37 and 1938 — were among the weakest in Australia's Test history, but for one factor: they had Bradman in them.

His advantage was himself. After Bradman, the next best batsmen in Test history fall into a bracket of averages between 45 and 60. Bradman on average made 40 to 55 runs an innings more than this group. In effect, he was worth two of the best of the rest since the inception of Test cricket. 'Worth' is the key word here, for it would be misleading to claim he was twice as good, other than in statistical terms. Nevertheless, if you picked any great team in history, from the first-ever Test in 1877 through more than 140 years to the present day, he would be equal in value to any two other batsmen chosen.

Any team containing Bradman would win a series, given the rest of the two squads chosen were more or less of the same standard. When the big match or series-winning innings was needed, Bradman would deliver it.

In 1936–37 and 1938 particularly, he could have led Australia's second XI and the series result would have been the same. He won one series and saved another. After World War II, when he led three stronger sides against England in 1946–47 and 1948 and India in 1947–48, the distance between Australia and the opposition was huge. At 40, Bradman's output remained more or less the same with a better batting line-up around him and a far better, more rounded bowling array to throw at the opposition.

After a rotten start in his first series as captain in 1936–37, in which Australia lost the first two games to England, he scored 270, 212 and 169 to dominate victories in the last three Tests. In the drawn (one-all) 1938 Ashes, he scored a century in each of the three Tests in which he batted. In the last game at The Oval, captain Wally Hammond let England bat on to a record 7 for 903. He feared that Bradman, given two innings, would make a huge score in at least one of them. The game ended in anticlimax when Bradman tore ankle ligaments in the field and did not bat. He was disappointed he could not contribute, yet observed some amusing moments during the match.

When the score was 7 for 876, debut England keeper Yorkshireman Arthur Wood was dismissed for 53. As he returned to The Oval dressing room, a spectator called: 'Well batted, Arthur!'

Wood responded in his Yorkshire brogue, which Bradman imitated: 'Yes, I'm always at my best in a crisis!'

When Hutton was 290 en route to a world-record Test score of 364, he received a long hop from Chuck Fleetwood-Smith. Hutton tucked it away for a single.

Fleetwood-Smith said to him: 'You could have hit that anywhere for four!'

Hutton replied: 'Aye, but there may have been a trap.'

*

Bradman had more 'control' over events and the environment he worked in than any other skipper in history. He only experienced three match losses over five series. Two of those were his first games as leader when the weather, not the opposition, beat Australia, which was caught on sticky wickets. The third loss was that game at The Oval in 1938. Then Bradman didn't have Bradman to score a double or even a triple century to force a draw.

There was never a shrewder leader than The Don. He supported Bill Woodfull when he opposed Jardine's Bodyline tactics. When he became skipper, his attitude was more flexible. He included bowlers in his line-up who could intimidate the opposition.

On the boat to England in 1948, Bradman discussed tactics with his main weapon, fast bowler Ray Lindwall. He would be used in an attempt to destroy England's trump, Len Hutton. Bradman wanted Lindwall confident and prepared for the Tests. He didn't want him to be a spent mental force before the Test matches, as speedster Ernie McCormick had been in 1938, when he was no-balled 35 times in his first game at Worcester.

Lindwall had a suspect 'drag' of his trailing foot through the bowling crease (where the stumps stand) when delivering, which made him liable to no-balling. Umpires had the toughest of jobs in glancing down at the trailing foot to make sure it landed behind the bowling crease, and then watching the bowler's arm to ascertain it was a fair delivery, and not a throw. Bradman told Lindwall to concentrate on passing the umpires in the opening games. Taking wickets was of secondary importance until the early umpires passed his 'drag'. The captain told him his place in the Test team was assured, no matter what his figures were early in the tour.

Lindwall did as instructed and kept his back foot a long way behind the bowling crease when he let go of the ball. He was 'passed' by the umpires. Lindwall went on to play a significant part in the Tests. (The rule was changed decades later to beat the 'drag'. The heel of the bowler's front foot had to land on or before the popping crease — the front line of the batting crease.)

Bradman also let Lindwall bowl bouncers at Hutton at Lord's. The star opener was troubled and dropped prematurely by selectors after failing in three of his four innings of the first two Tests. By the time Hutton was restored to the Test side, Australia had retained the Ashes.

In the Third Test, Lindwall felled Denis Compton (en route to 145). When Australia batted, Bill Edrich then bowled five bouncers at Lindwall, hitting him once. When Edrich came to the wicket in England's second innings, Bradman told Lindwall not to bowl any bouncers. The captain allowed intimidation, but would not cross the line into a bumper war that would 'not be in the spirit of the game'. Bradman was also aware that the media would pounce on the swapping of throat balls.

There was evidence of more subtle use of psychology in the way he handled Lindwall in 1948. The bowler strained his groin in the First Test. Bradman gave him a tough physical examination at Lord's before the Second Test. He passed, but Bradman, who knew all about leg injuries and recovery times, was sceptical.

'Leave me out on form if you want to,' Lindwall said, 'but not fitness.'

Bradman picked him. When he bowled, he pulled up during the follow-through of his first delivery. Lindwall tried to hide his discomfort. Bradman, who never missed a trick on the field, pretended he hadn't seen anything. Lindwall did everything to cover up his problem, including taking wickets — five of them — for 70.

Years later, Lindwall, on prompting from Bradman, admitted he had hurt his groin again with that first ball.

'Why didn't you say something at the time?' Lindwall asked.

'I noticed that you were trying so hard to hide it from me,' Bradman explained, 'and I reckoned you might bowl better if you thought I didn't know about it. I wasn't far wrong, was I?'

Bradman was also the pragmatist's pragmatist. He more than once rearranged the batting order to preserve his own wicket and those of his key batsmen when his team had to bat on a poor wicket. He had no time for the 'heroic' skippers, such as Joe Darling, who would go in first on a sticky to set an example to his men. Invariably, this was a suicide mission. By contrast, Bradman dropped himself down the list to avoid the worst of the wicket. Invariably, he succeeded. His mind, unfettered by conceit or egotism, the need to preserve an average, fear of failure, or bravado, speared right to the heart of the matter. He had to give his best batsmen a chance to win a game on a better wicket.

*

Bradman also dispensed advice, sometimes gratuitously, usually when asked. He kept it simple, often getting to the point in a word or two. If an individual absorbed what was said and acted on it, he was better for it.

In 1948, Neil Harvey, the 19-year-old 'baby' of the squad, had a shaky start to the tour. He was too nervous to ask Bradman himself for advice, so he prevailed on his Victorian friend Sam Loxton to intervene with 'the boss' and find out what he should do to improve his batting results.

Bradman told Loxton to tell Harvey to keep the ball along the ground.

The teenager was baffled. Was that it?

'That's what the boss said,' Loxton said, with a head tilt and a shoulder shrug.

A bemused Harvey took the advice. Bradman's reasoning as ever was pertinent. There was nothing wrong with Harvey's batting at all, and Bradman regarded him highly and without any weaknesses. To confuse him with unnecessary science about strokeplay on low, slow wickets, which he knew anyway, would be superfluous and counter-productive. To say nothing at all might lower the young man's confidence. Bradman's minimalist edict caused Harvey to concentrate on a basic. His scores improved. He was selected for the Fourth Test and hit 112 in his first-ever Ashes match and helped Australia to one of the great wins in history. No observer could recall any lofted shots from the teenage star.

During the 1970–71 season, Bradman met a youthful Dennis Lillee at a function just before his first Test at Adelaide. There was much media and paper talk about Lillee being selected as a counter to the aggressive fast-bowling of England's John Snow. Lillee was not quite sure what his approach should be.

The 62-year-old Bradman took the new demon bowler aside and said: 'Forget about all the newspaper talk about bowling bumpers. Concentrate on what you've done. It's got you into the Test side.'

'It was a good, logical piece of advice,' Lillee remarked in his book *Over and Out*. 'It relaxed me for the huge job ahead. I was 21 and the responsibility of opening the bowling for Australia was bigger than anything I had shouldered before. My chat with Bradman eased the inner tensions but put me in deeper awe of the man himself.'

Lillee bowled brilliantly in his first effort, taking 5 for 84, and never looked back.

CHAPTER 22

The Statement

Over the six-year relationship I had with Bradman, I got to know him and his character well. The event that reflected his integrity and character the most was his handling of the apartheid issue and the all-white South African cricket team that was scheduled to tour Australia in 1971–72.

I believe it was his greatest achievement and legacy, beyond cricket, his grand administrative skills in the sport and his monumental letter-writing.

The controversial issue began with Basil D'Oliveira, a so-called 'Cape Coloured' (a racial classification under apartheid of someone of mixed ethnic origin) who was born into a Catholic family of Indian–Portuguese descent in Cape Town in 1928. He was a talented all-rounder, who, with the help of famous English commentator John Arlott, emigrated in 1960 to

England, where a place was found for him at Middleton, a team in the Lancashire League. He was surprised to see white people doing menial tasks and was stunned when they waited on him in a café, something he had never experienced in South Africa. D'Oliveira felt he was more comfortable living in England. He was selected to play for England against the West Indies in 1966 and was made one of *Wisden*'s five cricketers of the year in 1967.

In 1968, South African cricket officials put pressure on the MCC, which ran England cricket, not to select him in the Test squad to tour South Africa. Apartheid's opponents were angered. A player in the squad dropped out because of injury and D'Oliveira, whose form more than warranted selection, was chosen. South Africa's prime minister, John Vorster, objected. The tour was cancelled. This brought world attention to apartheid.

Bradman was anti-apartheid, yet felt that South African cricketers were exempt because they had shown their opposition to racism.

'They have tried harder than our protestors to do something about it,' he wrote in 1971 in correspondence with Melbourne *Herald* journalist Rohan Rivett (which was later placed by his family in the National Library, Canberra). 'Why should they be crucified? I cannot see why they [white cricketers] should be blamed for attitudes of a Government with which they disagree.'

Bradman, accompanied by the South African ambassador, witnessed a rugby test between Australia and South Africa in Sydney. He abhorred the violence of protestors.

'The ground was protected by barbed-wire barricades,' he told me, 'and the police were ready for smoke bombs and flares. But the barricades didn't stop the protestors. They invaded the pitch.'

Bradman left that scene concerned that it would be hard to police a cricket match. He knew the sport would be the worse for it. Yet the protest didn't make him change his mind. Bradman was in his last year as Australian Cricket Board (now Cricket Australia) chairman. The South African government, by inviting him to watch the game, was preparing him for what to expect in the coming summer of 1971–72, when the South African cricket team was scheduled to tour Australia. The protest had the desired effect from the South African government's point of view. Bradman stood firm. The tour was still on.

Bradman pointed out to Rivett that the rugby team 'comprised mainly of [apartheid-supporting] Afrikaners'. The white cricketers were 'basically of English descent and a minority group among the whites. Their party — the United Party — is not opposed to mixed sport as are the [Afrikaner] Nationalists.'

'Politics should not come into sport,' he concluded. This placed Bradman in the 70 per cent majority of Australians polled at the time who favoured white-only cricket tours and who felt that Australia should not interfere in other nations' internal problems. He believed the South African cricketers should be 'encouraged to pursue their opposition to racism in sport'.

Yet the young protestors on the barricades caught his attention. Bradman was challenged. He had a flexible mind when he applied it. He decided to go beyond conventional opinion and investigate the issue himself. He wrote to the anti-apartheid protest movement in Australia, asking them why they were demonstrating. Meredith Burgmann, then a protest organiser, later in life president of the NSW Legislative Council, was astonished to receive such a request from someone she regarded as typically, trenchantly establishment.

She recalled: 'We had this dialogue, which went on for some time, and I'd send him information about what was happening in South Africa.'

Bradman was intrigued. He flew to South Africa to meet with John Vorster, a former wartime political extremist, who supported and admired the Nazis and Adolf Hitler. Vorster was concerned about meeting Bradman because he was unsure what he wanted. Vorster knew that Bradman was an enormous figure in world sport and he needed to have him 'on side'.

A witness to the meeting told me in 1974: 'I have never seen our very tough leader of the Republic so nervous. He literally sweated before the meeting. And it proved to be with good reason.'

Bradman was his usual direct self and the meeting quickly became tense, then turned sour. Bradman asked why the black players had not been given a chance to represent their country. Vorster suggested that they were intellectually inferior and could not cope with the intricacies of cricket.

Bradman laughed at this. He asked Vorster: 'Have you ever heard of Garry Sobers?' Bradman regarded West Indian all-rounder Garry Sobers as the leading cricketer of all time.

Vorster's racist attitudes, which Bradman thought 'ignorant and repugnant', led to Bradman's change of mind, which had been precipitated by Burgmann and Rivett and others with whom he corresponded. He flew on to the UK.

'You met the MCC president?' I asked Bradman, when we covered this issue in 1995.

'No,' Bradman said, 'why would I see him? He had no power over this. I met with [British prime ministers Harold] Wilson and [Ted] Heath, who had dealt with the problem [concerning D'Oliveira] in England.'

Bradman returned to Australia with his mind made up. He spoke to fellow members of the ACB. Despite some ill-informed commentary to the contrary, Bradman was not dictatorial. Neil Harvey and Sam Loxton told me that he did not always get his way at the Test selection table. If someone else put a cogent argument, Bradman allowed himself to be overridden. I had first-hand experience of this over six years of discussions where we did not always agree. Bradman was flexible and not dogmatic, but you had to have a watertight case, or at least strong enough points for him to relent from his view. It was the same on the cricket field when he was captain.

Bradman explained: 'If a bowler came to me and said, "I can get this fellow out," I'd ask him how he intended to do it. If it was not just chest-beating or bombast, and he had a sensible tactic, I'd let him have a bowl.'

The obverse was true. If a player was given his chance and fluffed it, then Bradman might not turn to him again in attempting to dismiss a particular batsman.

In the apartheid situation, Bradman put his views to each member of the ACB individually. They chatted until there was agreement. He then called a media conference at ACB headquarters in Jolimont, Melbourne. After a short preamble in which he announced that the South African tour had been cancelled, Bradman made a simple one-line statement: 'We will not play them [South Africa] until they choose a team on a non-racist basis.'

CHAPTER 23

Nelson Mandela's Hero

In 1971, I was a journalist at *The Age*, and I recall Peter McFarline, a notable sports writer, returning from the ACB media conference and slamming a file on his desk.

'Bloody Bradman!' he said, loud enough for me to hear from a few metres away.

'What's wrong, Peter?' I asked.

He told me about the conference and how Bradman had made the statement, turned on his heel and disappeared into the ACB building.

'He wouldn't take any questions,' McFarline complained. 'He makes a bloody important statement like that and won't give any explanation!'

Just about every top editor in Australia had Bradman's phone number. He made himself available, sort of. Everyone knew you did not waste his time. The reason for a call had to be valid and 'important', otherwise you would receive short shrift and risk not having access if something big happened and you wanted his comment.

The reverse was interesting. If Bradman wished to make a statement about a cricketer's milestone or the passing of a star, he would call one of the big dailies in Melbourne or Sydney and his comments would be taken down and published. I remember sitting at my desk and watching editors running across the floor in a commotion. I asked an editor what was going on.

'Bradman's on the line,' he replied in a reverential tone. 'We can't find [Graham] Perkin [*The Age* editor-in-chief].'

In 1959, Perkin had built trust with Bradman after first interviewing him in the lounge of Bradman's Adelaide home. He then observed that Bradman had been an 'imponderable personality' through his entire cricket career.

'No one knew what he was really like,' Perkin wrote, 'though many thought they did ... He was an ordinary small man [of 51 years] in a grey suit. But as he sipped his tea, another impression came through strongly ...' Perkin imagined that if his subject put on flannels and pads and walked out to the wicket that day, 'he would surely get a fast hundred'.

*

On the occasion of Bradman's one-line apartheid statement, Perkin suggested McFarline ring Bradman. In his eagerness to speak to him, McFarline was rude to Jessie. Bradman told him off for that and refused to talk to him. Discourtesy to his wife was a major sin in Bradman's eyes.

In South Africa, Vorster vented his anger publicly against Bradman while the main anti-apartheid organisation, the (black) African National Conference, rejoiced.

Burgmann, unaware that Bradman had met Vorster, Wilson and Heath, was again surprised.

'We expected him to use the excuse of not being able to guarantee the safety of the cricketers,' she said, 'but he made this wonderful statement, which pleased us [the protestors].'

Burgmann and Rivett congratulated him.

'I appreciate the compliments,' he wrote to Rivett in September 1971, 'but, no offence meant, I'm not really in the mood to feel elated. I've seen too much of both sides of the issue [which included the impact on the banned, innocent white cricketers], the good and bad of each. I was not cut out to be a politician or banner-carrier.

'In my few moments of triumph (if any) in the modern arena,' Bradman lamented, 'I have sought seclusion and peace — not publicity. But hate it as I might, publicity seems to be my lot.'

*

There were contrasting reactions, some positive, some unfortunate, to Bradman's humanitarian action that began the process which would help lead to the end of apartheid. First, the ACB had a major financial problem. Having 'killed' the international season of 1971–72 by stopping the South

Africans from touring Australia, Bradman had created the prospect of a gaping financial hole in the ACB coffers. He felt obligated to help and came up with the idea of inviting a squad of international cricketers to tour as a World XI (also known as the Rest of the World, or ROW) that would play Ian Chappell's Australians. It needed his pull and motivation to bring about. Only eight of the 17-man squad were white. Of those, three were South African. Tony Greig of England was formerly South African.

Bradman, then 63, and South Australian cricket official Phil Ridings made a point of meeting the chosen players coming into Adelaide Airport. Bradman was wearing glasses and a button-up cardigan when he greeted Tony Greig and South Africa's Hylton Ackerman. Bradman introduced himself, saying 'I'm Don,' but neither player had a clue who he was.

'They [Bradman and Ridings] looked like a couple of boring cricket officials,' Greig told me in a 2002 interview, 'and we wanted to avoid them. We gave them our suitcases to carry and went to the washroom. We had no choice but to meet these two elderly gents in the airport coffee shop.'

Making banal conversation, Greig asked what Bradman had to do with local cricket.

Bradman, delighted he had not been recognised, replied: 'Well, we sort of run the local scene.'

They chatted on until Garry Sobers walked in.

Greig recalled: 'He ignored us and went straight to the little chap in the cardigan and pumped his hand, saying, "Good morning, Sir Donald."'

Greig said he'd never been quite as embarrassed.

Bradman laughed when I mentioned this incident. 'It was a funny moment,' he said, 'and I never let Tony forget it. I think he has dined out on it ever since.'

*

The series was a success with the World XI winning the five-match series, 2:1.

'I wondered about the [World XI] selections,' I said to Bradman. 'Were they to further wound apartheid?'

'No, that was not the intention,' he replied. 'We had to work hard to secure the players we did. It turned out that the best squad available included West Indians, Indians and Pakistanis.'

'And South Africans?'

'Yes, each player was not obligated to represent his nation. He represented himself. The Tests were not official, although the standard was often higher than an average Test series.'

'It seemed you were making a point by choosing Sobers as captain ...'

'He was the greatest player in the world, and a natural captain who led by example.'

'I watched his 254 at the MCG,' I said. 'The best innings I have ever seen.'

'I have never seen a finer performance. Only Stan McCabe in 1938 ranks with it from my viewpoint.' (Here, Bradman was referring to McCabe making 232 at Trent Bridge in the First Test of the Ashes.)

'Ian Johnson [former captain of Australia] told me that you did not move from your seat at tea during Sobers's innings ...'

'That's right,' Bradman said with a smile, 'I was enthralled. I sat there contemplating the enormity of what I had just witnessed. The brilliant, cavalier shotmaking, especially through and over point, was breathtaking.'

'How do rank him in the history of the game?'

'Greatest player of all time.'

'Better than you?' I asked, genuinely surprised.

'I just told you. He is number one. He excelled in every facet of the game — as a batsman, bowler of pace and spin, and as a magnificent fielder. No one ranks with him.'

'What stood out for you in that knock?'

'His absolute mastery of power over technique.'

Bradman observed Sobers' long grip on the bat, high backlift and free swing of the blade. He had never seen anyone hit the ball harder.

'The emphasis is on power and aggression rather technique,' he said, 'the latter being the servant, not the master.'

Bradman admired Sobers's flexible wrists in driving wide of mid-on, and also his forceful cutting; he was exciting to watch.

In Perth, Dennis Lillee took 8 for 29 against the World XI. He captured six wickets for no runs in his last 13 deliveries in one of the most devastating spells of bowling ever. Bradman had seen plenty of ferocious, brilliant performances: Frank Tyson at Sydney and Melbourne in 1954–55; Harold Larwood at Adelaide in 1933; and Ted McDonald anywhere between 1921 and 1930 — and many others. But he put Lillee's effort in the top bracket, especially as it was against the best the world could offer in the early 1970s.

'He came of age in that performance with a combination of accuracy, blistering pace and control,' Bradman told me. 'It was the best bowling effort of the series.'

*

Bradman could not evade the limelight for the entire summer, attending all the unofficial five Tests. The ROW held a farewell dinner in private with just one guest: Bradman. But still the media dogged him. He was given credit for stopping the white South Africans, and for the fall-out for apartheid, and for the success of the 1971–72 series. After it, his second term as Chairman of the Board was up. His service to the game had gone well beyond the call of duty, but he stayed on as a Board representative for South Australia. The accolades and positive comments for his efforts kept coming. It was too much for Bradman's son, John, then 32 and a tutor in law at Adelaide University.

Lady Bradman described his reaction: '... a legal VIP from the UK was visiting in March [1972 — straight after the ROW summer]. When he met John, he was introduced as "as the son of Sir Donald Bradman". That was the last straw for John. He went out and changed his name by deed-poll to Bradsen.'

The 'last straw' in this case may well have been John believing he should have been given some credit for his father's change of mind over apartheid. John would never comment on this, but it seemed obvious that someone of his liberal-left persuasion would have been hard against apartheid. John was living with his parents at the time and I would be surprised had this topic not been 'hot' at the dinner table on occasions. I believe John would have swayed his father from a conservative position, even if it were a subconscious influence.

I put the argument about John's influence over his father concerning apartheid to him in a phone conversation in 2004. I wanted his input for an article I was writing for *The Australian* on the subject. He refused to comment. Finally I copied the method of American reporters Woodward and Bernstein, when they were trying to elicit more information from 'Deep Throat', their Washington DC insider, concerning the Watergate Affair.

'I'll give you 20 seconds to respond,' I said. 'If you don't answer, I shall regard that as tantamount to you admitting you swayed him.'

I waited 20 seconds. John did not say anything. We both laughed. I took that as a positive response.

There is strong evidence that Rohan Rivett had the biggest intellectual impact on Bradman over the issue. Others such as former prime minister Bob Hawke claimed to have had some say in Bradman's thinking. Yet, even if Don was reacting against his son, John's contrary thoughts would have stayed with him. Don had great respect for John's intellect, and had high hopes for him.

Bradman himself was especially bright, but regretted his lack of formal education. Several times in our chats he referred to this, and when I knew him well, I remarked: 'Don, you have educated yourself far beyond most people with PhDs. Look at what you have achieved in sport, as a stockbroker, an investment adviser, a cricket administrator and what you did for the anti-apartheid movement.'

I said this in as many words on another occasion and received the same response: he just shrugged each time and moved on. I believe Bradman would have made a superb professional at whatever vocation he chose.

*

On the bigger apartheid issue Bradman had succeeded where politicians and protestors had failed, by going beyond entrenched arguments to discover the integrity of the matter. His reputation and fame meant the unexpected move was a blow to apartheid on the international stage.

Yet the issue remained. Slow progress was made. In April 1986, a group of 70 world 'eminent persons' — including former Australian prime minister Malcolm Fraser — was allowed to visit the imprisoned deputy president of the African National Congress, Nelson Mandela. Despite being locked up from 1962 to 1990 at Robben Island Maximum Security Prison, Pollsmoor Maximum Security Prison outside Cape Town, and Victor Verster Prison near Paarl, he had a commanding presence.

Mandela's first question to the group was: 'Is anyone here from Australia?'

Fraser put up his hand.

To everyone's surprise, Mandela then asked: 'Is Don Bradman still alive?'

Bradman had been Mandela's sporting hero, and he had been endeared further to him because of his 1971 decision. Fraser was able to assure him that Bradman was definitely still functioning, and he arranged for a bat signed by him to be sent to the African leader.

A few years later, Mandela was released and apartheid was over. In late 1993, a South African team, chosen on a non-racist basis — 22 years after Bradman's one-line official directive — began a tour of Australia.

Mandela visited Australia in 2000 and wanted to meet Bradman and thank him for his courageous act in 1971.

I chatted with Bradman, then 92, about this.

'I'm not well enough to see him,' he told me, 'and I just don't want the media attention. I'm well past it.' Instead, he wrote Mandela a note.

Bradman was humbled by the regard from one of the most outstanding individuals of the 20th century, and someone he 'admired greatly'.

Mandela remarked: 'Don Bradman is one of the Divinity.'

I asked Bradman for his thoughts on that comment.

'Not sure about that,' he said with an embarrassed laugh. I thought it may have stumped him, until he added: 'You know, he was rather fond of Colonel Gaddafi as well.'

CHAPTER 24

The Compassionate Benefactor

Bradman's diligence in responding to letters produced a big part of his legacy. He usually replied using his battered old typewriter, but he also wrote in longhand, and had the help of a secretary only in the last year of his life. His output was up to a staggering 80 or so letters a day and every recipient holds the communication dear, usually forever.

Occasionally his letters appear at auctions, but not as much as other memorabilia such as books or bats. There was something endearing about his crisp, inimitable style, honed over his life, that made people treasure his epistles. Bradman would have disdained the semi-literacy and shorthand that tends to feature in emails and phone texts today. He would have been fine with 140-character tweets, though, as long as they were grammatical and meaningful — not a common feature in this modern form of communication.

Sometimes charlatans sent him items to sign, usually bats, that they would then sell off, and this upset him. But generally the public only wanted his precious name, and not to profit from it.

Bradman often did deeds for charities, particularly, but not exclusively, for the disabled. Having been through much with his own children, he was always sympathetic to those sorts of causes and was the quiet aid behind many fundraisers. Bradman joined Rotary, partly because of its support for the Crippled Children's Association in South Australia. He gave speeches where all proceeds went to it.

I had many people approach me in order to reach him for various causes. I would suggest that a woman head any delegation to him, but always to write first.

'Why a woman?' I'd invariably be asked.

I would explain that he couldn't stand the adulation of middle-aged men. Women in general were less interested in his sporting achievements and more interested in his character. He appreciated that.

On one occasion, Bradman sat for several sessions for a portrait. The artist would bring his most attractive wife to the sittings at Holden Street. Bradman was happy and chirpy with her.

'One day near the end of the sittings, I didn't bring my wife,' the artist told me, 'and he seemed quite grumpy. Apparently he enjoyed her company more than mine!'

Bradman, without prompting, told the story from his point of view.

'I disliked having to sit for the painter,' Bradman said, 'but he had a stunning wife and this made it all palatable.'

'No pun intended?'

'Oh, yes, "palatable" [palette-able],' Bradman laughed. 'But then one day he didn't bring her and I was most disappointed.'

It was one of those rare moments when two sides of a story matched perfectly.

*

Bradman, as far as I know, never knocked back writing a foreword for a book on a cricketer or other sportsperson he knew, and while this does not sound like much, such activity is always time-consuming. He had to think about what to say, and I would be surprised if he asked for payment for such labour.

The ultimate expression of his charitable nature, which he kept secret from the wider public, was the Bradman Museum at Bowral. There is a fair range of Bradman's own items donated and on display, but not as much as in the significant collection of his papers and memorabilia at the Mortlock Library, in the State Library of South Australia.

In the 1970s, Bradman struck up a friendship with the State Librarian Hedley Brideson, who asked for and received newspaper and other reports on him, which Bradman's mother had kept. The cuttings ran to 52 volumes. Brideson had them bound in leather. Later they were edited and stripped down to two published volumes — *The Bradman Albums* — by publishing house Rigby, where Bradman was a director.

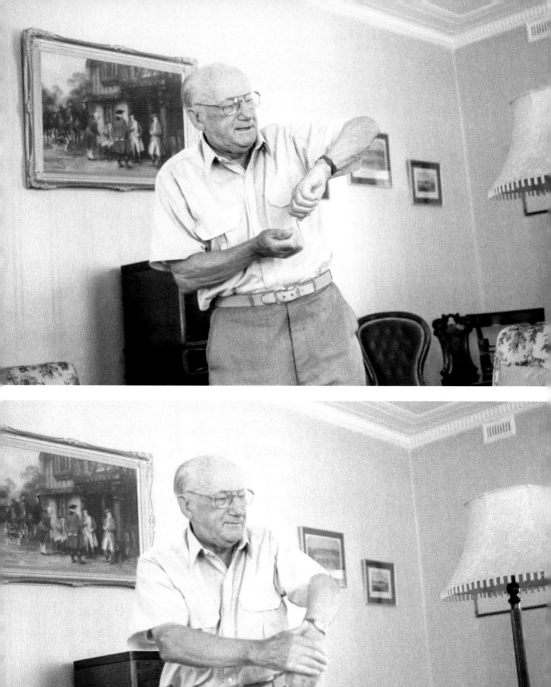

Instead of hoarding his many items of fame, performance and achievement — items that if auctioned today would attract big bids — he gave them to the library and museum. His bats, for instance, would be desired by many cricket fans, especially the English willow by London's William Sykes that Bradman used at Leeds to make 334. It sits with other mementoes — books, scrapbooks, Test jumpers, balls, tapes of his speeches and newspaper photographs.

In February 1998, Prime Minister John Howard opened the library's 'Bradman Collection', which was funded by industry, a $500,000 South Australian state government donation and a public appeal called 6996, his Test run aggregate. It was housed on the ground floor of The Institute, a restored 19th-century building on Adelaide's cultural boulevard, North Terrace.

The Bradman Museum in Bowral and the South Australian State Library in effect became rivals for anything he wore, used or kept. He happily allowed himself to be stripped of his possessions without any financial gains for what amounted to many tens of millions of dollars' worth of objects and items. This way, Bradman ensured posterity for himself and the game and, in the case of the Bradman Museum in Bowral, helped raise funds for charitable causes. The museum at the Bowral Oval has become one of Australia's top tourist drawcards.

*

As a key administrator, Bradman led by example rather than exhortation. Yet there many instances of his behind-the-scenes compassion. He had a soft spot for Terry Jenner, a battling spinner, who felt badly about being dropped from the Test team in the early 1970s.

Jenner's skipper, Ian Chappell, gave him permission to vent his spleen to the press. Jenner made a statement, saying: 'Obviously the selectors don't think I can bowl. Well, if I can't bowl, there are 280 batsmen who can't bat.' (This was roughly the number he'd dismissed in First-Class cricket to that point. He ended with 389 wickets at 32.18.)

The Cricket Board sent him several 'please explain' letters over breaching the player/ writer /media comments rules. Jenner ignored them. He arrived at his job with Coca-Cola and there was a message telling him to 'ring Don Bradman'.

Jenner thought it was a hoax.

'Oh yeah,' Jenner said to the secretary, 'please ring Mr Lyon at the zoo, and Mr Fowler at the chicken yard.'

Out of curiosity, he phoned the number. There was no mistaking the voice on the other end. Bradman asked him politely to come to his office. Jenner dutifully did so.

At their meeting, Bradman told him he thought he had been handled harshly, given that others had also breached these rules and had not been charged with anything. He handed him a letter that he had typed up himself. It aired Jenner's grievances.

Bradman had him read and sign it. He suggested Jenner send the letter to the Board after 1 June, when Bradman himself would be Acting Chairman of the Board.

'I'll receive the letter,' he said, 'and will ensure it is properly dealt with.'

Bradman accepted Jenner's written excuse and no charge was laid.

Jenner was astonished that Bradman would do that for him out of fairness and kindness, without prompting. It was Bradman's way of showing care, which he did often.

*

Another form of Bradman's generosity towards other people occurred when they were going through sickness or hard times. He was from a generation of males who did not show public affection with hugs and kisses. Yet he showed concern and care when it mattered. I've met many people over the years who told me how Bradman turned up unexpectedly at hospital when they were ailing, with a mission to encourage and cheer them up. It was a gesture that stayed with them for life.

I recall in 1998 he learned through a mutual friend that I was struggling with pleurisy. I was not doing well and had lost 12 kilograms rapidly. My then doctor had tried to handpass me to another medico.

'Why?' I asked.

'Because earlier in my career I had a patient with your symptoms and he died. I don't want that to happen again [on my watch].'

After that startling and less-than-reassuring comment, I found another doctor and recovered.

During the illness, I received a letter from Bradman wishing me well, and, a week after that, a phone call.

The man had a compassionate side and his love for family and friends was palpable. Even his medical friends were boosted when ill. In a memorial article in the *Sydney Morning Herald* in March 2001, his friend Dr Donald Beard told how he was in hospital in the late 1990s. He was feeling down after an operation. Like most doctors, he was not a good patient.

He received a card from Bradman. Bradman would never send just a 'get well' card. There would always be a comment meant to inspire. He said he was sorry Beard hadn't been well. He added: 'I suggest you put your pads on, go out in the middle, put your head down and play the innings of a lifetime.'

Beard was chuffed and felt uplifted. He also had a laugh. An 'innings of a lifetime' was unlikely since he was a bowler and a recognised 'bunny'.

The man who had motivated millions on the cricket field was still doing it in private in his nineties.

CHAPTER 25

Meet the Mogul

Bradman became acquainted with Clyde Packer in 1932 over the Radio 2UE contract and spoke to him only a few times. But 47 years later, he was to have more extensive dealings with Clyde's grandson Kerry.

It was early 1979. Packer's breakaway World Series Cricket (WSC) competition had been going less than two years, but was destroying the traditional Test competition. Packer had started the competition because he was angry that the Cricket Board had refused to give his Channel 9 network the TV rights for Test cricket in Australia. They had always gone to the national broadcaster, the ABC. He had also responded to top-line players, including Dennis Lillee and Ian Chappell and their representatives, who thought a breakaway competition would be worth the risk. They were underpaid and being asked to perform more and more at the Test level, including internationally, with poor remuneration. The coincidence of the rejection of Packer's TV rights and the players' revolt had led to the split.

After two years of WSC, the Australian Cricket Board was struggling with a lack of incoming revenue.

Packer was also losing money. Cricket was generating less than three per cent of his income as a media mogul. But he had deep pockets, and was preparing for a third round of international games in 1979.

Nevertheless, he hated the concept of endless losses and there was a danger that his WSC would lose momentum. There were plenty of players from all around the world willing to forsake their formal, traditional series. Cricketers from India, Pakistan and the West Indies had never had it as good as with WSC. But there was a danger that WSC was becoming more of a circus than a viable competitive environment, where nation was pitted against nation. Packer and his executives knew that they could never really manufacture the fierce competition of the Ashes, India versus Pakistan or, at that stage of cricket history, the great West Indies side versus anyone. Packer's men knew they could buy the players, but they could not make the profits he wanted. Packer and his WSC managers talked up their determination to 'win' and dominate world cricket, but there would be a limit to his willingness to pour good money after bad in maintaining a flagging WSC competition. Insiders were suggesting that Packer would hang on for another two or three years and then pull the plug.

The battle for the game itself was becoming one of stalemate, bluff, recrimination and bad blood among former friends.

Bradman was unhappy with Richie Benaud who had been seduced by Packer's funds to consult for him on WSC. Bradman saw it as an act of betrayal. He was annoyed with Greg Chappell for captaining the Ashes team to England in 1977 after secretly having signed up to WSC matches, which he denied to the ACB.

Near the end of the 1978–79 season, Graham Yallop's traditional Test team was in the process of being walloped 5:1 in the Ashes. No home crowds wished to see their team — effectively a second XI — being humiliated. Gate takings were falling off alarmingly. Meanwhile, the Australian WSC team was preparing to tour the West Indies. Packer was willing to take a big loss. He had no TV rights. Gates were good, but not better than that for a traditional series. Packer considered early 1979 was the time to strike again. He had failed in the early 1970s to gain the rights, but had failed.

By that stage, WSC executives had been getting nowhere in dealing with ACB representatives Bob Parish and Ray Steele. In January 1979, Benaud advised Packer to work something out with Bradman.

'Nothing at the highest level is done without his approval or initiation,' Benaud told Packer. 'He is shrewd, highly intelligent and with the finest mind on the game of all time.'

Benaud told me during a phone interview for my biography of Keith Miller, in 2005: 'Both Packer and Bradman were fair-minded and straight shooters. They effectively wanted the same thing. I expected the meeting to be successful, but it was really in Kerry's hands. He could already foresee the end of WSC.'

'Did you know how Bradman would react?'

'We had some idea. We knew that at the time [early 1979] he was of the opinion that the TV rights were open to negotiation.'

'That the ABC would lose them?'

'Yes. Nine would be in a position to secure them, if Packer played his hand well with Bradman.'

Bradman was no longer Board Chairman, but had become embroiled in the behind-the-scenes struggle against the impact of WSC. Among many things, he had personally brought Bob Simpson, 41, out of retirement to captain the traditional Test team. Simpson had not played Test cricket for a decade, yet he had maintained his form by playing club cricket in Sydney.

Bradman was on a three-man emergency committee with Bob Parish and banker Tim Caldwell, dealing primarily with issues from the WSC business. Caldwell happened to be one of Packer's bankers. Packer wanted a direct, secret meeting with Bradman and used Caldwell to arrange it. It would take place on 13 February 1979, at Bradman's home on Holden Street.

*

'Do you recall your first meeting with Kerry Packer?' I asked Bradman in a phone interview in 1996.

'He flew from Sydney in his private plane and came here.'

'What was your impression of him?'

'A big fellow in more ways than physical size. Much like his father, Sir Frank. Very much to the point.'

'Not into small talk?'

'No.'

'And a very good salesman?'

'Oh, yes, and that too.'

Bradman would not go into details of their two-hour discussion, saying that it was private. He did say that the business side of it was done in a few minutes. For the rest of time, they discussed families, and the past, including Bradman's relationship with Clyde, for whom he had worked for a short time in 1932 as a journalist on radio station 2UE and on the Sydney *Sun* newspaper.

According to Benaud, who had discussed the meeting with Packer, the encounter went off 'swimmingly'. Packer, the super-salesman in action, started with a clever opening gambit.

'We [WSC] have won, but that is not the main issue. I only ever wanted the TV rights, as you know.'

Bradman said nothing.

Packer continued: 'The cricket establishment should take over the game again, completely. I want to give back to you, and the people you represent, every part of the game we have at the moment. I want you to run it as you have always done.'

'And you want just the TV rights?' Bradman asked.

'That's it. I've been trying to do that for some time [seven years]. We'll guarantee you [the ACB] a minimum amount [payment] each year of our agreement.'

'OK,' Bradman said. 'There is a Board meeting in three days' time. It will be done.'

They shook hands. After a war that had annoyed and distracted both sides for some time, the former antagonists received what they wished.

*

Packer now had a more than satisfactory financial interest in the game he loved. He would have one of his executives, Lynton Taylor, on a five-man committee with Parish, Steele, Caldwell and Bradman to oversee the deal. WSC became PBL — Publishing and Broadcasting Limited. PBL Marketing would become the commercial agent for the ACB for a decade, with an option for another five years. It would chase sponsorship and broadcast deals beyond Australia. The ACB was guaranteed much more revenue a year than they had ever had under the previous ABC arrangement.

Bradman could see that the game in Australia would be much better off than ever before and that the ACB would have increased power.

The committee discussed various Packer demands, including coloured uniforms for one-day games, but Bradman cut through it in a discussion with Parish, which Parish relayed to me.

'You don't have any concerns over coloured uniforms?' he asked Bradman, who knew more of the game's history than anyone.

'Why should I?' he replied. 'The Pinks played the Blues in 1892. If they want to wear coloured clothing, even pyjamas, they can have them. We want this deal done.'

That elicited laughter. Yet his position was clear. Packer had guaranteed minimum amounts of money flowing to ACB coffers, and that was going to mean a boost for cricket in Australia. Bradman did not want quibbling over what he saw as inconsequentials.

He retired from the ACB soon afterwards at its next meeting, comfortable in the sense that the game would continue as it had, and that it would thrive. Packer's love of the game and punch-through style had revolutionised and revived the sport. Its prime custodians post the Bradman-influenced administrative period of three decades were pushed or dragged into a new era of commercialism and quasi-professionalism.

But not even Packer could have envisaged the bonanza that would flow to him because of the ACB deal. The next time the 'arrangement' was negotiated in 1994, the ACB (now Cricket Australia) was able to make the terms much better for itself. If the Packers wished to control the TV broadcast of the Test game, they had to go along with ACB demands, which they did. Consequently, the game's development accelerated into a second period, where Packer controlled TV broadcasts, and promoted the short form of the game.

A third era was the evolution of the Twenty20 domestic and international series, which has made more than cosmetic changes to the face of cricket. A less definitive fourth era has begun with the retirement of Cricket Australia's CEO James Sutherland after 17 strong years at the helm and his negotiations with Channel 7 and Foxtel taking over TV broadcasts from Channel 9 after four decades.

The public in general, especially children, have gravitated to the short game, notably Twenty20, which they relate to naturally as an extension of street, park, beach and school cricket with its 'slather-and-whack' attraction of action.

During my writing of the *The Don* in 1995, I discussed with Bradman the gravitation to the more action-oriented short game. He reminded me that he had begun the one-day format during the 1971 Ashes Test at the MCG that was washed out. Bradman hastily arranged a one-day game between the two sides on the scheduled fifth day. Forty-six thousand spectators turned up and enjoyed it. The match hardly covered the losses of the missing first four days of play, but it provided some revenue. By chance, and Bradman's quick-thinking, the international one-day game was born, eight years after England's domestic one-day Gillette Cup began in 1963.

Did he enjoy it?

'It was entertaining.'

'And now?'

'It's a development in line with society's needs for fast-food.'

'Do you see it as developing further?'

'It will become more like baseball in terms of marketing and structure. I said that in 1932 after playing a season in the US.'

'An even shorter version?'

'Club cricket on Saturday afternoons used to attract good crowds, which gives an idea of where one aspect of the game could go.'

We talked about stroke play and what that would do to batting techniques. Wouldn't the shorter game (that is, batting skills and techniques) kill finer strokeplay?

'Not as long as Test cricket is played,' he said. 'The shorter forms will augment the basic skills with innovations.'

Bradman himself had been criticised for unorthodox shots in handling bowling that was directed at the body to intimidate; that is, Bodyline.

We discussed the drift in the 1990s to over-use of coaches. (Two decades later, it has become an avalanche; now there is every type of instructor for every facet of the game.)

Bradman believed that 'young players should be left to work out their own styles, provided it did not perpetuate restrictions [in their strokeplay]'.

'Do you foresee Test cricket being usurped or even replaced?'

'I hope not, but it will have to evolve too, to survive.'

Bradman himself would have been a star in the modern format. He scored at a faster rate than Kevin Pietersen, Brian Lara, Sachin Tendulkar and Steve Smith, and for twice as long as them all on average in every innings. His capacity to carve through the field and contrive innovative, unorthodox shots was evident throughout his career. Bradman could turn it on at will. For the sake of winning Tests, and big Shield matches, he usually put away the lofted shot. But a closer look at his accelerated rates of scoring late in his big First-Class innings showed a willingness to hit over the top, although he rarely let loose in Test cricket, scoring a handful of sixes in his 80 innings. There was no question that he would have adjusted in a heartbeat to the demands of the modern short competition.

CHAPTER 26

Comprehension for Life

Bradman was outstanding at all the other sports he played, from golf to billiards, tennis, golf, squash and royal tennis. But cricket was his first choice. He sat an umpire's exam at 24 years and qualified to stand First-Class matches. It's not surprising that his book *The Art of Cricket*, first published in 1957, is still the finest instructional work on the game. Having studied the game as if he were creating a PhD, Bradman then reduced it to its basics in demonstrating how it should be performed.

His total command of cricket gave him outstanding vision. He showed this early in his career, when comparing baseball with cricket in a discussion with American star baseballer Babe Ruth in 1932. Ruth wanted to know what impressed Bradman, then 22, about the American game. The reply surprised Ruth. Bradman thought the skill levels were comparable. It was the professional presentation of baseball that attracted him. He predicted cricket would have to be better marketed to survive.

Bradman made himself a master of the game's knowledge by reading about its history and how it developed. His study gave him ideas — an annoying thing for cricket establishments that were slow to change. In 1933, he wrote a humble letter to the MCC, suggesting that batsmen using their pads against balls pitched outside the line of the off-stump should be judged LBW, if, in the umpire's opinion, the delivery was going to hit the wicket.

This suggested law was not in a batsman's interest, but it made for far brighter cricket. Batsmen were forced to play the ball and not use pads. It was several decades before his advice was belatedly heeded and his rule was introduced. Now if a player has not deemed to have attempted to hit the ball and is struck on the pad or anywhere on the body outside the line of the off-stump, he is given out, if the umpire and technology judges the ball would have hit the wicket.

Bradman wrote books on the game and did a fair amount of journalism over the decades. This and his experiences on the field, as a selector and as a member of Australia's Cricket Board, widened his comprehension of the game and its influences. This was especially beneficial when he had to analyse such things as the throwing controversy of the 1960s and the South African apartheid problem in the 1970s. It also gave him exceptional vision. Bradman was often decades ahead in his thinking with suggestions on marketing and, for instance, the use of video and camera technology to help umpires make quick, accurate decisions.

Bradman had few peers, if any, on his comprehension of cricket history.

I rang him in 1998 at the height of the match-fixing fiasco with Hansie Cronje (and others), thinking he would tut-tut the entire episode. Given his moral outlines for the spirit in which the game should be played, I expected a comment on how to restrict or end such practices. I often received the opposite response to that expected.

'You have to read the history,' he said. 'The game grew rapidly in the early 1800s based on gambling and betting. It's nothing new. It has never died away and will not. This current episode will pass. There will be admonishment and sanctions and the game will move on. Then in a decade this blight on the game will rear its head again.'

As I write this two decades on from that discussion, Bradman has been proved correct again.

(Bradman was not around for the 2018 ball-tampering fiasco, but I believe his reaction may have been similar to his view of the gambling issue. The action of 'planning' the tampering was wrong and needed to be sanctioned. He would have agreed with that. But perhaps not with the overreaction from Cricket Australia (CA), which saw three of its Test players humiliated and then penalised heavily with suspensions from playing. Various forms of scuffing up the ball — 'tampering' — have been going on since the game began. A few hours watching most local games would see a fielder approach an umpire to change a ball in the hope of dismissing a batsman. On occasions, the fielding side has 'helped along' the ball's deterioration. It is not new and will continue when the storm in a teacup has blown over.

The timing for Steve Smith, David Warner and Cameron Bancroft was unfortunate. CA was in the process of organising sponsors and selling the rights to media broadcast and coverage of the game. CA felt compelled to make examples and scapegoats of these three members of the national team.)

*

Bradman didn't confine his reading to cricket. He also enjoyed political tomes and biographies, and had just finished a book on France's Charles de Gaulle when we met. He enjoyed my book *The Fifth Man* and said he had long been intrigued by the British traitors in the Cambridge University ring recruited by the KGB. Bradman mainly liked non-fiction. His fiction reading was sporadic, beginning with Thomas Hughes' *Tom Brown's School Days*, when he was a teenager, along with some of Charles Dickens' works. He liked comprehending the Victorian era (1837–1901), which was the backdrop to cricket's accelerated development. It also gave him an idea of the environment he may have experienced in England had his family stayed there. Bradman's paternal grandfather, Charles, a farm labourer, emigrated to Australia from Cambridgeshire in 1852, with nearly 100,000 other free-settlers, attracted to the news of gold discoveries in the colonies.

I asked Don if he'd read popular 20th-century fiction writers such as Ian Fleming or John le Carré.

'I was given some of the James Bond series by a friend,' he said, 'but only liked one, *From Russia with Love*. I enjoyed [le Carré's] *The Honourable Schoolboy*, and *Tinker Tailor Soldier Spy*, which I never understood fully until I saw the BBC TV series starring Alec Guinness.'

In the early 1980s, he and Jessie watched the television miniseries *Bodyline*, in which they were both represented. I could not gauge if they liked it or not, but they watched all of it. They made some critical comments about facts and characters. Bradman was not overly impressed with the batting technique and footwork of actor Gary Sweet, who played him. He would have preferred Sachin Tendulkar or Michael Slater, both as yet undiscovered for their thespian abilities. But Bradman agreed on the near-impossibility of re-creating the game in such dramatic settings.

Jessie noted that the show had her dancing with Douglas Jardine, the MCC (England touring) captain in the 1932–33 Ashes.

'I would never, ever have danced with that man!' she told me in a tone of distaste during our first interview in 1995.

Bradman, as ever, did not bat an eyelid during this intervention.

The series was a hit in Australia and elsewhere, especially with younger audiences or those outside the cricket fraternity who had no idea of the furore the actual events caused.

CHAPTER 27

The Raptor

English county court circuit judge B.J. Wakley wrote a book on the statistics of Bradman's career and found his 'wagon-wheel' — the sketch of his shots around the wicket during an innings — 'varied more than any other cricketer' from innings to innings. Bradman had his favourites, but rarely indulged them if the conditions were not right. This is another demonstration of him not letting arrogance get the better of him.

He reset his mental computer and range of shots for each visit to the crease to meet the needs of the moment, always with the aim to attack and score fast, unless in a rear-guard action.

It helped that Bradman was a natural athlete. He had a small, compact, lithe frame, which was deceptively powerful. For the first decade of his Test career, he was considered one of the best, if not *the* best fielder in First-Class cricket. He had a deadly, fast throw and moved like Neil Harvey, Jonty Rhodes, Ricky Ponting and Glenn Maxwell. Bradman's strength came out of early 20th-century country boy development and hardiness. That background built in him an endurance and constitution that helped him survive severe illnesses and to live a long, mainly healthy life.

In his school years, Bradman was a good runner in sprints and long distance, a top cricketer and tennis player. He was a NSW country under-16 tennis champion, but had to decide at that age if he would pursue it or cricket. Tennis lost, but Bradman beat every Australian Wimbledon player of his era in 'friendlies', even though he never played in an official competition after he was 16.

He first took up golf, his second sporting love, on the Ashes tour in 1930 and regularly drove the ball more than 260 metres. He was impressive for his concentration, consistency and precision from tee to the green. Yet once on the green, his putting, according to former Test player Arthur Mailey, 'tended to be erratic' early on. Nevertheless, Mailey suggested he would have been a champion if he had put his mind to it.

'It was incredible to watch Don if he pushed one into a sand bunker,' Mailey said. 'He would never get despondent and drop his game. Instead, he would enjoy stroking his way out of the predicament and the challenge not to drop a shot.'

Mailey criticised that strange grip and his stance, and observed that his batting strokes 'would take a while to iron out of him ... when he's driving, his left foot is well forward, as if he's hammering a straight boundary'. There would be no major changes while he played First-Class cricket, and his golfing technique would have needed much work if he were then ever to challenge the world's best. Still, in 1935, at the age of 26, he won his first major trophy — the Mount Osmond (Adelaide) club championship — while recuperating after his life-threatening peritonitis. By 1940, he had reduced his handicap from 14 to 5.

In 1949, after retiring from cricket, he wanted to take golf more seriously.

'Did you get coaching?' I asked him.

'No. I took a golf manual onto the course and ironed all my cricket shots out.'

I was saddened to hear this. He wrote what is still the finest manual ever on cricket, one that such dynamic players as David Gower carried everywhere with them in their kitbags. Yet here was the finest all-round strokemaker in the game downgrading them all in his muscle memory in favour of the mechanics of a different game.

Bradman worked hard on looking like a golfer, not a brilliant batsman who played golf as a leisure-time interest. By 1960, at 52 years, he reduced his handicap to scratch and was playing his best golf at pennant level. Bradman aimed at beating the course par rounds wherever he played and achieved this at Kooyonga (par 73) with 69, Peninsula (in Victoria, par 73) with 69, Victoria (in Melbourne, par 73) with 71, and Kingston Heath (in Victoria, par 74) with 70. He retained his scratch rating well into his seventies.

More than 60 years after his first championship win, he was still winning at the club based on an age handicap. Until the age of 88 years, he played rounds twice a week at Kooyonga off 23. He occasionally beat his age.

*

Yet Bradman could turn on his cricket technique at will. An instance of this occurred on the practice pitch in the back garden of the Adelaide home of Dr Donald Beard. It was during the 1977–78 season and Australia was playing India. There were half a dozen players there, including Indian captain Bishen Bedi and Australian speedster Jeff Thomson.

One of the Indian players said to Bradman, then 70 years of age: 'Sir, we would love to see you bat.'

Bradman smiled, but didn't reply.

Another Indian player then commented: 'It would be such an honour to witness you batting, Sir Donald. Just a few shots ...'

Bradman put down his cup of tea and accepted a pair of pads from one of Beard's sons, who had been playing on the pitch. He faced up with that familiar stance. Beard's son and Thomson bowled to him.

'Now I wasn't bowling flat out,' Thomson said, 'but I was sending them down [with some pace] all right. He flicked and drove me everywhere. His enormous talent was on display. Those dancing feet were something to behold.'

*

Test cricketer Ian Johnson related a story about his father, Bill, watching a private billiards game between Bradman and professional billiards champion Walter Lindrum. This was in the winter of 1935 at the Adelaide home of Bradman's sharebroker boss, Harry Hodgetts. Lindrum was so well thought of in his game that Neville Cardus, tongue in check, called Bradman 'the Walter Lindrum of cricket'. Lindrum was the number-one player in the world from 1934 to 1950, when he retired.

In this friendly encounter, Lindrum made a break of 100, which Bradman couldn't match. It riled his competitive spirit so much that he had a billiards room built into his new Adelaide home that was being constructed at the time. Bradman bought a table and, according to Jessie in a phone chat with me in 1996, 'practised every night for the next year', until, like Lindrum, he was able to break a 100 with ease.

'Then he challenged Walter to a game,' Jessie said, 'and he beat him.'

That disclosure put me in terrific company. Walter Lindrum and I had been thrashed by Don Bradman in a game of billiards.

Lord Colin Cowdrey told me a similar story. It happened when he (aged 35) asked Bradman (aged 59) to play him at royal tennis in 1968 in London. It was the original racket game that led to lawn tennis and was often played for the amusement of France's royal court until near the end of the 18th century. It has been played in France, England and other countries, including Australia, ever since.

Cowdrey was a superb player.

'But I don't know the rules,' Bradman responded when challenged to a game. 'What are they?'

Cowdrey gave him a rule book about the ancient, elitist game. Bradman studied it overnight, which always meant he would read through until dawn.

'He knew the rules better than I when we played,' Cowdrey remarked. 'He picked me up on errors and beat me.'

Len Maddocks, former Test wicket-keeper and director of the Australian Cricket Board, tells of playing Bradman at table tennis on the ship to England for the 1956 Ashes. Maddocks could beat all the Australian squad members on board at the game. One day, Bradman challenged him and won easily. He had thrashed Maddocks, a very good billiards player, at that sport too.

(In November 2018, I played Ron Barassi, then 82, at table tennis, and he beat me easily.)

Bradman was tenacious at whatever he did, whether he was playing a game of any type socially or in a Test match. To him, competition was not worth bothering about unless you were prepared and played to potential, always aiming to win. He was obsessive. It didn't always please those pitted against him. Keith Miller, for one, thought him too competitive when they played billiards.

Sometimes it spilled over into a ruthless streak. Pacemen Ray Lindwall and Miller gave Len Hutton a torrid time in 1948 in bad light near the end of a day's play. Bradman did not ask them to relent. Hutton protested to him as they were leaving the field.

'C'mon, Len,' Bradman said, 'I used to love bumpers.'

'You wouldn't have liked that lot!' Hutton replied.

Bradman was one of the best players of the short ball the game has seen and he did enjoy facing bumpers, except for the Bodyline methods in the 1932–33 Ashes. Bradman liked the post-war Miller–Lindwall combination. They provided the speed and intimidation he had not been able to fire back at England in the 1930s.

Though there was no denying his competitiveness, Bradman always took a loss at any sport well. Win or lose, he was never other than generous and honest in remarks about opponents. Though he performed for the moment as if his life depended on it, at the end of the day, he competed for enjoyment. Despite a fierceness that would have made him a formidable performer in professional cricket ranks today, he was forever an amateur at heart.

*

Bradman's strong forearms were developed in a country environment, which was his natural gymnasium where he chopped wood daily from age eight to 18. Later in life, he had a farm in the Adelaide Hills, and he cleared the land as a weekend hobby. In his fifties and sixties, he was still chopping down trees and clearing land. It kept him fit and he loved it.

In the late 1950s, he wrote to Rohan Rivett:

Axemanship has become a speciality. I enjoy the ring of steel on wood and get the thrill of a forester in a fine, clean cut. It has put thirty yards on my golf drive for sure. I am meeting the challenge of the land with fortitude. Other people have a different name for it but I can afford to pity their ignorance and go on revelling with my joust with nature.

The country lad was back in his element and enjoying the solitude and challenge, as much as he did in his Bowral boyhood doing family chores.

CHAPTER 28

The Private Man

Bradman hated his privacy being invaded, mainly because if he had not guarded it, he would have had none at all. One day, as I walked with him to the nearby post office, where he went daily to send off his scores of mail items, he spoke of his irritation that even this simple chore could run the gauntlet of fans. We were in the main street and he told me of an incident there where a car came to an abrupt halt on the other side of the road. A man of about 60 years alighted, left the driver's door open and hurried across the road.

'Are you Don Bradman?' he asked.

'Yes,' Bradman replied.

'I want your autograph,' the man said.

'Have you got a pen … a piece of paper?'

The man slapped his pockets.

'You can get them there,' Bradman said, pointing down the street to a newsagent.

The man bustled off down the street. He returned with a notebook and pen. Bradman signed a page.

'Do you always leave your car like that?' he asked, nodding to the car, with the door open.

The man hurried off, mumbling a 'thank you', satisfied with his acquisition.

*

On another occasion Bradman and I were on the front doorstep of his home, chatting as I was about to catch a waiting taxi. A middle-aged man walked in the front gates, stopped, and looked around at the garden.

'Can I help you?' Bradman said.

'You're Don Bradman?' the man asked.

'Yes, and you're on private property ...'

The man nodded and walked out.

It reminded me of another incident that occurred in 2000. I was working with the media pack at that time, covering Tests and writing biographies on Shane Warne and Steve Waugh. I was also researching a chapter for *Bradman's Best* that included Sachin Tendulkar, who was a selection in his best-ever cricket XI. I was in discussion with several Indian journalists. One told me how he had wanted to give Bradman a gift of a miniature grandfather clock in 1991.

'I was told that he always came out to pick up milk bottles from his front porch at 6 a.m.,' the journalist told me. He waited for hours several mornings, but Bradman did not appear.

Finally, the journalist plucked up his courage and pressed the doorbell. Bradman came to the door. The journalist prostrated himself at Bradman's feet.

'What are you doing?' Bradman said, surprised, as he helped him up.

'I just wish to say how much I admire you, Sir Donald,' the journalist said, 'and I have a gift for you.'

Bradman accepted the clock. The journalist backed away, bowing.

Nine years later, in 2000, the same journalist had caught John at the front door to Holden Street and had given him a wristwatch for Don. It was an example of how Indians venerated Bradman. He was viewed as a cricket god, despite never having played there.

*

Bradman's attitude in public to autograph hunters depended on the situation. There are plenty of photos in any newspaper file of him signing. He preferred people to send items in the mail rather than accost him in the street or at a sporting event or function, although the huge number of letters and packages he received were a burden to him over his lifetime. He spent many Mondays at the South Australian Cricket Association offices signing endless lines of bats and memorabilia. As ever, he received nothing for his 'volunteer' efforts.

His rejection of an autograph hunter would often mean a negative attitude towards Bradman for a lifetime. I came across two instances of this, both by elderly adult men, who recalled Bradman refusing to sign autographs in the members' enclosure at the Melbourne Cricket Ground when they were boys of nine and ten.

3AW Melbourne radio personality Neil Mitchell told me his brother Ross had disliked Bradman ever since Bradman rebuffed him when he approached him in the Members' Pavilion. In October 2016, I was introduced by journalist Tony Walker to another man of about 70 at the South Yarra Tennis Club. In 1956, he was about ten when he also spotted Bradman inside the adult male-only reserve at the MCG. The adventurous lad climbed over the fence and approached Bradman.

'You're not supposed to be in here, son,' Bradman said, waving away the autograph book.

Both rejectees had been hurt, but they had never stopped to think of Bradman's position. He was not then a current player. If he allowed everyone to seek his autograph in the Members', especially the then stuffy Melbourne Members', he would be drawing attention to himself, which Bradman never wanted.

It was not the same for ten-year-old Ricky Scheeren. Bradman, 55, was playing his last-ever international match in 1963 when Robert Menzies drew him out of retirement to captain the Prime Minister's XI in Canberra against England.

'I was one of six kids, the only one to get polio,' Scheeren recalled in a *Weekend Australian* article in 2001. 'My brother and I went together [to the game] and he couldn't get any autographs.

I said, "Don't be silly, there's no such thing as 'can't'." I hate anyone telling me I can't.'

Scheeren, on crutches and wearing calipers, climbed the two-foot-high fence, and, armed with his brother's bat and their autograph books, he knocked on the dressing room door. Bradman came out, chatted with the boy and signed the items. The meeting was captured by photographers in one of the most memorable shots in Bradman's life. Both were oblivious of the cameras. The difference from the MCG incidents was that Bradman was in a match and therefore more open to autograph hunters. No doubt young Scheeren also drew out his compassion, and the memory of his son, John, who had also had polio a decade earlier.

*

In general it was clear that Bradman did not enjoy the ongoing adulation. He took it in his stride, but was uncomfortable. This was in contrast to Ron Barassi, the most successful player and coach in the history of Australian Rules Football. Barassi had been in the public eye since he was 17. He, too, took the public attention in his stride, but was more comfortable with it.

I have been a friend of Barassi's for decades. I have been a Melbourne Football Club supporter since 1953 and was fortunate to grow up supporting a team that won six premierships in a decade to 1964. Barassi was a mainstay of the club, perhaps the best big-occasion performer in the history of the game, having been best-on-the-ground in three, arguably four grand finals.

Barassi is a larger-than-life character admired for his achievements, determination, readiness to laugh and integrity, which made him similar to Bradman, apart from how he took public adulation.

I recall being with Barassi to visit former Melbourne premiership captain Noel McMahen at Melbourne's Box Hill Hospital. We had been having lunch at the nearby RSL. When we walked into the hospital foyer, it was as if we were suddenly in 'freeze frame'. A score of people, from young nurses to other medicos, patients and visitors, stopped, whispered and pointed at Barassi.

We approached the reception desk to find out McMahen's room number. Aware of the reaction, and noting that Barassi seemed oblivious of it, I said: 'Do you realise that everyone here is suddenly conscious of your arrival?'

'Don't forget I was at four football clubs [Melbourne in two eras, Carlton, North Melbourne and Sydney].'

To Barassi, this explained it. After all, Australian Rules is the most popular sport in Australia. This is just part of it. Barassi's drive, character and success are closer to the answer.

Unlike Bradman, Barassi embraced the situation rather than avoided it. I was with him at a football match in 2009 at a Melbourne coterie lunch. We were in the lift after the game with a group of suited coterie members. The lift stopped at a floor. A Collingwood supporter, about 40, replete with black-and-white beanie, scarf and footy jumper, stepped in. He stood nose to nose with Barassi. The supporter was suddenly startled.

'You're Ron Barassi!' the man said loudly in a hitherto silent lift.

'I know,' Barassi said.

'You are a fucking legend! A fucking legend!'

'How'd you know about my sex life?' Barassi said.

The suited coterie members laughed.

The supporter was so pleased with meeting the football superstar that he was not aware of Barassi's quick-witted response. The supporter insisted on several selfies with Barassi, who simply rolled with the moment without a hint of rancour.

This moment was particularly poignant. Barassi had been the single biggest reason for Collingwood's lack of premiership success over a quarter of a century. He had played in or coached teams that had defeated the Magpies on six occasions in grand finals. If there was one individual who was Collingwood's nemesis, it was Barassi. In football terms, he was hated but greatly respected. With the passage of time, that respect had morphed into admiration. Barassi's reaction to being 'crowded' by fans was not because he craved this fervent attention. He simply dealt with it, although I had been with him once when we slipped out of a cinema before the end of a film to avoid a rush of fans. He had the personality to absorb the attention and saw it as part of his life in the public domain.

Bradman was different. He wanted space at all times when in the public eye, although it was almost impossible to attain. He thrived on anonymity and privacy.

He and Jessie drove from Adelaide to the Bradman Museum in Bowral in 1996. He rang me from a hotel they were staying at en route to discuss something. Bradman was delighted.

'We checked in as "Mr and Mrs Smith" and no one recognised us,' he said, clearly pleased that they were incognito and would not be harassed.

On another occasion, he was on a boat trip on the Murray River with friends. They stopped to buy petrol at a jetty. Bradman volunteered to fill a can.

As he was doing so, the bowser salesman scrutinised him and commented: 'Has anyone ever told you that you looked like Don Bradman?'

'No,' Bradman said, 'they haven't.'

Again, he was chuffed that he did not have to lie and there was no further chat.

*

Bradman and Barassi had many characteristics in common. They both had modesty. Their egos were intact and strong. They were both well rooted in who they were and what they stood for. However, despite countless opportunities over six years of discussions with Bradman, not once did he puff out his chest and tell me how good he was, or how much better he was than others. When we discussed his great innings, he spoke of them from a perspective of his own inner measure. His 254 at Lords was 'my best-ever innings', he said, but not the best-ever performance by a batsman. *Wisden*, the cricketing bible, said Bradman's 270 at Melbourne in the 1936–37 Ashes was the best-ever Test innings.

I chose his record-breaking 334 at Leeds in the 1930 Ashes as his best innings and opened the Bradman biography with a chapter on it. To me, his 309 not out in a day, including a century before lunch and another between lunch and tea, against one of the two best bowling attacks England ever put in the field, deserved the highest recognition. Bradman disagreed. I asked why him why he chose his 254 at Lords in the same series.

'I was dropped on 273 [in the Leeds knock],' Bradman replied, 'but did not make a mistake at Lord's. Even the shot I got out on [caught in the covers] was a good one.'

So there it was. Bradman's measure of performance was perfection and in not giving a chance.

After that chat, I still opted for the 334. As I write this in 2019, no Test batsman has ever scored more runs in a day of Test cricket. That magnificent record has stood 89 years, despite today's massive bats when Bradman used a toothpick by comparison. He also had to reach bigger boundaries and had next to no protective padding or helmets, and the gloves would be scorned today by an under-12 player. Furthermore, the opposition teams today can be decidedly weak. Bradman was also in an era of uncovered wickets, where rain impacted on pitches and often caused batting collapses.

I would be surprised if someone such as David Warner did not break that record, despite the hiatus in his career forced on him over the ball-tampering affair. His brilliant performance with a pre-lunch Test century against a sloppy Pakistan attack on 3 January 2017 looked promising, but he fell at 114. Interestingly, Warner hit 17 fours in that enthralling effort and no sixes. Bradman always tried to keep the ball along the ground and it was a clue to his fast-scoring, big innings. Warner is one of a handful of the world's top heavy hitters who could get 310 in a day. If so, I hope I see it.

Bradman's modesty, threaded with a shrewd competitive edge, was evident when questioned by the press after his Leeds knock of 334.

'I consider I was lucky to strike my best form on an ideal batsman's wicket.'

He was not lucky because dame fortune smiled upon him. He was 'lucky' to strike his *best form*, on a good wicket. This was a message to England that if he was on the job, it could expect plenty grander, crushing performances. He was just 21 years old and at an early peak. He would go on to make 12 double hundreds (including two triples and a 299 not out) in Test cricket, a feat not equalled over the next nearly nine decades, despite other players having two or three times the number of innings as him. In short, Bradman knew how good he was and didn't have to tell anybody.

Barassi had the same attitude. I recall him talking only about his average effort in the 1964 Melbourne grand final win against Collingwood. He never spoke in public about his best-on-ground and top-line efforts in five other premiership wins.

I said to him once, 'Don't you recall your match-winning efforts in grand finals? I remember you dominating games, say, in the 1959 grand final when you kicked three goals in three minutes ...'

'Of course I do,' Barassi said in practically a whisper.

Again, there was no need to push the chest out and boast. It was not in the nature of either of these legends in sport.

CHAPTER 29

The Underside of Fame

Phenomenal developments on the cricket field go some way to explaining why Bradman's image was so outstanding over the last seven decades of the 20th century. But there were other traits and issues at play that would sustain it.

Over the decades, his principles helped him through rough patches and attacks by bowlers trying to bring him down by foul means or fair; by envious cricketers who hated his amazing performances with the bat; by religious bigots; by journalists he had snubbed for one reason or another — usually valid; and by hack reporters taking cheap shots at one of the nation's tallest poppies, for which they would be paid 'nice little earners' in books and articles.

One surprising discovery was the animus displayed by a few journalists with English backgrounds. At first I couldn't believe that someone's roots would determine their professional analysis of Bradman's career or even his character. But on reflection, most people's support for nations and individuals depends on where they were born. Any international soccer tournament is testimony to that. I expected a higher standard from observers, but instead found a handful were intellectually soft. They just could not stomach the superiority of Bradman, an Australian, over, say, W.G. Grace. It coloured their every account.

Bradman was diplomatic in public. There may not be a public record of his criticism of any other person. Even in private, he rarely directly expressed ill feeling towards anyone, although he had his dislikes. You don't become the most famous person in Australia without creating enemies.

He was aware of which members of the media or the cricket fraternity were against him. When Bill O'Reilly and Jack Fingleton tried to get rid of him as captain of Australia in 1936–37, Bradman went public and called for unity in the fight against the common foe — England. This defused the issue and Australia united to defeat England 3:2 (thanks mainly to Bradman's great batting). Yet undercurrents flowed for decades afterwards. Long after Fingleton's death, someone sent me lawyer-like letters demanding I change what I'd said about him in my Bradman biography. They were threatening but anonymous.

Fingleton blamed Bradman for his non-selection for the 1934 Ashes tour of England and was viewed as 'the ringleader' of a minority cabal against the captain in 1936–37.

Fingleton was supported by O'Reilly. Their dislike for Bradman was precipitated by cricket events rather than the sectarianism of the time, and differences between Catholics and non-Catholics. Within the non-Catholic sector were Freemasons, who formed a secret society and pledged their allegiances to 'King and Empire'. Bradman, aged 21, at the direction of his state skipper, Alan Kippax, in 1930, had become a Freemason. But he was never a very active member. When he moved to less sectarian-split Adelaide in 1935, he let his Freemason connections lapse.

O'Reilly had never come to terms with the thrashings he had taken from Bradman at the wicket, beginning in a country match when they were both still youths. His disgruntlement was exacerbated by Bradman's early wowserism. After belting O'Reilly around the park, or when dismissed on occasions by the 'best bowler' he ever faced, he didn't wish to 'mix with the boys' and have a drink after stumps were drawn. You received the impression from O'Reilly that if Bradman had been a mixer, the leg-spinner may have been better disposed towards him. But his aloofness at first bothered and later rankled O'Reilly.

There is no doubt that O'Reilly had an obsession with Bradman. I experienced it twice in discussions with O'Reilly. Many others did too. Commentator Alan McGilray even rounded on O'Reilly once at the Sydney Cricket Ground (SCG) in front of Bruce Collins (a Sydney QC who later set up the Bradman Museum), telling him that if he didn't stop attacking 'the little fella' (Bradman), he and other journalists wouldn't speak to him (O'Reilly) again.

Despite O'Reilly's over-the-top mouthing off against Bradman, there is nowhere on the record that O'Reilly or Fingleton implied that Bradman's lack of post-match socialising was connected to his being a Mason. Yet somehow that connection led to baseless rumours about him being anti-Catholic.

In the Australia of the 1920s, bigots appeared on both sides of the religious divide, which went back hundreds of years to England when Henry VIII broke from the Catholic Church and Rome and set up his own Church of England. Post–World War I, mistrust developed on both sides.

Bradman never concerned himself with the background of a player, although as a non-Catholic, and a non-religious person (I believe he was an atheist), he would have been aware of the solidity of the Catholics within the Test team, and perhaps even intrigued by it. Yet the facts are irrefutable. He argued for the selection of talented players with Irish Catholic backgrounds, purely on merit. Like him, they played it hard but fair. They put serious passion into playing against England.

In 1936–37, Bradman was a selector who backed seven Australian Test players of Irish Catholic descent — the most in cricket history. In the case of rugged Victorian speedster Laurie Nash, he argued strongly at the selection table for him and won. Nash's biographer, E.A. Wallish, claimed that Bradman threatened to resign as a player and selector if Nash was not picked.

Rumours abounded at the time that the Board was against Nash's selection. But if some of its members were not happy with him, Bradman's argument for him won them over. Having experienced Bodyline, he wanted to make sure he had the aggressive, in-form paceman in the team for the Fifth and deciding Test of the 1936–37 Ashes. Besides this, Bradman was fond of Nash because of his character and courage.

'He wanted to perform even when fatigued,' he told me. 'He carried injuries from his [Aussie Rules] football but never complained.'

Skipper Bill Woodfull refused to consider Nash in 1932–33 because it would have started a tit-for-tat Bodyline war. But Bradman wanted him in as both an insurance policy against Bodyliner Voce being tempted to use it again against Australian batsmen, and an intimidatory weapon. Bradman played psychological warfare games with the English over whether he would select Nash for the final Test on the MCG. They only learned on the day of the match that he was playing. They were beaten before the contest began.

Any accusations against Bradman's position concerning Catholics did not wash with Catholics in the side — such as Leo O'Brien, Chuck Fleetwood-Smith, Ernie McCormick, who all liked and respected Bradman, and Stan McCabe, who regarded Bradman as a 'mate'.

Fingleton seemed ambivalent about Bradman. He wrote a book that suggested Victor Trumper was a better batsman. Yet he also produced a compelling tome, *Brightly Fades the Don*, on Bradman's triumphant all-conquering tour of England in 1948. Although O'Reilly was open about his dislike for Bradman, he was always quick to say he was the greatest bat who ever lived. As the decades rolled on, the bad blood created by him and Fingleton surfaced and was carried to their graves. In O'Reilly's case, it went beyond it.

In the mid-1990s, information in tapes made by O'Reilly that were critical of Bradman was released posthumously by a journalist. The tapes were long on hyperbole and devoid of specifics, but received wide publicity.

Bradman at the time asked me how I thought he should react to the article. I advised him to write a reply to *Wisden*, which he did.

He appeared the statesman, while his detractors were reduced to appearing like miserable hatchet men.

When questioned (over five years) about certain individuals, he only once replied with open criticism of a cricketer.

'Oh, him,' he said, 'he's hopeless, always has been, always will be.'

The rest of the time he made his point by a subtle remark, a look or a non-comment, or he rationalised why someone was against him.

Bradman let his guard down once on Clarrie Grimmett, the great leg-spinner, who wasn't selected for the 1938 Ashes tour of England. 'He was difficult to captain,' he remarked, intimating that he wanted loyalty on the tour and that Grimmett would give him trouble.

Bradman saw his former NSW skipper Alan Kippax as 'jealous', which may well have been true. The Bowral Boy came along in the late 1920s and overshadowed his record (and everyone else's) to such an extent that Kippax, who had a fair Test record (34 innings at an average of 36.12), felt he didn't receive the accolades he thought were due to him. His sports store in Sydney also struggled against that of Mick Simmons, who employed Bradman.

You couldn't say Bradman loved to hate like, say, writer Patrick White or NSW premier Jack Lang, men who bore grudges and honed them. Before he stopped playing, he said nothing and let his blade and leadership do the talking, which made fools of critics for two decades. On retirement, he received criticism and was the subject of rumour-mongering — some of it malicious, most of it empty. But, as he said, he had to 'take it on the chin'. If he judged it fair and factual, he didn't let it bother him.

*

Perhaps the most ridiculous Bradman rumour was that he'd had a love affair with a Board member's wife, and this was why he had not been chosen to tour South Africa in 1935–36. In 2012, I gave a talk on Bradman and his character to the Roaring Forties Club, a group of Melbourne businessmen born in the 1940s. I took questions after the speech.

One member asked: 'I heard from one of the Invincibles that Bradman had a girlfriend on the 1948 Ashes tour. Do you know anything about that?'

I had come across this chestnut before. I answered, in a voice and manner mimicking former US president Bill Clinton: 'I can tell you that Don Bradman did not have sexual relations with that woman!'

It got a laugh.

I did not really care to know anything about Bradman's private life unless it interfered with his sport or work or family. I would doubt that he had much privacy at all on that tour, when he was on duty all waking hours. Any woman spirited into his hotel suite at night would have been noticed and such information would have been tabloid fodder. There were plenty of British journalists willing to derail The Invincibles Express, which was steadily mowing down county and England Test teams in 34 consecutive matches.

*

Perhaps the most nauseating attempted slandering occurred posthumously. I was being interviewed in 2002, a year after Bradman's death, by a TV researcher for a documentary on Australian communist journalist Wilfred Burchett. I was Burchett's biographer and it seemed to me that the aim of the research, as I read her questions, was to gain dirt on the Americans during the Korean War.

At one point, she said in a phone interview after quizzing me: 'Ha! Ha! I know something about Bradman that you don't know!'

It was a childish comment but I was intrigued.

'What?' I asked.

'Not telling,' she replied, keeping up an infantile manner. 'We are making a documentary about it. You'll see.'

A few weeks later, I rang John Bradman to ask what she was getting at. He told me that the documentary makers had taken a blood sample of one of Don's close relatives to see if a certain individual's claim of being Bradman's love-child were true. John told me that the tests had proved the claim was false. The documentary was never made. Nor was the one on Wilfred Burchett, which was based on a further false premise that the

Americans had used biological weapons in the Korean War. Even the Chinese said this was untrue. Burchett had spread the fake propaganda.

I wondered what could be the reason for such pernicious activity concerning Bradman. Apart from the tall poppy syndrome, what else was relevant in the early part of the century?

One suggestion put to me by a media observer was that 'getting at Bradman indirectly hit John Howard' because of their friendship. It was possible. Howard was riding high as prime minister at the time.

There were a couple of other made-up tales or delusions about Bradman's love life. There were other bits of scuttlebutt about his business, about what he said or did not say in the dressing room. All were run down by me and other writers and found to be baseless.

I chatted to John Bradman about this in the year after his father died. I was getting caught up in responding to Bradman's critics, all very brave after his death, and the false news about him.

'Go fishing,' he said, 'take a holiday.'

It was good advice.

I also learned from the way the family of B.A. 'Bob' Santamaria handled his death three years earlier than Bradman, to the day, on 25 February 1998. Santamaria was a Catholic anti-communist, political analyst and journalist, who had started the Democratic Labour Party in the 1950s. I'd had many conversations with him because of our mutual interest in Burchett, and the Cambridge University ring of spies, my research trips to Russia and dealings with the KGB old guard.

Anti-Santamaria journalists attacked him for the first few years after his death, vented their feelings and disappeared. I worked with Bob's barrister son, Paul Santamaria, on the Advisory Council of the National Archives Australia (2006 to 2012) and observed how he and his family had positive books published about Santamaria a few years after that. It reminded me of boxer Muhammad Ali's 'rope-a-dope' tactics in the ring, when he took punishment until his opponent was spent. Then he delivered the knockout blow. Bradman, like Santamaria, had weathered the storm of the 'intellectual pygmies', as Sam Loxton called the detractors.

CHAPTER 30

George Burns – Without Cigar

I was thankful for Bradman's humour. He liked to tell jokes and hear them, and he always punctuated his speeches with comical asides or witticisms. For a few seconds at every meeting (and in almost every phone call, unless it was a solemn discussion), his impassive, impenetrable visage would transform into the late American comedian George Burns, sans cigar. If anything, Bradman was quicker, funnier and more spontaneous. Unlike Burns, he didn't need a script.

This feature became apparent early in our first interview in 1995 in his lounge room at Holden Street. Halfway through the eight-hour session, I asked him how he would go batting against the recent (1980s) crop of great West Indian fast bowlers. 'What would your average be?' I said.

'About 50.'

'Why 50? That's half your actual average ...'

'Well, I will be 87 next birthday.'

We — including Jessie — discussed the then contemporary republican debate. I mentioned that newspapers had listed him as being a suitable choice to the fill the role of first president of an Australian republic in 2001. 'How do you feel about that?'

Bradman replied, 'I'll be 93 in 2001. I might be getting a bit old to run the country, don't you think?' (He died in 2001, aged 92. The republic is yet to materialise.)

*

Bradman's humour ranged from the risqué and rustic to something dry, subtle and witty. More often than not, it had a certain ambiguity that confounded me and I am sure others. *Was he kidding or not*?

For instance, I asked him how he kept fit as a youngster.

He replied: 'I chopped a lot of wood.'

Photographer Dean Golja laughed at this as he took shots. I remember not responding. I was unsure whether it was meant to be amusing or not.

However, Dean and I both laughed at his answer to a follow-up question about fitness: 'Modern top cricketers do a lot of training to keep fit: weights, sprints, distance running, callisthenics, diet and so on. How did you keep fit as a First-Class cricketer?'

Bradman's rapid-fire response was, 'I did a lot of running between the wickets.'

This was true and also funny, and the interesting point was that few others in the history of cricket could get a laugh from replying that way. He just made so many runs at such a clip that he had to be fit.

More than two decades later, I received a clue to this ambiguity. Sydney barrister and cricket tragic Thos Hodgson arranged a lunch for Neil Harvey's 88th birthday at Sydney's Australian Club on 8 October 2016. I gave a brief talk about Harvey to the guests, and when chatting with him after the lunch, I mentioned this confusion about some of Bradman's comments, such as the one he made about the flowers I had brought for Jessie.

'Was he always fair dinkum or not?' I asked Harvey.

To my surprise, I found that he also had often been in a quandary over Bradman's remarks and responses. Bradman clearly had some perverse delight in keeping his interlocutor guessing.

More easy to discern were straight jokes. On one occasion, when discussing Keith Miller, Bradman mentioned that Miller had been having an affair with a well-known English countess, whose husband had been in the House of Lords.

'She was known as "Tug-boat Annie",' Bradman said. 'She moved from peer to peer.'

We calculated he received upward of five million letters in his lifetime. Given his sense of noblesse oblige in answering them, I asked: 'How do you manage that?!' I was exhausted at the thought. After a day's writing, I always loathed the idea of answering even a couple of letters and half a dozen emails.

'I respond to the sensible ones,' he said, again deadpan.

'How many would that be?'

'About one in five.'

This amounted to about a million letters written by him. He did his correspondence most mornings, taking three or four minutes on average for each of the 80 letters a day, meaning at least four hours' labour, either at his battered portable typewriter or by hand.

The vast majority of the less sensible ones, about four million all up, no doubt ended up in the bin. He did hold on to some wonderful examples, though, and loved letters from children. A nine-year-old boy wrote to him: 'I have a big interest in great people, like yourself. Johann Sebastian Bach is a great musician and worked hard. He had nine children. He used to practise on an old spinster in the attic.'

*

Every friend had an amusing tale about Bradman and, from my knowledge of him, they were mainly authentic. One of his best mates in England, the *Daily Mail*'s Alex Bannister, had engineered a job for him covering the 1953 Ashes in England. They were driving back from the north of England one day and passed the outdoor zoo, Whipsnade, which had a few kangaroos. Bradman was dozing in the front seat.

'It's amazing what goes through your mind when you're half asleep,' Bradman said. 'I could have sworn there were kangaroos in the field back there.'

'Come on,' Bannister said. 'Kangaroos in Bedfordshire?!'

*

Bradman originally hated the idea of public speaking. Yet similar to everything he did in life, he rehearsed until he could match the best on otherwise daunting Ashes tours of England, where he would be called on many times to 'perform' at lunches and black-tie dinners. Invariably, he would be introduced by a sparkling, often brilliant speaker.

'He responded with panache and his own style,' Arthur Morris said.

'I was just 19 [in 1948] and it was all a bit off-putting,' Neil Harvey commented. 'But when the boss [Bradman] got up and spoke so well, it added another dimension to what it meant to be "captain" on tour. He was terrific.'

In 1938, when Bradman captained Australia for the first time, the team were guests of the MCC at Lord's during the Middlesex match. Lindsay Hassett, himself an excellent speaker, recalled the British prime minister Stanley Baldwin making a first-class speech in which he told the assembled diners his ambition as a youth was to be a blacksmith.

Bradman then stood up and replied.

'He had a small page of bullet-point notes,' Hassett remembered, 'but had the presence of mind to slip in that as a youth he had wanted to be a house painter. Then he added while facing Baldwin: "You see, sir, we have both been thwarted in our ambitions."'

As Bradman grew in confidence on his feet, he was becoming a gentle iconoclast.

'George [Bradman's middle name, used by a few close friends] held his own everywhere,' Sam Loxton recalled. 'In April 1948, Prince Philip was in the audience when he [Bradman] told the guests that England had missed a rare opportunity to select an obviously fine off-spinner. George then demonstrated a royal wave that could have doubled as a spinning action. The audience loved it. All eyes turned to Prince Philip. He enjoyed it.'

Bradman told me about a satirical comment by a writer, paraphrasing dialogue between the inmate of a mental asylum and the captain of Worcester, who was visiting during the lunch break. The inmate asked the skipper what he was doing and he replied that he was playing Bradman and the Australians. The inmate asked who was batting. The captain said that the Australians were. He'd won the toss and sent them in.

The inmate shook his head and said: 'Come inside.'

Bradman spoke at functions until about the time I was first interviewing him in the mid-1990s. His knowledge of the game was always evident. It was clear that he loved the numbers and statistics and he could regale rapt audiences with them, which made him the hero of any accountants present. Bradman's leisure-time included spending hours each week devouring books, looking at *Wisden*, and reading obscure articles and in fact anything that related an unusual cricket tale. This, along with his enormous chest of personal anecdotes, formed the basis for his speeches.

He peppered them with jokes relevant to the audience, whether it be an umpire's dinner, a Lord's Taverners function or a ten-year reunion of the 1948 Invincibles.

A favourite was the tale about Bert Ironmonger, a batting bunny from the 1920s and 1930s going out to bat, just when his wife rang the dressing room.

'He's just at the wicket now,' the manager said, 'could you call back later?'

'No, I'll hang on,' she said.

'The story goes,' Bradman added when relating this one, 'that when Len Hutton's wife rang and was told he was batting, she said: "I'll call back tomorrow."'

Then there was the tale of Napoleon III visiting England with his stunning Spanish wife, Eugenie. They were entertained by a game at Kent involving The Gentlemen of England. A fielder took a spectacular, acrobatic catch. Napoleon III sent his equerry out on the ground to ask him to do it again.

Bradman always got a laugh when telling the tale about a game between Victoria and NSW. Victoria was piling up a huge amount of runs and nothing was going through to the keeper Andrew Radcliffe. The bats were hitting everything coming at them. At one point, the keeper's box slipped. Other fielders gathered around to give him privacy to adjust his box. As he did so, a stentorian voice from the outer called: 'That's the only ball you've touched all day, Radcliffe!'

Bradman had a fine friendship with writer Neville Cardus, who was both a cricket and music critic for the Manchester *Guardian*. Their relationship was therefore rich and they appreciated each other's humour.

'He [Cardus] wrote one of the shortest music reviews ever,' Bradman told me. 'He was at a Birmingham concert hall writing about a Mrs Brown who was playing Brahms. The headline said "Mrs Brown played Brahms". The review said simply, "Brahms lost."'

That ambiguous wit, which occasionally baffled, was ever present, even during setbacks. In 1996, he was picked up in his car by radar for doing 72 kilometres an hour in a 60 zone. The cop didn't recognise him until Bradman produced his licence.

'It's an honour and pleasure to meet you,' the cop said.

Bradman replied: 'Under the circumstances, I am very sorry I can't say the same to you.'

He was given a $173 fine.

*

Halfway through the research for my biography on him, Bradman asked me what I was going to use as the book's title.

'*The Don*,' I said.

After a slight pause, he said, 'You know, I am thinking of writing a book on you. Do you know what I'm calling it?'

I laughed. 'No, what?'

'*The Rol*.'

*

At age 89, in Adelaide, he won the Mount Osmond Club's trophy on handicap. He beat his age by nine despite having had a stroke a few years earlier. In the early 1990s, Australian batsman Dean Jones played Bradman in a round of golf at Bowral, Bradman's hometown. Jones got into a bit of trouble and hit the ball the wrong side of a clump of tall trees. He was in a quandary.

'Sir Donald, you've played here a lot,' Jones said. 'How did you manage a shot from here? I can't see the green for the trees.'

'I hit the ball over the trees, Dean.'

Jones considered the trees, played the shot and smacked the ball into foliage.

'How did you do it?!' Jones asked.

'The trees were a lot smaller in the 1920s, Dean.'

Jones was the witness to several Bradman asides and was able to incorporate them into speaking engagements. For instance, in the Fifth Test of the 1988–89 series against the West Indies in Australia, Jones scored 216 and Merv Hughes managed 72 not out. Merv was a bowler who could bat a bit. He didn't take a wicket in this game. So naturally, he was very pleased with his batting effort against the dominant West Indies. Their captain, Viv Richards, invited Bradman into the West Indian dressing room to meet his team. Merv Hughes and Jones tagged along, feeling triumphant.

The West Indians lined up to meet Bradman. Viv introduced him along the line. They reached the 200-centimetre-tall fast bowler Patrick Patterson, who had crushed Australia in the previous matches in the Test series. Patterson remarked in his broad West Indian accent: 'So you dah great Don Braarrdman … you just a little guy … I get you out no problem!'

Bradman looked up and snapped back: 'Get me out?! How are you going to get me out? You couldn't even get Merv Hughes out!'

I have used this one in my own speeches. It always gets a big laugh, especially if you do the voices. All professional writers, especially of fiction, are third-rate mimics, and after six years of talking to Bradman I had that piping, jockey-like voice down fairly well. Despite its high pitch, he still managed to make it sound mellifluous and at the same time authoritative. It was definitively Bradman, and full of verve and character.

CHAPTER 31

The Deal

By 1996, Bradman had never granted a commercial TV interview in the 40 years of the medium in Australia, except for 22 minutes with Doug Ring on Channel 7 in 1963. The extent of his accepting offers to appear on electronic media had been in 1988 in radio tapes with Norman May, as part of the Bicentennial Project; often on Alan Jones' Sydney radio program (Jones was his favourite broadcaster); and a TV interview with Jack Egan for ABC TV in 1990. Bradman had rejected approaches by several personalities, including former prime minister Bob Hawke on *60 Minutes* (when he had TV aspirations after he left politics), Ray Martin on various programs, and Mike Munro on *This is Your Life*. They had offered record amounts of money, but Bradman said No to all of them.

I was in his study with him on two occasions when he had a big offer, and I knew about the previous attempts to induce him to appear.

'I understand your reasons for not appearing [on TV],' I remarked when we discussed the offer, 'but a million for 20 minutes! What about your family, your grandchildren?'

'Don't worry about them,' he said, 'they're catered for.'

Bradman did say to me, 'Don't call me a millionaire' in the biography, which was his way of explaining he was not a wealthy man. He certainly did not live an ostentatious life, but I was not about to pry into his finances. In any case, he would not have let me do it.

I imagined, however, that as a broker with unsurpassed comprehension of the share market, he may well have put away investments in blue chips for family members. But we never discussed it, so I didn't know. However, towards the end of 1969, Rohan Rivett wrote to Bradman for advice about settling some funds on his own children.

'Better done while alive, heading off probate,' Bradman replied. 'The plan seems sound ... As you know I've done this for John and Shirley, and they are now settled and can take care of themselves.'

Shirley had been ill in 1969 and 1970 and Bradman admired her pluck.

'She remains sweet and brave despite her burdens,' he told Rivett. But Bradman and Jessie remained concerned about how she would cope, not with money, but with life in general once they were gone.

'I'd like to outlive her [Shirley],' Bradman told me when he was 88, aware that this was unlikely. She came to Holden Street with her small dog during the interviews. Shirley was vibrant and happy. When she had left, Jessie said proudly to me: 'She can do her own accounts.'

'Oh, yeah?' Bradman said, indicating that he had to check them. But knowing him, he would do that anyway.

*

During those attempts to persuade Bradman into appearances, I realised that he had another reason for rejecting direct money offers. *He could not be bought.* I could tell that he had pleasure in his blunt rejections without explanations. It was another admirable measure of the man. It was partly based on him not being acquisitive or greedy. It was also to do with his pride as an individual who did not have a price, no matter what was on offer. This made him stand out in an era of materialism.

That was why, when a senior Channel 9 producer rang me twice to ask my advice on how to convince Bradman to appear on commercial TV, I suggested it would be better to offer money to the Bradman Museum Trust that had been set up by others in his name.

Consequently Kerry Packer didn't attempt to throw money at him for a TV appearance, but instead offered to pay $1.2 million to the Bradman Museum Trust at Bowral. Neither Bradman nor any of his dependents would ever see a cent of this, which was the way with all deal payments to the museum, now one of the nation's top tourist attractions.

Packer had never been The Don's favourite media person after the attempt 20 years earlier to take over world cricket. So I also told the Channel 9 producers that it would be best if Packer visited Bradman in Adelaide, which he did in March 1996.

The meeting took place in the Bradman living room at Holden Street.

Packer needed all his powers of persuasion to have Bradman agree to a TV interview.

'You can have any interviewer you like,' Packer said at the convivial meeting. 'Who would you prefer?'

'Ray Martin,' Bradman said. He liked Martin. After Bradman had rejected an earlier offer from Martin for an interview, he said he would have Martin do it if he (Bradman) ever changed his mind.

After Packer returned to Sydney, he called Ray Martin to his office to discuss the TV interview.

'Did you enjoying meeting The Don [again]?' Martin asked.

'I loved it, son,' Packer said. 'It was truly one of the greatest days of my life. Now listen, son. I promised him, when the show is cut and before we put it on the air, he can have a look at it. I told him that if he doesn't like it, for any reason, then we'd burn the bastard. OK? So don't fuck it up, son.'

*

I wished I had been a fly on the wall at that meeting between one of Australia's greatest sons and one of its richest citizens.

I rang Bradman and said I'd like to write something about the second meeting in 17 years with Kerry Packer. I received a hostile response.

'Oh, would you now!' he snapped. 'And how would you do that? It was a private meeting like the first one [in February 1979] you asked me about last year. Packer won't say anything and neither will I. Are you going to make it up like that Indian journalist?'

This was a reference to an earlier conversation we had had about an Indian journalist who had tried to interview him and failed. 'He wrote a full page based on the interview that did not happen,' Bradman had told me at the time. 'I must say my answers were superb.' Even though he joked about it, it was clear the experience had upset him.

'No ...' I began and my mobile phone rang. I excused myself to answer it. When I got back on the phone to Bradman, he asked: 'How many phones have you got?!'

I couldn't help laughing, which cooled his irritated manner.

I noted he had not said, 'You can't write that piece.' Nor had he said he would prevent it being published, which I am sure he could have done with one phone call to the chairman of Fairfax.

'Well, how are you going to write it?' he persisted.

'I'll find a way,' I said, without letting him know that I had a potential observer in Bob Mansfield, who had been the middleman in taking Packer to the Bradman home. I rang Mansfield and he was happy to talk about the meeting and believed it would be 'in the public interest'. I wrote the piece and had it published in the *Sydney Morning Herald*.

I flew to London soon afterwards and did not speak with
Bradman for several weeks. While at Lord's watching a Test, I
took photos in the Long Room of interesting juxtapositions of
portraits. Bradman was at the apex of a triangle of three, with
Douglas Jardine and Len Hutton below him. There was also a
portrait of Keith Miller hanging above the door to the dressing-
room steps. I sent the photos to Bradman. I spoke to him again,
six weeks after the article had appeared in the paper. It did not
come up in discussion and, if he saw it, he was not offended.

*

Ray Martin kept the eventual TV interview innocuous and non-
confrontational. Anything else would have seen Bradman walking
off the set. He was not above rebuffing journalists, an attitude
which had bruised some big egos in the media. Martin did as well
as anyone could under the restrictions in three hours of questions.

Bradman wrote to me about the interview: 'I agreed most
reluctantly and it was a terrible ordeal for me — especially coming
so soon after I had had this wretched stroke, but Ray Martin was
wonderful to work with.'

*

In early 1997, I tried to persuade Bradman to have some of his
letters published in book form. But he would have none of it.

Early in 1998, the Becker Film group and I began discussing
a film on Bradman's life. The Bradman Museum was supportive,

but Don was ambivalent. He worried about the further run of 'publicity' a cinema release would bring. I tried to talk him around and got to the point where he said he would 'think about it'.

I began writing a script.

Later, I received a note from Bradman about an unrelated issue. At the end of the letter, he said: 'I hope you don't go ahead with the film idea. In my brief time remaining on earth I was hoping for a period of rest and privacy.'

Put in those terms, I couldn't go on with the project. I rang him, then Becker, to say I was pulling out.

*

Two of Bradman's final classic responses to the media and public exposure came on his 90th birthday. A black-tie celebration was held at the Adelaide Convention Centre in his honour. Bradman did not bother to go. He respectfully declined the invitation to the party, which was emceed by his friend and broadcaster Alan Jones, whom Bradman had wanted to do it.

'I had trouble speaking as clearly as I would like,' he told me. 'It would have been an ordeal for me. I just didn't wish to do it.'

People often forgot that he was a declining old man. He seemed to many to be an ageless mythical figure, above serious human frailty.

However, on the same day as the dinner, he took up an offer from Terry Jenner to lunch at Government House in Adelaide with the Invincibles. Bradman drove himself to the function, stayed two hours, and told me he had enjoyed every moment of it. He spoke to all his former team-mates, some of whom he had not seen for 20 years.

'His hands were very arthritic,' Jenner said, 'and he was frail. But he was terrific. He signed all the things he had to for the dinner.'

Bradman also had expressed a birthday wish to meet Sachin Tendulkar, the brilliant Indian batsman, whom Bradman (and his cricket expert wife, Jessie) thought most resembled the style in which Bradman played cricket. Somehow, Shane Warne managed to go with Tendulkar to Holden Street for the meeting on the morning of Bradman's birthday.

I rang Bradman the day after his birthday, knowing that on the day, 27 August 1998, the phone would run hot with calls from all over the country and the world, wishing him well on this milestone occasion.

I asked him how he found Warne and Tendulkar.

'Oh, Shane is a good bloke; I like him,' Bradman replied. 'But that Sachin, he is something special as a man and character. He will go well beyond cricket in life.'

Commentators liked to compare their batting styles. Both were adept at playing speed bowling; they were unsurpassed at handling spin. Yet there were other more personal characteristics that they shared. Both were highly intelligent, private individuals who knew what it was like to lose their privacy. Tendulkar, idolised by 1.4 billion people and admired wherever cricket is played, had similar pressures to Bradman. If Tendulkar wished to go and see a movie in a cinema, he would put on a wig for disguise. Bradman never risked such a luxury, or wore a wig.

On the day, when seeing off Tendulkar and Warne at the front of his home, Bradman faced a barrage of TV and newspaper cameras, and journalists. One intrepid young female TV reporter had the courage to ask: 'How do you feel on your 90th birthday?'

Bradman, who could play the curmudgeon if the mood struck, replied: 'How do I feel? I'd feel a lot better without all these cameras outside my house.'

He refused any other questions, turned on his heel and disappeared into his castle to avoid the media siege.

CHAPTER 32

Running from 'Bradman'

Fame can be unreasonable, even cruel, for the sons and daughters of those celebrated for their prowess and achievements. I have seen it so often in Australia that I am surprised if I meet an offspring in that position who has not been impacted by it. No name has been elevated above that of Bradman in sport or any other aspect of life in Australia.

John Monash's accomplishments in war, construction, law, music and education put his name over all others in the 1920s and the resonance into the 1930s brought an unwanted spotlight on his grandsons, even though they bore their mother's married name, Bennett. But Monash did not enthral huge crowds of spectators over two decades, in state and international contests. Bradman left an unmatched gold standard of fame and demeanour based on the principle 'seeing is believing'. The comment 'I saw

Bradman bat at ...' was a legacy that is only now beginning to fade. Yet the name has transcended time and made it difficult for his children and grandchildren.

John Bradman described his experience as 'the son of': 'I was popped in a metaphorical glass cage to be peered at or discussed. I was no longer prepared to accept being seriously introduced as simply someone's son. I am an individual, not a social souvenir.'

On a 2015 episode of ABC TV program *Australian Story* titled 'Being Bradman', John's first wife, Judith, said: 'We'd go to [South Australia's] Government House, to a ball. People would treat him as though he was just an object. They would point at us.'

Not many people could really relate to John, as very few had his experience.

There have been countless other examples of offspring who have had to carry the weight of public expectations brought on by the simple fact that they possess a certain name. I have dealt with many of these families in my biographical books, including Monash and his grandchildren; the Fourth Baron Lord Rothschild and his famous/ infamous father, the Third Baron; Barry Tasker and his roguish and bold sportsman/ businessman father, Rolly; and Keith Miller, the brilliant flamboyant cricketer/ footballer and bomber pilot, and his sons.

Not surprisingly, Ron Barassi's children were also unsettled by the huge 'name' they carried. His son, Ron Junior, said in Peter Lalor's excellent biography *Barassi* that he 'disappeared' with most people he met when they started talking about his father. As with John Bradman, Ron Jr became a non-person, except to be 'the son of'.

'It's kind of like you are invisible,' Ron Jr said. 'You are not an individual.'

Barassi's daughter Susan recalled an afternoon in a New South Wales pub where their father was not recognised. It was a novelty.

There is nothing new in sons or daughters of the famous undergoing serious soul-searching over their birthright and finding their own way in life. Yet the experience for John Bradman was another level above the rest in Australia, from John's birth in 1939, and over the following 40 years that Bradman dominated cricket on and off the field.

From the age of consciousness about his environment, John was made aware of his father's 'fabulous', 'legendary' status. All this was an albatross too much for him and he suffered from it. No matter what he did, how could he live up to his father's reputation. By all accounts, John was a very good schoolboy batsman. He played for Kensington, but he could never hope to better his father's record, and thus would fall short of expectations. He gave away a promising career with the bat early.

He concentrated on athletics, a different field from any of Don's sporting endeavours, and became a top state hurdler. But it could never be enough for a curious, over-inquisitive media and public. In Australia, where sport is overrated compared with, say, the arts or politics, John was mentally hemmed in to a point of distraction, which depressed him.

He told friends that his life was so suffocating as 'the son of', he wished as a boy that he would not recover from polio. That way he would not have to bear the pressure of always consciously or subconsciously competing with his father.

*

Bradman did not push his son in his sporting endeavours, but there would have been an underlying stress on John to be educated and to 'achieve' in some form of professional career. Bradman's own disappointment about being under-educated in a formal sense would have been transposed to some extent into expectations for John. Ways were opened up for John to take up membership of the Adelaide Stock Exchange. Bradman kept his seat after he had retired from the business. But broking and the relatively anti-intellectual establishment environment were never going to suit John. Realising this, Bradman sold the seat in the 1960s.

*

Jessie said they 'were in full support' of John's decision to change his name. It was an unfortunate by-product of the legend; the other side of fame that never sat well with the family. However, Bradman, in private, was not at ease with his son's move to seek anonymity.

'He really only went halfway, didn't he?' he said. 'Why not "Smith" or "Jones"? "Bradsen" indicated indecision and some pain.'

'You had little choice but to go with it …?'

'We [Jessie and I] gave it our support. We hoped it would help him over the problem.'

Bradman had deeper concerns as the ramifications of John's decision widened. John continued to live with his parents and accept the inherent benefits of this. Bradman favoured what is now termed 'tough love' and thought it might be better if John left home and sought the individuality he craved. Jessie took a softer line. As the months slipped by in 1972, Bradman became hurt and embittered over his son's decision, although he kept this to himself, apart from some heartfelt comments in letters to close friends. John moved to a Bradman-owned farm and married first wife Judith as 'Bradsen'. It gave him a sense of independence.

John did not lose contact with his parents, particularly because of his close relationship with Jessie. The locational separation of John from his parents, Bradman thought, was 'not all that bad a thing' for John. He was appointed a full-time member of the Adelaide University's law school staff. He went on to have a successful academic career with a strong publishing record.

Yet Bradman never quite came to terms with John abandoning the family name. It seemed that Don would be last in his line to carry it.

*

By 1990, the Bradman Museum at Bowral was a developing concern, but without the finances that would make it like no other museum in the country: independent and solvent. Bradman had at first been ambivalent about its existence. Yet the first curator, Richard Mulvaney, demonstrated so much professionalism and enthusiasm for the project that Bradman got behind it. That was the turning point for the museum.

'You became concerned about its viability?'

'Well, no museums make money,' Bradman said. 'I began to think about how it was going to survive.'

'Is that when you turned your name over [legally] to the museum?'

'It was.'

'That was a most generous act. I know that Richard Mulvaney appreciated it.'

At that point, John and his family had been called 'Bradsen' for nearly two decades. The museum offered a way to keep the 'Bradman' name alive, and to do perpetual charity works, and good acts for cricket. In a moment of typical creativity, Don wrote to his good friend, businessman Ron Brierley, who was on the museum's board, asking him what he thought about the concept.

Brierley fully endorsed the idea. With pro bono legal support, the museum began to register 'Don Bradman' as a trademark in every cricketing country in the world. Then his image and name appeared on Weet-Bix packets. This was followed by the Australian Mint putting his image on a coin. In 1997, Australia Post placed him on a postage stamp. He was the first living Australian to have this happen.

I rang Bradman and asked him how he felt about it.

'It's quite an honour,' Bradman replied. I knew from his tone that he was chuffed.

'Only fitting,' I said. 'No one has written more letters to fans in the nation's history. It justifies you licking all those hundreds of thousands of stamps!'

*

The museum began to make more deals with licences.

'When he saw the money we were making,' Mulvaney said, 'he was really very pleased. He was clearly happy that the museum would go on with strength. I think he dreaded it would fold. He had done so much that survival was assured.'

Rina Hore, who succeeded Mulvaney, has kept up the good work he started. The museum is one of the nation's most attended and admired institutions and tourist attractions.

*

In 1999, John changed his name and that of his children back to 'Bradman'.

'It must give you a good feeling?' I said to Bradman in a phone chat.

'Yes, it is good,' he said, 'a bit overdue, but nevertheless, not too late. I'm still here to appreciate it, although Jessie isn't.'

More important than anything in Bradman's mind was the fact that his three grandchildren would now carry his name forward. For a man from his generation and grand record in life, this was especially important.

CHAPTER 33

What's in a Name?

Juliet in Shakespeare's play *Romeo and Juliet* asks:

> *What's in a name? That which we call a rose*
> *By any other name would smell as sweet.*

That's a laudable sentiment, but she may have seen a different set of complications if she had been Juliet Bradman in the 20th century.

John struggled with it, found a solution, and to a point overcame the dilemma of wanting to be known as his father's son, while at the same time desiring to be appreciated for his individuality and achievements. For a simple man, it may not have been an issue. For a highly intelligent, sensitive individual, it was tough. In this respect, John was his father's son. Bradman had forced himself to perform herculean shows on the sporting field. He pushed his small, compact body to do what those twice his size could not. Bradman presented a macho image in the man's world that was Australia for most of the 20th century. Underneath, however, his love of privacy and the finest music ever produced, his bristling intellect and his selfless generosity to others were not entirely of that world. It was one reason he stepped away from it as much as he could when not performing in front of packed houses. John is similar, and because he has a strong mind of his own, he craved to be his own man.

John's children with Judith — Tom and Greta — escaped the scrutiny. The name change in their early years was fortunate for their own development. They had anonymity.

'That was a great thing,' Tom told ABC's *Australian Story*. 'I wasn't under particular pressures to be a certain way; achieve certain things. I was simply me.'

Tom was shaped in his formative years without the sense of having to live up to a name before he knew where his life was heading, which is the norm for 99 per cent of the population. Furthermore, the early years on the Bradman farm in the Adelaide Hills assisted Tom and Greta with a natural upbringing. They worked on the farm, clearing and improving it. They were in touch with nature, which was not unlike the life of both their grandparents. Bradman had been from rural Bowral. Jessie was the daughter of a farmer from nearby Glenquarry.

'We knew where food came from,' Greta said in summing up that farm life. Tom, in fact, after studying law and doing legal policy work at Canberra's Agriculture Department, switched to running a farmer's workshop. Genial and bright, he had found his niche and was more or less comfortable being a Bradman. He understood the bizarre side of it.

But it wasn't all a smooth path for Greta. She saw that her parents were not completely compatible. Looking back, Judith admitted that she and John were 'two very dysfunctional people at war with each other'. Greta, in her early teens, tried to mediate but failed. She suffered from glandular fever, which could have been partly psychosomatic, and missed most of her school years eight, nine and ten. An additional problem was that Judith and Jessie did not see eye to eye. Greta found herself avoiding Jessie, with whom she was very close, and Don, to avoid upsetting Judith. She did herself physical harm and contemplated suicide.

Her depression impacted on John. But he found a clever solution by taking her on a tough 65-kilometre walk over several days on Tasmania's Overland Track. Greta and John came out of it mentally stronger.

Less than a decade later, in 1999, when the family decided to change their name from Bradsen back to Bradman, Tom, then aged 18, had an amusing moment when he wrote out his name-changes forms for his bank account. He handed all his forms to a female teller at his bank.

She took him in for a moment and remarked: 'You must be a really big fan!'

Greta, then 20, found people changed their attitude to her. She was not 'Greta' any more in restaurants, but 'Miss Bradman'. She found that young men were far more interested in her, or perhaps this was just an impression. Like Jessie and Judith, she is most attractive. Photographs of a young Jessie and Greta have a strong likeness and their singing skills are similar. *Australian Story* told of how Greta walked into a boyfriend's home and it was festooned with Bradman memorabilia. He had forgotten to tell her how he was obsessed with her grandfather. The relationship was doomed before it got going.

Greta wrote to Don, telling him that she understood what it was like to have people look at her differently. She could comprehend why it would have been really tough for him.

After high school, Greta studied music and trained to become a soprano of note. I attended the Adelaide memorial for Bradman in March 2001 and, like everyone else in the audience, was impressed by her singing of 'Pie Jesu' from Andrew Lloyd Webber's *Requiem*. It took courage. To prepare for the event, when the eyes of Australia, and many parts of the world, would be on the family and her performance, Greta sat in front of a portrait of Bradman and kept singing until she could perform it without bursting into tears. After that, she faced the moment and performed faultlessly.

Listening to her, I thought of Don. Like him, she had willed herself to perfection. Similar to him, she suffered from tension before an event and a letdown after it. But during any performance, they took control of themselves, the moment and the audience.

*

John too faced the ordeal of acute public scrutiny as the family spokesperson after his father's death. John did not crave media attention, but suddenly he had more of it in one feverish burst that lasted a couple of months than his father ever had in a similar period. It was a fortunate thing that John wore sensible shoes and had everything in perspective.

He summoned all his considerable resources and met the demands of a needy media and public with aplomb, as if he had been bred to it like a worthy prince taking over from a mighty king. John came across as articulate and refined. He was not dazzled by fame and, having suffered from its excesses, disdained it.

John wanted to stop the deification of his father. But no matter what laudable logic was uttered by Don in the past and John in this respect, the legend and myth would remain as long as cricket is discussed and outstanding Australian characters and achievers in any field are examined. All nations need 'heroes'; there is a constant, daily media search for them. Transient examples come and go, but those with lifelong substance and integrity remain.

In a sense, the father's passing liberated the son — not an unusual event when it came to a famous, strong or overbearing individual dying. The son was now the head of the family.

*

After the memorial service, fame's fickle finger touched Greta. The Adelaide Conservatorium fielded scores of calls asking her to perform at various functions. She refused them. She had been exhausted by the memorial effort. Greta did not have the clichéd build of a big-lunged, busty opera singer. Nor did Don have the powerful build of many of his fellow cricketers. They both performed beyond the limits expected. They were strong-willed and determined. Both were left wrung out after their performances.

Greta appreciated the public reaction, but thought it was because she was 'the granddaughter of'. Like her father, she felt she would never be able to surmount the expectations.

But she was two generations removed from Don and in another field of endeavour. Had she wanted to be a cricketer, it may have been different, but less difficult than for John and his two sons, Tom and Nicholas. Greta was a gifted singer with that amorphous, catch-all description: 'potential'. Groping for what a future would look like at that time, Greta was not confident or satisfied with the idea of a singing career. It was a bit dreamy, a bit too fantastic to consider seriously. But deep down, she wanted it badly.

She regretted missing so many years of her early secondary-school education and decided to prove herself with study of substance, beginning a PhD in psychology. Greta worked hard and was tough on herself. She wanted first to prove herself academically, which again seemed similar to Don, who remained frustrated without formal academic training all his life, and John, who did find himself in academia.

This presented a second hurdle after facing what her 'new' name would mean for the rest of her life. Greta now saw her voice as a drawback. If it lured her into a life in the singing artist's glittering spotlight, then her more 'serious' career might not happen. She returned to a less severe form of self-harm by drinking saltwater on an empty stomach to make herself vomit. This way she hoped she would destroy her vocal cords.

Fortunately for herself and her singing, she did not damage them.

*

Years later, settled, married and with children, a more mature and secure Greta decided to make a full effort to be an outstanding soprano. Again it took intestinal fortitude. She would have to face the naysayers, those who were jealous, and those who would sneer that she could only 'make it' because of her name. But she did not wish to later regret not making a full-on effort. In that respect once more, she had her grandfather's gene. It was this rather than his surname that mattered. If Greta had stayed with 'Bradsen' or taken her husband's name, she still would have been outed quickly as 'the granddaughter of', so it was of minor consequence. Greta had that exceptional 'will' that so enchanted philosopher Brian O'Shaughnessy.

A big step forward for Greta was winning the Australian International Opera Award. She took her husband, Didier Elzinga, and sons with her to Wales and began training at the Wales International Academy of Voice. In this way, she and her supportive partner were the modern reverse of Don and Jessie. In their era, the man's interest usually came first, and he needed the backing of a 'good woman' to reach serious heights in any endeavour. In the 21st century, Greta is fulfilling her dreams and ambitions with the support of an understanding husband.

Greta had some expert coaching in Wales and her singing went up another notch. She then sang for the octogenarian conductor Richard Bonynge, who is the widower of Australian operatic superstar Dame Joan Sutherland.

Bonynge is one of the world's foremost conductors and he had, in his words, seen too much of the great singers to be impressed any more. But Greta amazed him with the quality of her voice that was peculiar to her.

'[It was] a luscious, velvety, round sound which comes from inside her,' he told ABC TV. 'There's heart in it and I loved that.'

Bonynge collaborated with her on *My Hero*, a 17-track album featuring compositions by great composers including Strauss, Bellini, Verdi, Mozart, Haydn and Handel. I listened to this on a flight recently. The blurb describing the album read: 'Sliding between ethereal and intricate, Greta Bradman is a ferocious talent, described as having vocal abilities similar to the late Dame Joan Sutherland.'

By 2018, Greta was living with her name and giving a whole new dimension to it, which would have brought her beloved grandparents to tears of joy.

*

They would also have been proud of their third grandchild, Nicholas (the son of John and Megan), who made headlines himself at age 18 early in 2017 by scoring 99.95 in his International Baccalaureate results in South Australia. The media, predictably, made much of Nicholas scoring 0.01 more than Don's Test batting average. Nicholas, being raised as 'Bradman', was forced to give up cricket because of the same expectations, watered down by a generation.

Yet he seemed undaunted in his response to journalists' questions. With that exam score, any profession he desires will be his. Nicholas was planning to do a double degree in law and arts or politics.

That would have been music also to Don's pleasantly envious ears.

CHAPTER 34

The Hobby

During a set of questions for my Bradman biography in 1995, I asked him if he had ever thought about a best-ever, no-restrictions world team. He gave me that characteristic half-grin and replied intriguingly: 'Often.'

'A sort of hobby?'

'More an interesting exercise.'

He revealed he had drawn up a 'dream team' 'every decade or so'.

I left it there as we were discussing another issue and we both wished to concentrate on that. But I was fascinated.

I began to wonder about his choices for a World XI, but did not get around to asking him about it until late 1998.

*

It has been said that Bradman was to sport what Einstein was to science and Mozart to music. Some sports fans might think that's a bit flattering to Einstein and Mozart. But allowing for the comparisons, I considered Bradman's selection for his best-ever cricket team one of his more creative formulations or compositions.

I had discussed Bradman with Richie Benaud, who was adamant about his capacity as selector: 'Sir Donald was the best selector I came across in the game anywhere in the world, not just Australia.'

Bradman watched Test cricket for 80 years, beginning in 1921 when, at age 12, he saw an Ashes match at the SCG. In that game, Charlie Macartney made a magnificent 170. This innings inspired the young Don to become a Test cricketer.

Bradman enjoyed roaming the eras choosing the finest side, without national boundaries or horse-trading between the states; without compromise or inhibitions. It exhilarated him. It was the most exalted level of thought in an unpaid job with few rewards and decades of criticism. Everyone knew better than the selectors. For every happy player chosen, there were three or four who were disgruntled with the selection panel. And as Bradman was seen as the game's supremo, he received the most flack. For this reason, he at first refused to give me his dream team. I suggested to him that it would only be published posthumously. In late 1999, I was thrilled to receive a letter, which Thos Hodgson referred to as 'the Magna Carta of cricket'. It was not quite King John's declaration at Runnymede in 1215. Yet in sporting terms it was a powerful statement in its own right.

The letter contained his dream team in batting order. It was, 1 Arthur Morris; 2 Barry Richards; 3 Don Bradman; 4 Sachin Tendulkar; 5 Garry Sobers; 6 Don Tallon; 7 Ray Lindwall; 8 Dennis Lillee; 9 Alec Bedser; 10 Bill O'Reilly; 11 Clarrie Grimmett; 12th man, Wally Hammond.

The living players selected and the families of those who are no longer with us ranked this honour from Bradman high in their illustrious records. Arthur Morris, for one, was chuffed.

Bradman said of Morris:

> I think Arthur, towards the close of the 1948 tour, was playing the finest cricket of any left-hand bat I've seen. He had that wonderful quality so noticeable in good players — plenty of time to play his shots. All strokes came alike — hooks, drives, cuts, glances. [He had]... powerful wrists and forearms ... Great team man; studious and intelligent observer.

Barry Richards, as much as anyone, comprehended the significance of his selection. Bradman indirectly helped to end his Test career. He was a member of the South African team in 1969–70, but played only four Tests, not counting his performances in World Series Cricket and for a World team against England in 1970. His placement in Bradman's best went some way to bolstering his strong claim to being one of the game's greats.

After Bradman's team was announced, I received a fax from Richards. It said:

It is indeed a great honour to be selected in a team by the ultimate peer within the cricket community. To be mentioned amongst so many legendary names has for me compensated in some way for the fact that I had such a small taste of international cricket. In many ways it is overwhelming, but it gives me a sense of great pride.

Bradman made all his choices without fear or favour. Three players selected — Clarrie Grimmett, Bill O'Reilly and Wally Hammond — were not fans of the Don.

*

One important factor in Bradman's selection process was that he didn't just choose a list of 12 outstanding players. The temptation in such an exercise is to pick names that you think *ought* to be selected, or *must* be selected. That wasn't Bradman's way. His approach was simple enough. I asked him to select a *team*, not a list of great players. He went for a winning combination. He chose aggressive batsmen who could score fast runs so that a penetrating bowling line-up could dismiss any opposition twice.

Bradman would always choose a left-hand, right-hand opening batting partnership if he had outstanding candidates for each spot. Arthur Morris, a left-hander, and Barry Richards, a right-hander, filled the bill. Bradman took the number-three spot (funny that). That left one recognised batsman to choose for the number-four spot. He couldn't go past Sachin Tendulkar, whom he admired for his shot production, compact defence and many other qualities.

Bradman selected only four specialist batsmen. Garry Sobers, the all-rounder, really made it five. Sobers averaged around 58 in Tests and was one of the finest batsmen of all time. Bradman's Test average of 100 made him worth two of the best of all time. This means the best-ever team, in effect, had the standard six batsmen.

He would always choose a brilliant keeper ahead of a batsman who could keep. That's why he opted for Don Tallon. And anyway, this keeper could bat. You have to look well beyond the stats with this selection and consider Tallon's batting displays in the 1930s. His Test average of under 18 runs an innings contradicted that. Yet if ever the figures lied, they did with this player concerning his batting skills. In the 1930s, he was judged as one of the most talented attacking batsmen in First-Class cricket. He made the Queensland state team at 17 years old, in 1933–34, and two seasons later, in 1935–36, impressed Bradman with a dashing 88 in a state game. It was just one innings among many in that season (and the next four before war stopped play) that stamped the young Tallon, then still a teenager, as a prodigious all-rounder. Another innings of 193 in 187 minutes against Victoria at the Gabba in 1935–36 ranked as one of the finest of the 1930s. Bradman didn't see it, but read about it and was informed of its outstanding class by witnesses.

Having experienced at first hand his ability (both with the bat and behind the stumps) early in the season, Bradman was prepared to consider fast-tracking Tallon into the Test team. Indeed, in the next season (1936–37) the way was opened up for him by

Bradman and the other Test selectors when Tallon was chosen to play in a trial game for a Bradman XI against Victor Richardson's team that had just had a most successful tour of South Africa. Bradman thought so highly of Tallon's batting that he placed him not at six or seven, but at five in his team's actual order.

After World War II, when he made the Test team, Tallon's chances were limited by the batting in front of him. Morris, Barnes, Brown, Bradman, Harvey, Hassett, Miller and Lindwall would variously, and in different combinations, build huge scores that would reduce the opportunities for the rest of the side, led by Tallon. Yet there were flashes of his 1930s brilliance, such as in Melbourne in the Third Test of the 1946–47 Ashes, when he managed 35 and a brilliant 92.

*

Choosing only four batsmen and an all-rounder allowed Bradman to select a brilliant bowling line-up. But how did he choose from the large number of champion pacemen stretching back to Fred Spofforth in the 1880s?

Ray Lindwall made it a less problematic decision. He could bat. Ray had scored two Test centuries, two more than any other pace bowler except Sir Richard Hadlee. But Don regarded Ray as a better bladesman than Hadlee.

Lindwall took the number-seven spot.

Bradman went for Dennis Lillee at number eight. Few would argue that Lillee was one of the best, if not *the* best, fast bowler of all time.

Alec Bedser was placed at nine. Bradman already had three pacemen — Lindwall, Lillee and left-armer Sobers. Instead of going for more of the same — think of the outstanding but metronomic West Indies foursomes of the 1980s — he decided on a brilliant swing-bowler. Unlike the others, Bedser preferred bowling into the wind. He could also become the work-horse as a stock bowler when required.

The Dream Team's speed quartet has variety. It has pace, guile, swing, bounce, right-arm, left-arm and strong elements of intimidation.

The number-ten position was also easy for Bradman. He regarded fast leg-spinner Bill O'Reilly as the best bowler he ever saw or faced. Bradman noted the spinner's individualistic grip: 'O'Reilly did not hold the ball in the fingers quite like the orthodox leg-spinner. It was held more towards the palm of the hand. He was advised by certain "experts" to change his grip but fortunately refused to do as advised.'

In this respect they were similar characters. They held to their ways and opinions, especially if their methods worked.

Number 11 was a tougher choice. He always favoured a left-arm orthodox spinner in any of his teams, if possible. But he already had one in Garry Sobers, who could also bowl wrist spin. This freed up Bradman to select another spinner. It got down to Clarrie Grimmett or Shane Warne. He bracketed them and O'Reilly together as the best three leg-spinners in history. Grimmett got the nod, mainly because he worked so well in combination with O'Reilly.

Bradman also witnessed Grimmett at his brilliant best in England in 1930. Wally Hammond had crushed Australia in 1928–29, making 905 runs at an average of 113.13. In 1930, Grimmett, with an unprecedented bag of deceptive deliveries, demoralised Hammond and often took his wicket. This left the way clear for Bradman to dominate. Against all odds, Australia won the series 2:1.

Bradman had many personal tussles with Grimmett in Shield and other matches, and knew his exceptional abilities at first hand.

Bradman's Best, then, in effect had eight top-line bowling options, given that Sobers was three bowlers in one. And if you like Sachin Tendulkar's style of spinning, you have a ninth alternative.

Compare this with the 2001 Australian Test team with its four bowlers — one of the best-ever attacks: Brett Lee, Glenn McGrath, Jason Gillespie and Warne. Bradman's dream team has twice the bowling options of a normal team, and therefore, on paper, twice the firepower.

Finally, Wally Hammond was picked as 12th man. Bradman found it tough to separate him and Viv Richards. Whenever Bradman couldn't separate the skills and records of players, he would look at something else on which to make a choice. Hammond was a more useful bowler.

Was his team a work of genius? It was certainly unique and, once it was in the public domain, I fully understood his reluctance for having it published while he was around.

CHAPTER 35

The Reaction

In mid-2001, it was made public that I would be publishing a book revealing Bradman's choices for his best-ever World XI. Mike Selvey, a cricket writer on the London *Guardian* newspaper, ran a competition to see if anyone could pick the same world team as Bradman before the team was announced. Selvey had a cute tie-breaker should more than one contestant pick the team.

They had to finish the sentence: 'Douglas Jardine should get a posthumous knighthood because ...'

I couldn't resist responding to this on email with: 'Douglas Jardine should get a posthumous knighthood because of his services to Australia, which, after the Bodyline series, lifted its rating against England and did not relinquish the Ashes for another 20 years.'

But Mike Selvey need not have bothered with the tie-breaker. I doubted that anyone in the world has picked the same team as Bradman.

*

Bradman's Best was published on 12 August 2001, with simultaneous publications in Australia and England, after a commendable effort by the publishers to keep the contents under wraps. It was not quite *Harry Potter*, but weeks before publication Norman Harris in the London *Observer* noted: 'The books containing the 11 precious names will be guarded like gold bars.'

The timing was fortunate. About a week before release, former minor media mogul Christopher Skase died in Spain. The media was swamped with the story. Most book publications were ignored. A few weeks later, the 9/11 hits on New York's Twin Towers occurred. Everything was pushed aside and there was no other major news worldwide.

As it turned out, Monday, 12 August was a slow news day and my book, *Bradman's Best*, had a very good run of media attention and a chance to stimulate much reaction. Competitions sprang up in both the UK and Australia with prizes for those who could pick nearest to Bradman's choices. (No one picked all the names.)

Newspaper columnists in both countries made up simulations of a game between Don's team and their own. Even London's venerable magazine *The Spectator* became involved when writer

Frank Johnson was inspired to choose his own Philosopher's XI, starting with Plato and Aristotle.

'Donald Bradman's posthumous ideal cricket XI of all time was revealed this week,' he wrote. 'Few political scoops have inspired so much conversation and argument ...'

The fact that Bradman had only chosen two English names — Bedser and Hammond — caused Johnson to remark:

> ... another humiliation for English cricket at Australia's
> hands in this dreadful summer [2001]. But at this point
> we English should stop conceding that, at this or that,
> we are not world class. What is the most important and
> hardest of man's functions? It is to think. The selection of
> an international, 'dream' thinking XI would tell a different
> story about the English.

Johnson, tongue firmly in cheek, finished his article with: 'So: five English speakers; three Frenchmen; two Greeks; one German. No Australians were selected.'

In response to this, I wrote a letter to *The Spectator* (published 1 September 2001):

> ... I agree with Frank Johnson's Philosophy First XI, except
> for a glaring omission which has overtones of vindictiveness.
> Surely England's most radical, and in my opinion best,
> modern philosopher, Professor Brian O'Shaughnessy, author
> of those weighty tomes *The Will* and *Consciousness and the
> World*, should be in the team, even as 12th man.

Has Professor O'Shaughnessy been left out for reasons not obvious from your clearly biased selection process? Is this the meaning behind Frank Johnson's rather pointed last line: 'No Australians were selected'?

Did the good professor's accident of birth in Australia cause him to be overlooked?

The fun continued.

Predictably, there was much criticism of Bradman's selections.

His choice of Tallon batting at number six raised many eyebrows. Yet it was noticeable that no critic seemed to take the time to analyse Bradman's assessment. Some ignored the fact that he had seen more of the great cricketers than anyone else over a long period. So if critics had not seen, for example, Tallon, they tended to avoid the fact that Bradman had been able not only to watch him, but to play with and against him. This in turn was one of the beauties of the selections. They covered nearly eight decades.

Matthew Engel, an assiduous Bradman detractor, felt he was given a free hit with the dream team. He commented in the London *Guardian*:

The odd thing is, that with the whole of history to go at — and without ever having to worry about Graham Thorpe and Michael Vaughan being out injured — the great man has come up with a side every bit as inadequate as England's [in 2001]. As an all-time World XI, it is surprisingly flawed and decidedly beatable ... the fact that he played in England and Australia is all too evident.

Engel then chose his own, not surprisingly flawed and decidedly beatable — yet still strong — team: Sunil Gavaskar, Jack Hobbs, Don Bradman, Viv Richards, Denis Compton, Garry Sobers, W.G. Grace, Les Ames (keeper), Malcolm Marshall, Shane Warne and Michael Holding, with Wilfred Rhodes 12th man.

Engel noted that Barry Richards played in only four Tests because of apartheid, saying: 'His ability at the topmost level was never fully tested. For all we know, he was another Graeme Hick.'

This comment smacked of selective amnesia. Richards acquitted himself brilliantly in World Series Cricket, which even Bradman, who disliked the concept even more than Engel, saw as a cut above official Test standard in the 1970s.

Mark Nicholas in the London *Daily Telegraph* made some thoughtful criticisms, saying: 'Imagine Tallon at six and Lindwall at seven scrambling for their helmets in the face of Andy Roberts, Michael Holding, Joel Garner and Malcolm Marshall.'

That mighty West Indian speed quartet would be hard to combat. But on Bradman's reasoning, his top five — Barry Richards, Morris, Bradman, Tendulkar and Sobers — would have scored enough runs for it not to matter. Nicholas pointed out that only Bradman and Sobers were chosen in both Bradman's team and *Wisden*'s five cricketers of the 20th century. Those who missed out (only just) on selection in *Bradman's Best* were Warne, Sir Vivian Richards and Sir Jack Hobbs.

'... the arguments rage,' Nicholas added. '... Wasim Akram picked his greatest team and could find no place for Sachin

Tendulkar. E.W. Swanton might arouse from his deepest sleep if he heard that Wally Hammond had not made it.'

Yet at least Wally got to carry the drinks in Bradman's team!

Nicholas also noted that Richie Benaud said that Warne is the greatest spinner he has seen, which reiterated a basic point about the choices. Bradman did see Warne, Grimmett and O'Reilly, and played against the latter two. Benaud did not play against Grimmett or O'Reilly and would have seen very little, if anything, of Grimmett and little of O'Reilly. Any selection, and thoughts, for that matter, would seem to have more credibility if the selector saw and/or played against the nominees.

'A billion Indians and equally vociferous Yorkshire folk might baulk at Barry Richard's four-match Test career being acknowledged before the lifetime achievements of Sunil Gavaskar and Sir Len Hutton,' Nicholas added. 'The fact that not one member of the West Indian juggernaut that flattened the rest of the world through the Eighties has made the final XI will spill a few rum and cokes across the Caribbean.'

Here Nicholas seemed to drift from a main plank in the Bradman approach. He was not looking to award 'lifetime achievements' but to select the best combination of cricketers in a team. And while no one could disagree with the devastation and brilliance of the awesome foursome from the West Indies, how would their penetration, variety and balance stack up against that of Lillee, Lindwall, Bedser, Sobers, Grimmett and O'Reilly?

Nicholas's nomination of Sunil Gavaskar as the unlucky Indian not to be recognised by Bradman in this team was a sensitive point. Gavaskar had been chosen by Bradman in a real World XI in 1971–72. He was so disappointed that he did not gain a place in the 'dream' team that he claimed it was not authentic.

'I refuse to believe the Bradman Dream XI was actually Sir Don's personal selection for the world's greatest-ever combination,' Gavaskar told the BBC. 'Even when he was the target of Bodyline tactics in 1931–32 [sic] he never uttered a word. I am sure he would not have stuck his neck out for something like this which is bound to give rise to a huge debate.'

Gavaskar added: 'Sir Don was a man who steered away from all controversies in his lifetime.'

Which is correct. That's why *Bradman's Best* was published posthumously.

*

In our discussions, Bradman said to me: 'You'll be sorry [when your book on Bradman's selections comes out].'

I asked why.

'There are 12 names involved. Think of the hundreds of players who have missed out, and the reaction of their families. It won't be pleasant.'

Another miffed player was Shane Warne. After being asked at several media conferences about how he felt concerning his non-selection, he suddenly let his mouth rule his brain: 'We don't believe the team,' he said, irritated, and added a few other pithy comments. His royal 'we' here were some members of the then current Australian team. There was some ill-feeling that no contemporary (2001) Australian was selected.

I recall being asked onto an ABC afternoon radio program where I was 'challenged' by a commentator who took up Warne's disappointment.

'Interesting that Warne's attacking the team when he has not even read Bradman's analysis,' I said. 'But I suppose this is understandable. Shane doesn't read. He has even boasted he has not even read his own [ghosted] autobiography.'

The BBC also reported: 'Gavaskar's sentiments contrast sharply with those of countryman Sachin Tendulkar.'

Tendulkar commented: 'It is a great honour to be among those names especially when Sir Don himself chose the team and made me bat at number four, after Sir Don bats and before Sobers. What else can you ask for? All I can say is that it is a great honour. There are a lot of great names that missed in that list, and my name was considered. I'm on top of the world.'

It's easy to understand Gavaskar's feelings. Yet he may have had some further reflection when he was called upon by the International Cricket Council to be a selector of the World XI that played Australia in October 2005, which was inspired by *Bradman's Best*. He and the other selectors were criticised for their choices after the drubbing by Australia, especially the tendency to go for 'name' rather than form players. The Gavaskar case further demonstrated the difficulty of choosing world teams, whether hypothetical or actual. Everyone — Bradman included — has a varying point of view in choosing a side, depending on their bias towards their own country or favourite individuals. They are also limited by the range of players they have seen.

*

Former Test cricketer David Hookes, in typical fashion, jumped in for a headline, damned the selections and wrote a rushed piece for the next morning's *Age*. He had not read the book and Bradman's thinking. He went on Neil Mitchell's 3AW morning program with his reaction, and seized on Gavaskar's attitude. I went on 3AW's sports program that evening and confronted Hookes.

'Did you say the team was not authentic?' I asked him as soon as I got on air.

'No,' he said, 'but Sunil Gavaskar did.'

After hiding from his assertions earlier in the day, Hookes proceeded to criticise the selections and I defended them from Bradman's arguments. Hookes was not a reflective type. He had not stopped to consider he was contradicting the selections of a far deeper mind on the game than his, let alone the thoughts of an infinitely superior cricketer. It was not that Bradman should not or could not be criticised. But the quick, dismissive points Hookes tried to make were predictably weak.

(In 2003, Derryn Hinch attacked him over a conflict of interest when Hookes was both a commentator on 3AW and coach of the Victorian state side. Hinch asked me onto his 3AW afternoon program. We discussed the conflict of interest. I agreed with Hinch.)

Most commentators were preoccupied with picking their own teams to rival *Bradman's Best*. Several newspapers and media outlets opened up the columns to readers for their opinions.

Those in *The Times* of London were especially entertaining, including the thoughts of Richard Penney:

> As someone whose career peaked with the Dublin Fleas
> XI, I hesitate to suggest that Sir Donald's judgment could
> be flawed. However, while I can live with the absence of
> Compton, Miller and S.F. Barnes, to include the inestimable
> Barry Richards ahead of the sublime John Berry Hobbs is
> evidence that Sir Donald needed stronger spectacles.

Perhaps Penney's respect for Bradman's eyesight may have been increased marginally with his selections for his best-ever Australian and England teams. They included his favourite Hobbs, along with his expendable Compton, Miller and S.F. Barnes.

Peter Crush would be given the humility/ humour/ generous and imaginative thinking awards after he wrote:

> Who am I, the cricketing equivalent of pond life, to be even
> asked to question the opinion of a cricketing god like Don
> Bradman? He clearly picked a side that he wanted to play
> in, and that alone should not be dismissed lightly as his
> happiness would probably ensure a double hundred.

After Penney questioned the Don's seeing capacity, two emailers to *The Times* went further, attacking his sanity.

John Cottrell wrote: 'Two specialist spinners when he has Sobers and Tendulkar? Bradders must have been bonkers.'

Giles W. Smith wrote:

Not much to quibble about but Tallon at number six with
an average of 18? Did the great man lose his marbles? He
isn't even close to Evans, Knott, Marsh. What would have
happened if Martian seamers produced five unplayable ones
at an overcast Headingley and Tallon had appeared at nine
(runs) for five (wickets)? Still the whole debate is a lovely
idea.

Edward Little, showing a certain perspicacity, was less concerned
with Bradman's mental stability, and more interested in how his
brain worked:

His selection shows a fascinating insight into his mind. The
balance is somewhat old fashioned and shows a degree of
arrogance that was his personal trademark. Who else would
pick only four first-line batsmen? Obviously he backed
himself to make most of the runs.

One observer's arrogance can be another's self-confidence.
Bradman's first five selections — it is misleading to leave out
Sobers — were made with the belief that they could do the job
enough in a five Test series to win against any other team, perhaps
with the exception of Mr Smith's Martian XI. This would apply
especially with these five superstars batting together in Don's
team and generating a celestial brilliance.

As Bradman remarked: 'If they can't make 500, who can?'

Perhaps *The Guardian*'s editorial of 17 August 2001 on the selections was as good a summary observation as anybody's:

Matthew Engel, unconcerned that his batting average
is 99.94 lower than the Don's, has already criticised the
composition of the Bradman team in this paper ... but
no two pundits will ever agree. Bradman allowed his
closeness to his teammates to influence his selection; ask a
Yorkshireman and it is a fair bet that the entire 'dream' team
would be from God's own county; and, as for computers,
they will rely on averages, an unreliable arbiter of greatness.
Would Spofforth have routed today's England, or Jessop
saved the day with a sparkling hundred? We will never
know ...

CHAPTER 36

Best Ashes Teams

After we discussed Bradman's best World team ever, I was keen to know his best-ever Ashes teams, aware that this competition was closest to his heart. He sent me a typed list of his Australian team in late 1998 (as he did with the World team), and later a handwritten note containing the England team. The resultant book, *Bradman's Best Ashes Teams*, was published in August 2002. These selections were taken from all players from the first international between England and Australia in March 1877, until the end of 2000. Bradman again did not select the best 11 players for each team. His decisions came from much thought into the combination of players, and with regard to their impact on the opposition team. Primarily the choices were made as the best to win.

He enjoyed the exercise and I was pleased to have unlocked the thoughts of the finest mind on the game of all time, for posterity.

As with the World team, Bradman's selections for the Australian and England Ashes teams contained plenty of surprises.

The Australian side in batting order was: Arthur Morris, Bill Ponsford, Don Bradman, Neil Harvey, Charlie Macartney, Keith Miller, Don Tallon, Ray Lindwall, Dennis Lillee, Bill O'Reilly and Clarrie Grimmett, with Richie Benaud as 12th man.

*

The name 'Victor Trumper' has a romantic 'winning' ring to it; someone who trumps others with style and grace. 'William Ponsford' is more solid and reflects something ponderous and safe. One is gay, in the old cavalier sense, and flamboyant; the hare in Aesop's fable in the losing race against the tortoise. In choosing his right-hand opening bat for Australia, Bradman sided with Aesop and chose Ponsford as the cricketer more likely to win you a series.

It was predictable. They had forged some of the biggest, most important partnerships in cricket history. Bradman had seen his choice's exceptional skills and big-occasion capacities at first hand. He did not see Trumper bat, and this swayed him in part to opt for the devil he knew. He read everything published about Trumper, listened to experts who saw him and studied the record.

'There is no doubt Trumper was a great player,' Bradman said, 'and one of the finest stylists of all time. By all accounts he would have been great in any era.'

Ponsford was a more reliable opener and a better performer when a series depended on him lifting his rating. His massive scores of 181 and 266 in the last two Tests of the 1934 series in England and his 110 at the Oval in 1930 were evidence of his temperament under pressure. Ponsford performed at his best when he had to make a big score to help secure the Ashes in England on both these occasions. He was no slouch when it came to the pace of making his runs either. In his big partnerships with Bradman and others, he blended solid defence with attack. He had a mind to go for his shots when he had set up an innings. Ponsford still holds the record for the most runs made in a day in First-Class cricket in Australia — 334 not out against NSW at the MCG during the Christmas match of 1926.

*

Ponsford's partner in the dream Australian team was the left-handed Arthur Morris. Bradman's selection of himself at number three was automatic. He would place at least one other left-handed batsman in the top six, *if* the player was superior or equal to right-handers vying for a place. He ranked only four other left-handers with Neil Harvey, his choice for the number-four spot. They were Arthur Morris, Garry Sobers, David Gower and Brian Lara. Bradman ranked Harvey with the finest batsmen — left or right — Australia has produced down the ages.

Bradman noted that Harvey was:

Strongly built in a compact frame. He had no technical faults. He was blessed with supple wrists and was a strong driver and powerful cutter. He could hook extremely well and enjoyed the shot. He appeared to struggle against spin early in his career, but mid-career became one of the best players of spin I ever saw. Neil liked to dance to the ball, and apparently his mastering of spin on tours of Pakistan and India was something special to behold. He was also one of the best outfielders of all time. His work in the covers, even late in his career, was sensational.

Harvey was very much in the Bradman mould. He liked to get on with the game. He was a naturally attacking cricketer, as was Bradman's choice for number five, Charlie Macartney.

*

Bradman's initial impression of Macartney was in the first Test he ever saw — at the SCG on 25 and 26 February 1921. It was the Fifth Test of the 1920–21 Ashes series. Macartney played one of his best innings, making 170. His timing for such a show was impeccable. The 12-year-old fan from Bowral would never forget the all-round display of stylish, powerful strokeplay.

Macartney scored seven Test hundreds in his 35-Test career, including a century before lunch on the first day of the 1926 Leeds Test. He was perhaps the hardest-hitting top-drawer batsman to play for Australia before the advent of David Warner, and he had all the strokes. The shortish, square-shouldered right-hander loved to improvise. He refused to let bowlers get on top and would always attempt to dominate early in an innings.

Macartney averaged nearly 42 runs in Test innings, which was six runs short of McCabe, but well short of Greg Chappell (nearly 55), and Steve Waugh and Allan Border (both 50 plus). Macartney's left-arm orthodox spin-bowling (45 wickets at the good average of 27.55) put him in the genuine all-rounder class, which provided the Bradman team with a strong third spin option of a different variety to support the O'Reilly–Grimmett combination.

At the beginning of his career, Macartney was selected more for his spinners than his batting. On his first tour of England in 1909, he took 64 wickets at 17.85 runs apiece. He took a long run for a slow bowler, and had a deadly quicker ball.

Macartney was one of five new faces in the Australian team, along with the seven players Bradman selected in the World team. The others were Bill Ponsford, Neil Harvey, Keith Miller and 12th man Richie Benaud.

*

Much has been written in the last 70 years about a feud between Bradman and Keith Miller, the choice at number six in the Australian dream team. There were tensions between them, but the real differences stemmed from the fact that they were two very different, great Australians and sportsmen from divergent backgrounds a generation apart.

Bradman found Miller irritating at times, but he did not let it interfere with his appreciation of him as a grand cricketing all-rounder. He was selected in front of a fine group of all-rounders including Richie Benaud, Alan Davidson, Monty Noble and Warwick Armstrong.

Bradman saw Miller as a 'dangerous' new-ball bowler who could swing it both ways, and was nearly as fast as Ray Lindwall. Bradman also admired his batting and his big-hitting ability, but was critical of his lack of application and concentration at times.

Miller had remarkable Test figures with both bat and ball. Performances under pressure or at key moments, and the strength of the opposition, should carry more weight. Yet over time, statistics are strong indicators of a player's capacities. Bradman's choice of Sobers as the number-one all-rounder of all time is hardly disputed by any astute observer or anyone who saw him perform. But Miller was close — perhaps equal — in his overall impact. His batting did not have the sustained brilliance that Sobers attained over 38 more Tests. Miller was more flamboyant and more likely to surrender his wicket attempting a big hit. In his prime, probably during the unofficial 'Victory Tests' in England just after the war, he was a magnificent performer. In a game at Lord's in August 1945, playing for the 'Dominions' against England, he smote seven sixes in a blast of 185.

Miller's bowling returns are far more impressive than Sobers', and because of this some have argued that the Australian was the more valuable player. He could be quick and lethal if in the right frame of mind.

*

Bradman again chose Lillee and Lindwall as his tearaway opening bowlers. He could also call on a third in Miller, which formed a trio that would put fear into any batting line-up. I could see that he struggled to leave out Ted McDonald, a speedster he also admired greatly.

'McDonald was tall and had a perfect rhythm,' Bradman recalled, 'rather like Larwood after him, and Lindwall much later. McDonald had real stamina and pace. Yet he didn't rely entirely on speed. He could swing the ball, cut back to medium pace and even deliver spin. I first saw him in 1921 [in the Fifth Test of the 1920–21 Ashes] and later batted against him in 1930 when he was playing for Lancashire. He was still very quick when he wished to be. He knocked my middle stump out of the ground.'

However, Bradman noted: 'McDonald had to make way on the score of fielding and batting.'

'In my judgement,' he was careful to say, thus emphasising it was only the opinion of one selector, 'Miller and Lindwall on their record [as all-rounders] just shaded the others. But Davidson's outstanding and versatile fielding entitled him to be in close consideration.'

The keepers were down to Bert Oldfield, Wally Grout and Tallon. Bradman had already chosen Tallon in the World XI and was not going to change his mind for the Australian side.

'They were all superb and fit to grace any side,' he said. 'Oldfield did so many brilliant things but he made more mistakes than the others. I felt Grout and Tallon were very similar, but Tallon was slightly quicker and certainly a better bat.'

Perhaps one selection that he may have changed had he lived a few more years was the position of Australia's wicket-keeper. But his cut-off point was the end of 2000. He chose Tallon as the best keeper he ever witnessed, and would not have changed his mind on this point. However, he did remark in *Bradman's Best* that if Adam Gilchrist 'maintained his batting average above 50 and his form behind the stumps, he would be the most valuable keeper-batsman in history'.

Gilchrist came close, averaging 47.60. Add to this his batting strike rate of 81.96 runs per hundred balls over 96 Tests, and an outstanding keeping record, and you have one of the most brilliant all-rounders of all time.

*

Bradman naturally opted for Tallon as keeper again. Tallon's selection at seven summed up Bradman's attitude to his batting skills, which he considered even ahead of the bowling all-rounder, Ray Lindwall, who stood at number eight.

After the 1948 tour, Bradman ranked Lindwall almost in McDonald's class, but thought McDonald, who was much taller, had a better bouncer because he didn't have to dig it in so short to get lift. However, as Lindwall's career progressed through the 1950s, Bradman acknowledged his ability with the short ball was as good as anyone he had seen. He admired Lindwall's courage, and was aware of his capacity, learned from his rugby league days, to carry injuries.

'Lindwall had wonderful stamina,' he said. 'He could swing the ball either way, and had a nice, deceptive change of pace. Ray also had great control over line and length.'

By the end of Lindwall's career, Bradman ranked him with McDonald as the best Australian fast man he had seen and had the advantage of having faced them both a generation apart. Then along came Lillee, and Glenn McGrath, the latter's record being incomplete when Bradman made his selections.

'Taking Lillee's entire career into account,' he said, 'he was the best paceman I ever saw. He showed enormous guts in returning from his serious back injury. Lillee was a dangerous bowler, who could both intimidate and out-think batsmen. He swung the ball both ways and had a magnificent leg-cutter.'

Lillee was one of Bradman's last official selectorial decisions in Ashes cricket, although he was not enamoured with the lanky West Australian at first. It was fellow selector Sam Loxton who opted and fought for the speedster's inclusion. The fast bowler didn't let him down. Lillee took 5 for 84 in an innings in his first Test in 1970–71, and a year later turned on a performance in Perth in 1971 against a World XI that changed Bradman's mind. When Lillee made a comeback after breaking his back in 1974, he was less the demon and more a threat to batsmen with his guile, accuracy and brilliance. He went on as the world's leading speed man for another decade.

*

Places 10 and 11 went to the leg-spin twins, Bill O'Reilly and Clarrie Grimmett, and 12th man was given to leg-spinning all-rounder Richie Benaud. Bradman preferred an all-rounder as his first reserve. He narrowed the choice down to Richie Benaud and

Alan Davidson, who could hardly be separated on the figures or performances over coincident careers. Bradman always looked for a 'breaking point' — an attribute such as a specialist fielding skill that gave one player the advantage over the other. In this case, it was Benaud's leadership abilities. Bradman regarded him as the best post-war captain he had seen.

Benaud was often a match-winner with the ball, most notably in England in 1961, but his aggressive batting also had its moments. In 1957–58 in South Africa he was instrumental in winning a series with two dashing centuries.

Bradman chose a strong, well-balanced Australian side with six talented batsmen, arguably the best wicket-keeper of all time, and a bowling line-up with plenty of options. The three pacemen — Lillee, Lindwall and Miller — were nicely complemented by a trio of spinners. Grimmett and O'Reilly provide two different kinds of leg-spinner, while Macartney delivers variety with orthodox left-arm finger spin.

*

Warne and Gilchrist were the only selections on which I tried, through discussion rather than argument or debate, to change Bradman's mind. But it was his team and he stuck with his reasons, despite having been thrilled and appreciative of what Warne and Gilchrist meant to the game.

This team would always be hard to beat, especially with Bradman in the line-up.

CHAPTER 37

England Reverie

Despite his many Ashes battles with England, Bradman was an Anglophile with great respect for all its institutions and history. When recovering from his appendectomy after the 1934 Ashes, he and Jessie toured England, avoiding the press. It was a rare idyllic sojourn for them.

Bradman remarked after the experience: 'Nothing in the world appealed to me more than England as nature made her, unchanged in centuries.'

He had composed World and Australian 'dream teams', but when I requested the England side from 1877–2000 (again, the best combination rather than a list of outstanding performers), he relished the challenge. It exercised his love of the UK and unmatched comprehension of cricket from just about every angle. Once more, he came up with a team unique in its composition and creativity.

The team in batting order was: Jack Hobbs; Len Hutton; Denis Compton; Peter May; Wally Hammond; W.G. Grace; Godfrey Evans; Fred Trueman; Alec Bedser; S.F. Barnes; Hedley Verity; with Ian Botham as 12th man.

The selection of W.G. Grace ahead of Ian Botham, spinner Hedley Verity instead of Jim Laker, and the choice of early-20th-century medium-pacer S.F. Barnes were the most controversial decisions. Bradman, as ever, was looking for the best team balance. When asked why he chose Grace as the all-rounder over Botham, he said that he wanted a batting all-rounder at number six. If he had been looking for a bowling all-rounder, he would have chosen Botham over Grace.

'The first five — Hobbs, Hutton, Compton, May and Hammond — are all top-line batsmen,' Bradman said, 'and Grace made up the complement of six.'

Bradman judged Grace a more effective batsman and leader than Botham.

'Many observers in England rate Grace the greatest cricketer of all time,' he said. 'He was certainly the most outstanding cricketer, character and leader of the 19th century.'

Bradman also judged him the best captain in the England team, ahead of Hutton and May.

'The other bowlers [Trueman, Bedser, Barnes and Verity] would be selected ahead of Botham, and Grace for that matter, taking into account their speciality and importance to team balance,' Bradman noted. He also pointed out that Hammond at times was a 'superb' medium-pacer, which gave England a sixth bowling option. This further off-set the need for Botham in the balance of this particular line-up.

*

Bradman was not inclined to leave out any of his three paceman choices —Trueman, Bedser and Barnes — which meant he could only select one spinner. He reduced his choices to either Verity or Laker.

Bradman batted against both left-arm orthodox spinner Verity and right-arm off-spinner Laker, but took into account that Laker was not at his prime during the 1948 Ashes, when Bradman faced him. Laker played in three 1948 Tests and his series figures of 9 wickets at 52.44 reflect the pasting he received.

'He was inexperienced then,' Bradman recalled, 'but developed into the best off-spinner of the post-war period along with [the West Indies'] Lance Gibbs. Laker managed outstanding accuracy and control. He had a nice high arm action and could spin the ball hard.'

Laker is best known for taking a world-record 19 wickets for 90 runs at Manchester in the Fourth Test of the 1956 Ashes. Bradman reported on that match where the pitch was described as 'a dustbowl, a sub-standard Test wicket, conducive to prodigious spin'. He recognised the performance as one of sustained brilliance, but ranked Hedley Verity's 15 for 104 at Lord's during the 1934 Ashes as an even more impressive effort, 'given the comparative conditions and batting strengths of the opposition'.

Bradman concluded that 'while it was testing for a period [on a rain-affected pitch] after lunch on the final day, I played on worse pitches. Hedley bowled superbly, taking advantage of the conditions. He kept a remarkable length, and, encouraged by some indifferent batting, made the ball spin and jump awkwardly.'

Bradman's decision to include Verity in his team may well have been influenced by the fact that the Yorkshireman dismissed him eight times in Tests — more often than any other bowler.

*

Bradman had been intrigued with the career of the dark, brooding S.F. Barnes ever since he could remember. The legendary English medium-pacer was very much in the psyche of Australian cricketers and fans in the early part of the 20th century. Bradman was only three years of age in 1911–12 when Barnes had a sensational Test series in Australia, taking 34 wickets at 22.88, and would have been too young to appreciate the bowler's effort in the Triangular Test Series in England in 1912. Then Barnes took 39 Australian and South African wickets at just 10.35 followed by 49 wickets at 10.93 in four Tests in South Africa in 1913–14. But at the age of seven or eight, Bradman became aware of the name Sydney Francis Barnes.

'When we played scratch "Test" matches in the schoolyard or the street, all the boys wanted to be Trumper when batting and the bowlers all wanted to be S.F. Barnes, even though he was English,' Bradman recalled with amusement. 'He was very much the talk among cricketers. His performances in Australia had given him legendary status here. He was the most respected English cricketer of the so-called Golden Era before World War I.'

When Bradman began playing First-Class cricket in 1927–28, the conversations he had with bowlers who had seen Barnes, and batsmen who had faced him, confirmed his genius. Bradman also read widely about Barnes' style, ability and record. Barnes could deliver swing and cut, and then spin, with such cunning that few batsmen knew what was coming from ball to ball. Like O'Reilly, he was tall, long-limbed and straight-backed, and with a short, springing run-up.

Bradman concluded in 1950 that Barnes and O'Reilly were the two greatest bowlers of all time, and maintained that view for the rest of his life. Yet he could not find a place for Barnes in his best-ever World team.

When asked about this, Bradman replied: 'My understanding was that they [Barnes and O'Reilly] were similar in style, aggression, intelligence and abilities. Barnes was probably quicker but did not have a wrong'un [googly] which gave O'Reilly the most marginal advantage. There was not much point in having two such similar players in the one team. I could only choose one. Another point for O'Reilly was his pairing with Grimmett.'

Bradman made this comparison to Neville Cardus in 1938, who informed Barnes.

'It's quite true,' Barnes said, 'I never bowled the googly.' Then with a glint in his eye, he added, 'I never needed it.'

This inferred that his hundreds of wickets were enough.

'He was not an easy man to handle on the field of play,' Cardus noted. 'There was a Mephistophelian aspect about him. He did not play cricket out of any green-field starry-eyed realism. He rightly considered that his talents were worth estimating in cash values.'

Barnes was one of just two players in the three best-ever teams (World, Australia and England) chosen by Bradman who he never saw play, which was a compliment to his reputation and record. However, Bradman and Barnes were playing in the same English seasons in 1930, 1934 and 1938. In 1930, when Barnes was 56 and Bradman 21, the press tried to arrange a match where they played against each other. Bradman would have loved the experience, but the long, tight schedule for the Australians on tour, and Barnes in the Lancashire League, didn't allow the confrontation.

*

Jack Hobbs was one of the many fine early-20th-century England players Bradman did not see until late in Hobbs' career. When Bradman played against him in 1928–29, Hobbs didn't have the force or stroke range of earlier seasons. Yet what Bradman saw was enough to convince him that Hobbs was one of the game's greats.

He had emerged as a Test player early in 1908, the year Bradman was born, and nearly a decade after Grace had bowed out at the top. It was a suitable time for someone to wait before challenging Grace's dominance of the game in England. Hobbs, a taciturn, low-key character, was a contrast to the forceful Grace, yet he was to develop as a batsman of greater quality. Bradman, ever the detective looking for clues concerning a player's technical faults, observed Hobbs, then aged 46 to 48, at close quarters in 14 matches, including ten Tests, in 1928–29 and 1930. He branded him without any deficiencies at all. He ranked him technically the best batsman he ever saw.

'I never saw him make an uneducated stroke,' Cardus noted. 'He not only enlarged and subtilized the art of batsmanship; he like, W.G. [Grace] widened and strengthened cricket's appeal and history.'

*

Bradman found his choice of the other opener, Len Hutton, similarly faultless with footwork, strokeplay and shot production, yet believed he could have been more aggressive in his approach. Bradman thought less of batsmen who were intent on keeping the ball out of their stumps and not giving a catch, than those who had a forceful way whenever they were at the wicket. He always believed it was necessary to take the initiative from bowlers, set a mood and pave the way for team-mates to follow.

The Don scorned 'stodgy' play. It left the bowlers in charge and 'fellow batsmen in the dressing room with an air of gloom'.

Bradman noted that Hutton eschewed the hook if bowlers tried to tease it out of him, but found him a good hooker when he wanted to use it. Hutton's dour character, lightened by a whimsical sense of humour, was too much in evidence at the crease for Bradman's liking, yet he recognised him as an outstanding cricketer.

Hutton was the first professional to regularly captain England, and the man who won back the Ashes in 1953, and successively defended them in Australia in 1954–55. He was also the first professional to be elected to the Marylebone Cricket Club before his career finished. He was the second (after Jack Hobbs) to be knighted for his services to cricket.

*

Bradman described his choice for the number-three spot in the England side, Denis Compton, as a 'glorious natural cricketer' and regarded the Middlesex champion as a master batsman, despite his occasional unorthodoxy.

'His left elbow does not always please the purists,' Bradman wrote in *Farewell to Cricket*, 'and in some respects his stroke production is not up to the standard of other masters.' Bradman thought he had a good cover drive, although he didn't rank it with that stroked by Wally Hammond. He liked Compton's daring in playing the sweep and his other improvisations, which some incorrectly saw as imperfections.

Bradman thought he had a weakness against the short ball after the 1948 series and put it down to indecision over how to play it — either by getting his back foot across in the technical prescribed position to hit it, or by a more 'stand-and-deliver' pull shot. However, that assessment was made when he had to face Lindwall and Miller, who peppered him with head-high bouncers. Then he won some or lost some, mainly because of inexperience in facing such a lethal delivery, at least as sent down by these two intimidators. Bradman considered that later in Compton's career he was more circumspect in playing the shot and more selective in his counter-attacking.

'He had another characteristic capacity common to all the masters — he played the ball late and had time to do it,' said Bradman.

Compton was a poor runner between the wickets. Trevor Bailey noted that 'a call from Denis was merely the basis for negotiation'.

Compton, barring injury, was an automatic pick for England from 1938 to 1956, and in the late 1940s was the most attractive of all the country's batsmen. At times Hutton, an almost exact contemporary, and later Peter May, were regarded as more effective batsmen, but Compton's aggressive yet cheerful and carefree demeanour at the crease made him one of the most attractive crowd pleasers of all time. He was a superstar drawcard of his day and also represented England in soccer.

Compton's only rival for the coveted number-three spot in England's team was left-hander David Gower, who Bradman regarded also as one of the finest natural talents in the history of the game. Bradman enjoyed watching him and ranked several of his innings highly, particularly his 123 at Sydney in 1990–91 and his 157 at The Oval in 1985. Gower scored 8231 Test runs at an average of 44.25 and made 18 centuries.

*

Peter May, the choice at number four in the batting order, superseded Compton as England's leading batsman by the mid-

1950s. May, at 183 centimetres (6 feet), was broad-shouldered and had strong forearms. Blessed with excellent timing, he was a superb driver, especially through mid-on. His polish and style was accompanied by a temperament that pulled England, Surrey and Cambridge University out of many a predicament. I witnessed his best 'hour' in this respect at Melbourne in the Second Test of the 1958–59 Ashes when he arrived at the crease with the score at 3 wickets for 7. Alan Davidson, swinging the ball prodigiously with his long left-arm, had England on the ropes under low cloud in one of the most exciting passages of bowling I ever saw. May weathered the conditions and the brilliant bowling and went on to a century.

'May was the finest batsman in arguably the best and most balanced line-up England ever put in the field,' Bradman said, referring to England's 1956 team. Its batting order through the Ashes series, which Bradman covered as a journalist, included Peter Richardson, Colin Cowdrey, David Sheppard, May, Tom Graveney, Cyril Washbrook and Compton.

Behind May at number five in the batting order was Wally Hammond, who Bradman regarded as the best bat England produced from 1928 until World War II. Hammond, according to Bradman, was the most majestic and graceful cover drive of all, whether on the back or front foot. His athletic build allowed him to deliver shots with timing and power. Hammond was balletic in his movements. He used his dainty feet to advantage, learning all the steps back and forward from the great Charlie Macartney on Australia's tour of England in 1926.

'There probably was never a more balanced player than Wally,' Bradman said.

Hammond was Bradman's biggest rival over the decade 1928–1938. Hammond, aged 25, on the tour of Australia in 1928–29, out-gunned the Test tyro Bradman, aged 20, in their first Ashes encounter, but Bradman was never 'beaten' again over the next six series contests. Honours were even during the Bodyline series of 1932–33, although considering England captain Douglas Jardine's tactics, Bradman with a marginally superior average (56.57 to 55.00) could claim to have done better, especially when his team was soundly beaten 4:1.

Bradman noted two areas to work on when attempting to deal with Hammond. One was his reluctance to hook or pull when 'bounced' or attacked with short deliveries. The other was his lack of attacking on-drive. But these were minor deficiencies in an otherwise near-perfect technique. Bowlers could only work on them hoping to force an error. The only factor that could beat such a champion was brilliant bowling. Leg-spinner Clarrie Grimmett delivered this in 1930, and gained a psychological hold on Hammond. Bill O'Reilly on occasions also challenged him with his exceptional skills, but that was it. No paceman ever really had his measure.

Bradman also noted that Hammond was at times a talented medium-pace bowler.

'He was most dangerous when he failed with the bat,' Bradman said. 'He liked to have some success, one way or another, in every game he played. If he had concentrated on his bowling, I believe he would have been bracketed with the best medium-pacers in history.'

Hammond took 83 wickets in Tests at 37.80. In First-Class cricket, he took 732 wickets at 30.58.

Bradman himself happened to bowl Hammond in a Test.

'How did he react to that?' I asked Bradman.

'Not well,' he replied. 'It was a full toss.'

*

Number six in Bradman's line-up was W.G. Grace.

When I received Bradman's handwritten letter containing his all-time England team, I at first had a little trouble deciphering it. I rang him, congratulated him on a 'work of art', and told him I wished to check who he had at number seven.

'Is it Godfrey Evans?' I asked.

Bradman replied sharply: 'He'll bat where his captain tells him to!'

'I'm not questioning his position in the order. It's just that I'm not sure of your handwriting.'

'Yes,' Bradman said, 'it's Evans.'

Godfrey Evans, the wicket-keeper, was a stocky extrovert. This man from Kent was a character with flair, who took advantage of his showmanship. He stumped with a flourish and caught with movements that reminded onlookers of a Catherine wheel. Bradman, as ever, chose the keeper for his ability behind the stumps rather than his batting.

'Evans was both spectacular and safe,' Bradman said. 'On occasions when Australia amassed huge scores, he hardly let a bye go through, which demonstrated his skill and concentration. [Alan] Knott and [Les] Ames were better batsmen, but Evans was the superior keeper. I also rank George Duckworth highly as a keeper, despite his raucous appealing!'

Bradman recalled that Duckworth was so deft down the leg-side that Australian batsmen refused to glance in case he caught them.

He regarded Yorkshire's Fred Trueman, at number eight, as the best England fast bowler ever. 'Fred Trueman was England's pace bowler with the lot,' he remarked, 'fire, courage, guile, pace, line, length, swing and cut. I don't think any batsman I saw was comfortable against him in his prime.'

Trueman began as a blustering tearaway, but when his career settled he emerged as a master bowler, who could lift for the big occasion, especially in Ashes contests. He was at times uncouth on and off the field, and this endeared him to cricket fans in Australia as well as England. I recall him throwing in from the third-man boundary in a Melbourne Ashes Test with his left hand. It was quite a feat, but an act designed to excite the Bay 13 yobbos in the outer and irritate his skipper, Peter May.

Bradman was not as impressed with Harold Larwood, the speed demon of the Bodyline series, as many would expect. He pointed to the statistics that show Larwood took just 31 wickets at 41.29 in Tests, apart from the 1932–33 series. Larwood's only other Ashes in Australia (1928–29) yielded 18 wickets at 40.22. Bradman had no trouble with him in his debut Tests for Australia. In 1930 in England, Bradman targeted him particularly, and went all out to remove him from the attack. Larwood then took 4 wickets at 73.00. In the 1932–33 Ashes, when he came to prominence armed with Bodyline tactics, he managed 33 wickets at 19.52. Larwood in all bowled in 21 Tests and took 78 wickets at 28.35.

Alec Bedser was Bradman's choice at number nine, with S.F. Barnes at ten and Verity last man in.

Bradman's complete England team was a combination of sheer class.

CHAPTER 38

Defying the Laws of Averages, Physics and Economics

I rank Bradman alongside Muhammad Ali as the greatest sportsman who ever lived. They were outstanding in their field and both figured in their own way in racial political developments that took nerve and commitment. Ali was a substantial figure in the American civil rights movement, more as a symbol than an activist like Martin Luther King Jr. Ali's refusal to be drafted to fight in Vietnam cost him dearly in his grand boxing career, and it took as much moral courage as physical to make his point. Bradman's stand against apartheid had a similar impact. He was the first non-politician, neutral international figure of integrity and weight to take action and it played a substantial part in the breakdown of the iniquitous South African system.

But in both cases, it was their chosen sport that brought them fame, prominence and the capacity to have influence, however originally unintentional. By any measure, Bradman is the greatest batsman the world has ever seen. If you don't like statistics or they bore you rigid, then look away now, for Bradman's figures are truly mindboggling. Here is just a skim across the surface of his dominance at every level of the game against all-comers. He batted 338 times in First-Class cricket over 22 years from 1927 to 1949, scoring 28,067 runs and averaging 95.14. He hit 117 centuries at better than one every three innings, a rate that no other batsman has remotely approached. He scored nine triple centuries, including six First-Class triple centuries, a quadruple (452 not out against Queensland in 1930), and 299 not out. He maintained a rate of 42 runs an hour. That's 84 runs a two-hour session, or 252 runs in a day — and at a strike-rate of 75 runs per hundred balls, which would be respectable even in modern *one-day* cricket.

Analysis of Bradman's First-Class innings shows that 75 of his centuries were chanceless, while 95 were chanceless up to 100. On top of that he threw his wicket away in at least 46 innings. He made only 16 ducks, six of them first ball, three second ball. In 52 Tests he managed 6996 runs at 99.94 — or rounded off, a century — every time he went out to bat in those 80 innings. He actually hit 29 Test centuries, including 12 doubles, two triples and that tantalising knock of 299 not out against South Africa in 1932. Even in grade cricket and what was once called 'Second-

Class' matches, he kept up this relentless run accumulation and average at a pace unmatched by anyone else.

Just to put Bradman's superiority in perspective, his nearest rival through a 20-year career, England's Wally Hammond, scored 36 double hundreds in 1005 First-Class innings at an average of 56.10. Bradman scored 37 doubles from just 338 First-Class innings at an average of 95.14. In all, he had 669 innings from school and country to club, First-Class and Test matches, scoring 50,731 runs at an average of 90.27 runs every time he batted over nearly 30 years.

This demonstrates a supreme power of concentration and controlled aggression in another dimension of performance from any other cricketer, or any individual in any other sport.

As mentioned earlier, he was worth two of the best batsman in history. Would any other sport have a player at the top worth the value of the next two performers together? In tennis, would Laver be worth Newcombe plus McEnroe, or McEnroe be equal to Becker and Federer? No. In boxing, would Muhammad Ali ever be considered the equivalent of Rocky Marciano and Mike Tyson together? Hardly. Or in golf, could Jack Nicklaus be the equal to Tiger Woods plus Greg Norman? Never.

South Australian biochemist Charles Davis went further in analysis and created a bell curve that weighted Bradman's average against the best of the rest in cricket. Bradman's record is so far from the norm that we would have to wait for another million Test batsmen before someone approaching it would emerge. The bell curve could be applied to all sports. Analysis shows that the best performers in other sports such as football, high-jumping, tennis, swimming and running could not get anywhere near Bradman's distance from the rest in cricket.

Bradman's attitude to his own average, and statistics in general, in which he revelled, is instructive. He loved the 'numbers' and had a quick brain with them. More than once we eschewed calculators and used pen and paper to do some large addition and long division together to calculate averages. His mind was nimble and fast. Yet he had the self-confidence to deny and defy the numbers when it suited him.

The night before the Leeds Test in 1934, Neville Cardus wanted Bradman to join him for dinner. Cardus was a wonderful observer and first-rate writer. He was also a friend of Bradman's, but the Australians viewed him as an adept fifth columnist for the England side. Whatever he could pick up in titbits and intelligence about plans or injuries or attitudes in the touring camp, he would report back to his fellow Englishmen, or resort to well-crafted propaganda that was meant to unsettle the Australians.

I asked Bradman for his thoughts on the Cardus invitation.

'We knew Neville was fair-minded, but of course he wanted England to win.'

'But you rejected his invitation.'

'I did and with good reason. I wanted to get to bed early and be fresh for what lay ahead. The Ashes were in the balance. We needed a win.'

'Cardus claimed he said to you something like, "C'mon, Don, you won't be getting 200 again"' (referring to what Bradman had done in 1930 — actually 334 — in the corresponding Ashes Test).

'He did say that.'

'And you asked him why?'

'He said getting 200 was against the law of averages.'

'And you remarked: "I don't believe in the law of averages"?'

'I did. He underestimated our determination to win the game and secure the Ashes.'

The word 'determination' is a euphemism here. Bradman was ill and underweight, with a yet-undetected burst appendix, which was slowly poisoning him.

As ever, he wanted to win for his country first with a gigantic score. He managed 304, thus defying the law of averages and Cardus's well-considered judgement.

*

It seemed Bradman was capable, or gave the illusion, of this defiance with other natural laws. It was often said by observers that his late cut was so late that it was 'posthumous'. To the naked eye, it appeared the ball was so far past him that it was impossible to strike. But he managed to steer, guide or nudge it through slips to the boundary with ease. Bradman had the gift of being able to play so late that it made observers gasp because it had to have slipped past his defensive or attacking stroke. (Another to have this eye-tricking capacity in recent years was the elegant Michael Clarke.)

Away from the sporting arena, Bradman also ignored a basic law of economics concerning supply and demand. He had 'saturated the market' with his signature on letters, memorabilia, bats, balls and any other piece of equipment in or outside of cricket. Yet the price for these items seemed to never fall. The more he signed (or 'supplied'), the more the price went up. With anyone else, this would not apply.

I discovered this with my Bradman biography. On 22 April 1999, I wrote to him:

> I was at a Variety Club function last Monday, emceed by
> Bruce Woodley, where an author-signed copy of The Don
> was auctioned for specific equipment at the Children's
> Hospital ... The auctioneer on the night was not certain
> the book would gain much without your signature [which
> Bradman later kindly supplied] ... the reserve price was set a
> $3340, an extra nought added to your highest Test score ...
> it went in twenty seconds. After the auction someone came
> in with a late bid of $5000, which was declined ...

I have heard many such stories and they have continued long after Bradman passed on.

*

Bradman never could explain why his record is so much better than anyone else's. He said he had seen 'plenty' of cricketers who looked better than him, even two whose natural home ended up as Grade cricket. One player who Bradman judged 'superior' was Rayford Robinson from Newcastle. He played just one Test, aged 22, at Brisbane in the 1936–37 Ashes series. He was caught by Hammond off Voce in each innings, making 2 and 3. Robinson was dropped and never played Test cricket again. He represented both NSW and South Australia, and scored 2441 at a modest average of 31.70. Robinson was judged by many to rank in strokeplay and timing with Trumper, Archie Jackson and Kippax.

Robinson's flaws were more character-derived than anything else. Off the field he worked on the wharves and preferred the company of gangsters and criminals to his cricket companions. He was once charged with stealing. He had a sad end sleeping rough in the parks and under bridges in his native Newcastle. Robinson died there aged 51 in 1965.

Other batsmen, Bradman said, lacked concentration or had never learned to pace an innings. If players with the finest style kept being dismissed early they would soon disappear. Indiscretion, lack of discipline, over-flamboyance or lack of concentration — one or all of these faults would often cause a downfall.

Rarely could a bowler con Bradman into a shot he didn't wish to play. Rarer still were rushes of blood to the head after, say, two well-hit fours.

In this respect, I recall my last game of cricket in 2000 at the Bowral Oval in that year's Lady Bradman Cup. I had just come to the wicket. A capable leg-spinner came on. I hit his first two loose balls either side of the wicket for four. In the sporting vernacular, I was 'pumped'. The leggie's third delivery was just outside leg stump and spinning away, providing a juicy opportunity for a left-hander. I swung under it sweetly and watched it sail away to the square leg boundary, a certain six. In my head I was already on 14. Out of the afternoon shadows came a fielder who caught the ball on the boundary. I was out for a bright 8. I had defied the laws of Bradman — (one) do not loft the ball early in an innings, and (two) do not get carried away after a couple of boundaries — and fallen ignominiously.

In part my fate in this instance was why good park cricketers remained park cricketers, and others went on to club, State and Test level. Players look like champions, until they get out. It's not a matter of luck. These types will spend decades displaying all the strokes for a bright 30 or 40 and then play a hopeless shot that will end their innings.

'Great players learned to avoid errors,' Bradman said, 'or they had innate intuition, which allowed them preserve their wickets without necessarily playing defensively.'

*

When Bradman bowed out in 1949, no one realised that a cricketer with a Test century average over a career would not be seen again for a long time, maybe forever. Fine players burst on the scene, were worked out by bowlers and pegged back to averages between 40 and 60. Some were dubbed 'the new Bradman' in hope and expectation. Less than a decade after The Don retired, the public was hungry for a new champion and the media fed it. Ian Craig, in 1953, was the 'baby Bradman'. He was promising and stylish, but the endless media need to compare someone with Bradman was too much of a burden. Illness and his need to follow a career as a pharmacist ended his playing days. Norm O'Neill was next, and he could certainly belt the ball harder than most. His scoring was heavy early and his Test start in 1958–59 against England hinted at something like the Bowral Boy's 30 years earlier. Yet he levelled out with a strong Test career and an average in the mid-40s.

Then in the mid-1960s, easygoing Doug Walters started with two terrific hundreds against England. He even looked like Bradman in the baggy green. Yet Walters also disappointed, not because he wasn't popular or attacking or first rate. The poor fellow simply averaged in the 40s rather than 100.

In the modern era, David Warner has been spared the 'kiss of death'. Observers have refrained from the thoughtlessness of branding him the new Bradman. That he is 'Bradmanesque' is a misnomer too. Warner is making his own mark.

Also recently, Adam Voges, who started his Test career at 35 years of age in April 2015, came out of the blocks fast with big Test scores that put his early average at more than 100. Commentators were quick to compare him to Bradman, at least with his numbers. Then the scores began to dwindle. He retired early in 2017 after 20 matches with an average of 61.87, leaving him second only to Bradman in Australian all-time Test averages.

As American Gore Vidal said about the death of rival author Truman Capote: 'Good career move.'

Recent Australian captain and star bat Steve Smith was the latest character caught in the 'could he be the new Bradman?' scenario; at least, before the over-blown 'ball-tampering affair'. One article I read in Thailand's admirable broadsheet *The Nation* in December 2017 commented: 'Smith is only one of three Australian batsman to have scored two Ashes double hundreds.'

The article failed to add that Bradman had hit eight (with Bob Simpson, the third batsman, with two). This is not to discount Smith. I would love to see an Australian emerge with better figures than The Don. But it's best to compare performances when the players concerned have completed their careers.

CHAPTER 39

The Greatest Australian?

The *Oxford Dictionary* definition of 'genius' is 'exalted intellectual power, instinctive and extraordinary imaginative, creative or inventive capacity'. The word is overused, but if ever it applied to anyone, it did to Bradman and his approach to cricket. Intellectual strength alone would mean little if an individual didn't have the innate and acquired physical skills to play at the top. If they happen to be coupled together, as they were in him, the result was an exceptional individual of brilliance and mental stamina. Add his exceptional character and the other features mentioned in this book and you have a big part of the package that made Bradman the true master of cricket in the 20th century. Yet examining his character and characteristics to fully explain his genius is a bit like a surgeon dissecting a brain to find a soul. It can't be done.

*

The Bradman legend, begun in the Depression, remained untouched by the behind-the-scenes battles over his style and early captaincy. His ruthless application of cricketing genius allowed him and Australia to rule world cricket from 1930–1948, except for the 1932–33 blip of Bodyline. This strengthened his image ever further until he retired in 1949 and was knighted. That accounts for his unshakeable hold on the title of 'Greatest Australian ever born' for half of the last century. But what of the other half?

His faults centred on a tendency at times to be unpalatably direct, especially for the pompous and wasters of his precious time. Yet overriding this was a person of exceptional integrity and character; one who was modest, and quick to make a generous comment about another, if merited. In private he was humorous with a sharp wit and interested in others' views. These features came through over the decades, coupled with other important factors that extended, maintained and built him as the leading legend of Australian 20th-century characters from 1950 to 2000 and beyond.

First, no one came remotely near Bradman's batting record. His average and big innings grew in proportion as the decades rolled by.

Second, he became the most prolific and expert letter-writer of the era, sending out an estimated one million letters in response to about five million he received in his lifetime. It was the only way Bradman could reach out personally to his correspondents.

Written responses became a habit — a self-imposed obligation to his countless fans worldwide. This developed into an obsession, even an addiction. Most recipients of any reply from him placed it among their most prized possessions. The result was a huge constituency of supporters, from the world's movers and shakers to the most humble. Bradman's clear, concise prose, often with a witty or penetrating line, reflected his outstanding mind, and made you comprehend in a small way what bowlers, or opponents in any competitive environment, faced.

Third, he did endless work for charity, mostly in private and without help, which he couldn't really afford. Apart from sitting down at his battered portable in his modest upstairs study every day for at least four hours, most days of every week would see him signing or writing something for worthy causes, or just fans. If that seems unimpressive on the surface, think of anyone devoting themselves to others half a day of every day for seven decades, even well into their nineties. How Bradman stayed sane and on top of this output is remarkable, especially when there was mail overload on his birthday and at Christmas. At those times of the year, an Australia Post truck would be dedicated to his mail.

Occasionally he wrote to me that the mail was 'driving him insane' as he tried to keep on top of it. On his 90th birthday he told me: 'I've a pile of mail you couldn't jump over.'

After that, it overwhelmed and depressed him, and he needed secretarial help, which was provided by the Bradman Museum. In the week after his death on 25 February 2001, the outpouring in the media of memories and references to the letters he sent to children, ordinary people and others reflected the inspiration he gave to millions over the last 72 years of his life.

Fourth, and most importantly, was his stand against apartheid.

Apart from all this, Australia never had a 'hero of the people' who quite matched Bradman, even in the second half of the century, although champion swimmer Dawn Fraser, in a decade burst, came close. She collected gold at three different Olympics from 1956 to 1964. Bob Menzies was a towering figure for two decades, but never had support from about half the constituency needed to challenge The Don. Bob Hawke's star flashed across the sky of popularity for a while in the 1980s, as did John Howard's over much of his prime-ministership and beyond. Malcolm Fraser did endless 'good works' for a foreign care agency and signed up for worthy causes at home, such as Aboriginal rights, support for Vietnamese immigration, and the republican cause, but it didn't bring him hero worship. Aloofness, patrician bearing and lack of charisma would never qualify Fraser as a 'man of the people'.

Labor politician Barry Jones was a popular figure, and a rare bird in Australia — an admired intellectual — after his gallant performances in Bob Dyer's *Pick-a-Box* TV quiz show. He disappeared from our screens about 1968, and later became prominent in state and federal Labor politics; the latter turning off half his 'fame' constituency.

Bradman was named by *Time* magazine (as was fellow Australian-born Rupert Murdoch) among the first 100 most influential figures of the 20th century. There was Bradman alongside Gandhi, Churchill and Mandela. Gandhi expressed a fervent hope to meet him, but was assassinated before he could.

Bradman did mix it with Britain's mighty wartime leader. He was leaving Victoria Station in London in 1934 when Churchill used journalist connections to arrange a meeting and a photo opportunity. Winston needed Bradman, but the latter would have avoided the meeting if he could. Bradman was also Nelson Mandela's standout hero before and after Bradman's adroit handling of apartheid.

Murdoch, a high achiever by any measure, never excited the masses, and harmed his popularity by becoming an American citizen. Swimmer Kieren Perkins, a wonderful modern role model, stopped the nation and caused the heart to beat faster during the 1996 Atlanta Olympics, as did Cathy Freeman at Sydney in 2000. Aviators Nancy Bird Walton, Bert Hinkler and Charles Kingsford Smith soared for short periods and caused hats to be thrown in the air.

Scientists such as pathologist Howard Florey and nuclear physicist Mark Oliphant had their moments, but their fine work with experimentation did not draw regular enthusiastic applause. Poring over penicillin dishes and magnetrons were not spectator sports. This did not invalidate them as 'greater' Australians than Bradman. They were. Florey had an enormous impact on medicine. Oliphant changed the course of World War II with his work on the atomic bomb and radar. But these high achievers were much less known.

Then there was General Sir John Monash, my choice for the highest-achieving Australian of all time. But winning big battles, except in movies, was never the same as dominating sporting contests.

Perhaps only Phar Lap, the fabulous stayer with the big heart, challenged Bradman as Australia's number-one icon. Yet he would be disqualified, not because he wasn't human, but on two counts. First, his winning record made him the punters' favourite for a few years, but his early death limited his claim. Second, Phar Lap happened to be a New Zealander.

If you were looking for one image, one face, one performer, one communicator that most represented Australia in the 20th century, it had to be Donald George Bradman.

CHAPTER 40

Final Days

Journalists would send Bradman his obituaries for approval. Not surprisingly, he hated these reminders of his mortality. People treated him as a mythical figure, more public property than human being. Bradman wrote to me about one obituary writer and remarked: 'His rationale for sending it to me was that he wanted me to know in what high regard I was held *before* I died, not afterwards. Strange how the minds of some people work.'

Bradman responded to another obituary:

My death has been reported prematurely on two occasions, once when it was announced in a North Queensland paper that I had succumbed to a bout of dysentery and once when I was hovering near death in a London hospital in 1934 after an operation for appendicitis. Now I'm sure you won't be surprised to know that I received your epistle with little enthusiasm. I had a close call in November [1994] when I had a serious throat operation but, having survived that, I hope your obituary won't be used for quite a while yet ...

That said, Bradman reverted to his pedantic form: 'You refer to my "padding a golf ball against the surface of a corrugated iron tank". Not so. I threw the ball against the circular brick tank stand (about 18 inches high) on which the tank rested.'

The obituary writer could take heart from the fact that he wasn't alone in this error. The *Encyclopaedia Britannica* has him hitting a 'soft ball against a corrugated metal water tank'.

Bradman's reply to this obituary writer added: 'You then go on "bouncing the ball off the twisted palings of a backyard fence". In fact I threw the ball at the rounded rail to which the palings (on the other side) were nailed.'

The biggest rumour about his demise came during the Sydney 2000 Olympics when the word that he had died swept the village. Les Carlyon, former *Age* editor-in-chief, was in touch with me to find out.

'I don't think so,' I said, 'I'll ring him.'

His housekeeper, Mrs Joseph, answered the phone.

'Is he in?' I asked.

'No,' she replied, 'he went out in his car and is expected back early this afternoon. Is there any message?'

'No, no,' I said, not wanting to say I was ringing to see if he were alive or not, 'just tell him I called.'

Bradman phoned back a few hours later. I told him of the rumour, knowing that I wouldn't be the last to call him over the non-issue. My instinct was correct. Richard Mulvaney at the Bradman Museum had had several enquiries and had to wait until Bradman returned from shopping.

'So you called just to see if I were alive,' he said to me with a chortle.

'Well … yes …'

'I told you about the many times these stories of my demise surfaced.'

In his 1996 TV interview with Ray Martin, he recalled an eight-year-old boy writing to him: 'I am sorry it has taken so long to write to you, but I'd always regret it if I was too late.'

Bradman wrote back to him: 'Not half as much as I would.'

He told me of a ten-year-old writing to him: 'I've been wanting to write to you for a long time, but my grandfather says you are dead. But recently my father told me you were alive. I am writing to find out the truth.'

'I suppose the rumours will be true one day,' Bradman said to me after that last rumour in 2000, 'so keep ringing!'

And of course, he was right, as ever.

*

Several comments that stay with me were uttered with some feeling by Bradman in his final years.

'The worst thing about getting old is that your friends depart,' he remarked, which was sad enough, but, also, as mentioned, he often expressed concern for daughter Shirley and her future. His deep love and respect for Jessie came up often. She had suffered for years with chronic leukaemia.

'She'll be telling people how well she is on the day she dies,' he said.

Bradman more often than not put his grief and sadness on paper. Whether it salved those feelings, I shall never know. I received several letters from him about Jessie when she was near the end of her life. Early in November 1995, her condition worsened. Bradman wrote to me:

> The most awful tragedy has occurred in that Jessie is in hospital with terminal cancer. My life is at an end and I just cannot explain my devastation and grief … a partnership of 70 years is ending and really a chapter in Australian life and history. It is so sad and unfair that this wonderful lady should suffer in this way.

Another letter of further poignancy followed in which Bradman said: 'Life without Jessie would be meaningless for me and I can only pray that medical skill and prayers will do the trick.'

Jessie died in September 1997 and Bradman went into his shell. He said in several phone chats that 'life was not worth living without her'. This was not meant to engender sympathy. Bradman was just stating the facts as he saw them. He did last another three and a half years and carried on as best he could, mainly responding to requests from others.

In 1997, he began to wind down his golf. I asked him, as I always did, how it was going.

'Terribly,' he said.

Why?

'I have to use a buggy,' he said, miffed by the realisation that he would never again be able to stride over 18 holes.

The Don was finding it harder than most to bend to the uncompromising forces of old age. He had a severe flu during a cold 1998 Adelaide winter and a torn calf muscle just before his 90th birthday on 27 August. Any exercise became unfeasible. He was dispirited in the knowledge that his golfing days were over after 80 years of playing. All his grand gifts and command of implements with which to hit spheres were being slowly, inexorably taken from him. Bradman's fingers became arthritic and he couldn't play the piano or Bridge. The things he loved most were slowly leaving him. The Don was letting go and ready to depart.

However, in late 2000, I was still receiving letters from him. His signature was still intact. The phone chats often revealed he was, not surprisingly, depressed. Yet still his clarity of thought in conversation and letters was evident. That very good memory also was still operating as ever. His stylish, occasionally sardonic wit was still present.

One example was a letter on 30 October 2000, in which Bradman wrote: 'Thank you so much for your book on Australia's captains [which was dedicated to him]. I look forward to it. If the inside is as good as the outside I will not be disappointed.'

Soon after that letter, Don caught pneumonia and was hospitalised. John Bradman and his family did much to ease his slow, brave exit.

*

I learned of his death on the morning of Monday, 26 February 2001, from ABC Melbourne radio commentator Jon Faine, who rang to ask me on his program to speak on the news.

After being stunned by this revelation, I asked: 'When did he die, exactly?'

'Five a.m. this morning,' Faine said.

'That's funny,' I said. 'I had a dream about him "departing" at 5 a.m. *yesterday* morning [25 February].'

In the dream, I was at Bradman's bedside. He smiled at me, left the bed in his pyjamas and dressing gown and beckoned me to follow him. He walked to wide wooden steps that led to a green garden. I stopped at the top of the steps and watched as Bradman walked down. People materialised from everywhere in the garden to greet him.

Then the dream ended. I awoke and wondered what it meant.

Later, while being interviewed, Faine informed me Bradman had indeed died at the same time as my dream — at 5 a.m. on Sunday morning, 25 February 2001.

Acknowledgements

I wish to thank Jude McGee for the opportunity to write this memoir.

Thanks also to publishing director Brigitta Doyle and my agent Jo Butler.

Those who contributed specifically on the topic with interviews, correspondence, files, information, photographs over 40 years include Sir Donald Bradman, Lady Bradman, John Bradman and the family, Dean Golja, Professor Mary Finsterer, Dr Felix Nobis, Thos Hodgson, Bruce Woodley, Neil Harvey, Keith Stackpole, Ron Barassi, Rosemary Long, Greg Thomas, Tommie Gregory, Lyn Thomas, Sam Loxton, Arthur Morris, Lindsay Hassett, Richie Benaud, Martin Ashenden, Alec Bedser, Eric Bedser, Denis Compton, Colin Cowdrey, Godfrey Evans, Gus Glendinning, Jack Grossman, Ian Johnson, Bill Johnston, Ray Lindwall, Tony Maylam, Keith Miller (also Miller's family, notably Denis Miller, Bob Miller and Miller's niece Jan Beames), John Miles, Mary Newham, Lady Pippa O'Brien, John MacWhirter, Rod Mater, David Temple, Alan Young, Ian Craig, Alan Davidson, Basil Grapsis, Peter Philpott, Doug Ring, Ron Hamence, Vicki Ritchie, Sachin Tendulkar, Barry Richards, Tony Walker and Tony Henningham.

*

Thanks to Carcanet Press Limited for permission to reproduce Robert Graves's poem 'At First Sight', from *The Complete Poems in One Volume*, edited by Beryl Graves and Dunstan Ward, Carcanet Press, Manchester, 2000.

Bibliography

Arlott, John, *Gone to the Test Match*, Longmans, Green and Co, London, 1949.

Barnes, Sid, *It Isn't Cricket*, Collins, Sydney, 1953.

Bedser, Alec and Eric, *Following On*, Evans Brothers Ltd, London, 1954.

Bradman, Don, *Farewell to Cricket*, Hodder and Stoughton, London, 1950.

— *The Bradman Albums*, Rigby, Sydney, 1987.

— *The Art of Cricket*, Hodder and Stoughton, London, 1990.

Bromby, Robin, ed., *A Century of Ashes*, Resolution Press, Sydney, 1982.

Davis, Charles, *Best of the Best*, ABC Books, Sydney, 2000.

Fingleton, Jack, *Brightly Fades the Don*, Collins, London, 1949.

Frindall, W.H., *The Wisden Book of Test Cricket 1887–1984*, MacDonald Publishing, Guild Publishing, London, 1985.

Geddes, Margaret, *Remembering Bradman*, Viking, Sydney, 2002.

Harvey, Neil, *My World of Cricket*, Hodder and Stoughton, 1963.

Heald, Tim, *Denis Compton*, Pavilion, London, 1994.

Howat, Gerald, *Len Hutton*, Heinemann Kingswood, London, 1988.

Lalor, Peter, *Barassi*, Allen & Unwin, Sydney, 2010.

Lillee, Dennis, *Over and Out!*, Methuen Australia, North Ryde 1984.

Lindwall, Ray, *Flying Stumps*, Stanley Paul and Co, London, 1954.

Martin-Jenkins, Christopher, *World Cricketers: A Biographical Dictionary*, Oxford University Press, UK, 1996.

McHarg, Jack, *Arthur Morris, An Elegant Genius*, ABC Books, Sydney, 1995.

O'Reilly, W.J., *Cricket Conquest*, Werner Laurie, London, 1949.

O'Shaughnessy, Brian, *Consciousness and the World*, Oxford University Press, Oxford, 2000.

Perry, Roland, *Don Bradman*, Hachette Australia, Sydney, 2014.

— *Bradman's Invincibles,* Hachette Australia, Sydney, 2008.

— *The Don,* Macmillan, Sydney, 1995.

— *Bradman's Best*, Random House, Sydney, 2001.

— *Bradman's Best Ashes Teams*, Random House Australia, Sydney, 2002.

— *Captain Australia*, Random House Australia, Sydney, 2000.

— *Miller's Luck*, Random House Australia, Sydney, 2005.

Pollard, Jack, *The Complete Illustrated History of Australian Cricket*, Viking Australia, 1995.

Preston, Hubert, ed., *Wisden Cricketers' Almanack, 1949*, London, 1949.

Rippon, Anton, *Classic Moments of the Ashes*, J.M. Dent, Melbourne, 1982.

Wakley, B.J., *Bradman the Great*, Mainstream Publishing, London, 1999.

Wallace, Christine, *The Private Don*, Allen and Unwin, Sydney, 2004.

Webster, Ray, *First-Class Cricket in Australia: Volumes 1 and 2*, 1991 and 1997, Victoria.

William, Charles, *Bradman: An Australian Hero*, Abacus, London, 1996.

Yardley, N.W.D. and Kilburn, J.M., *Homes of Sport*, Peter Garnett, 1952.

WHAT THE REVIEWERS HAVE SAID ABOUT ROLAND PERRY'S CRICKET BOOKS

The Don
'an unsurpassable record of a phenomenal figure'
— E.W. Swanton in *The Cricketer* magazine, UK

'a sterling biography ... and one can almost feel the excitement that gripped cricket fans when [Bradman] strode out to bat' — *Herald Sun*, Melbourne

'a magnificent book. Bradman's story is wonderfully related by Perry — a monument both to his research and his writing ... Perry's joy in relating [Bradman's] greatest innings is infectious' — *Total Sports Magazine*, UK

Waugh's Way
'Roland Perry is gloriously readable, always thoughtful'
— *Wisden Cricketers' Almanack*

Captain Australia
'Perry is a prolific, stylish writer'
— Robin Marlar in *The Cricketer International*

'a valuable addition to our cricketing canon'
— *Cricket Magazine*'s Inside Edge

Miller's Luck

'up there with the great cricket biographies'
— cricket historian J. Neville Turner, speech to the Australian Cricket Society

'an excellent biography ... an honest portrayal of the imperfect human being behind the heroic legend'
— Ron Reed, *Herald Sun*, Melbourne

'not just a great cricketing book, but also a complete portrait of a fascinating life' — Archie Mac in Cricket Web

The Ashes: A Celebration

'[Perry's] knowledge on the game is formidable ... he's an authoritative observer ... and a very entertaining read'
— Steven Carroll in *The Age*, Melbourne

Bradman's Invincibles

'a wonderful insider's view ... a great Australian yarn' — *Sydney Morning Herald*

'[Perry's] meticulous approach gives us a great understanding of the subtleties and room for instinct that were Bradman trademarks' — Adrian Nesbitt in *The Sun-Herald*, Sydney

'Perry's work, much like Bradman himself, is head and shoulders above the competition ... *Bradman's Invincibles* leads the reader into the dusty backrooms, on to windy training pitches and mid-Test; beautifully written'
— Teri Louise Kelly in *The Independent Weekly*